BLUE THINKS ITSELF WITHIN ME

ᐅᐢᑲᓇ

OSKANA POETRY & POETICS

Blue thinks itself within me

Lyric poetry, ecology, and lichenous form

KIM TRAINOR

Printed and bound in Canada.
The text of this book is printed on 100% post-consumer recycled paper with earth-friendly vegetable-based inks.

Cover art: Detail from photo by Natasha Lavdovsky
Cover design: David Fassett
Page design and layout: John van der Woude, JVDW Designs
Series Editor: Randy Lundy
Cody Editor: Kelly Laycock
Proofreader: Crissy Boylan

The text and titling faces are Arno, designed by Robert Slimbach.

Library and Archives Canada Cataloguing in Publication

Title: Blue thinks itself within me : lyric poetry, ecology, and lichenous form / Kim Trainor.
Names: Trainor, Kim, 1970- author.
Series: Oskana poetry & poetics ; 21.
Description: Series statement: Oskana poetry & poetics ; 21 | Includes bibliographical references.
Identifiers: Canadiana (print) 20250258226 | Canadiana (ebook) 20250262150 | ISBN 9781779401212 (hardcover) | ISBN 9781779401205 (softcover) | ISBN 9781779401229 (EPUB) | ISBN 9781779401236 (PDF)
Subjects: LCSH: Trainor, Kim, 1970- | LCSH: Lyric poetry. | LCSH: Poetry—Social aspects. | LCSH: Ecology in literature. | LCSH: Environmentalism—British Columbia—Vancouver Island. | LCSH: Activism–British Columbia—Vancouver Island. | LCSH: Civil disobedience—British Columbia—Vancouver Island. | LCGFT: Ecopoetry. | LCGFT: Literary criticism.
Classification: LCC PS8639.R355 B57 2026 | DDC C811/.6—dc23

10 9 8 7 6 5 4 3 2 1

UNIVERSITY OF REGINA PRESS
University of Regina
Regina, Saskatchewan
Canada S4S 0A2
TELEPHONE: (306) 585-4758
FAX: (306) 585-4699
WEB: www.uofrpress.ca
EMAIL: uofrpress@uregina.ca

We acknowledge the support of the Canada Council for the Arts for our publishing program. We acknowledge the financial support of the Government of Canada. / Nous reconnaissons l'appui financier du gouvernement du Canada. This publication was made possible with support from Creative Saskatchewan's Book Publishing Production Grant Program.

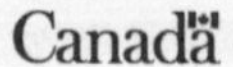

For the flying beings, the ones with sharp teeth,
the ones who swim, the fire stones, the trees, the rain.
For the mice, who come to scoop up lard with tiny nails.
For Ada'itsx, for Grandfather Tree, for Grandmother Tree.
For oldgrowth specklebelly lichen, for raven, for tree frog.

CONTENTS

LIST OF ILLUSTRATIONS

SEPTEMBER 30, 2021, 9:43 PM.
TREE FARM LICENCE 46, GRANITE MAIN

Two days after a renewal of the injunction requested by Teal-Jones was denied.[1]

Day of Truth and Reconciliation.

First day at Ada'itsx / Fairy Creek.

Some have been here a year, or more. But it is our first day. First day rebuilding Fairy Creek HQ, renamed HQO at the 7 pm campfire. We brought some supplies to share—rain jackets, tarps, freeze-dried meals, rope, warm layers of wool. We helped to unpack supplies from a car that was dropping more off and carried these to the new kitchen and gear pop-up shelters—across the mud, then a winding path through the forest to avoid a trench created earlier by Teal-Jones before the injunction expired. We helped to fill in a smaller ditch so cars could pass over, until a rumour circulated that the RCMP would arrest anyone digging for impeding the work crews, and the shovels were hidden under tarps. We climbed the steep grade of the mossy banks to secure a white tarp 20 feet overhead. We gathered stones to build a fire ring. We set up the kitchen, washed dishes, boiled water, made instant coffee in thermoses, heated leftovers of couscous and curry, served slices of cheese and bread and pie. We pitched our tents in the dark, in rain, by the side of the road. The creek rushing past, far off. At the 7 pm meeting, Hazelnut told us,

---

1 Cordasco, "BC Judge Refuses to Extend Court Injunction at Fairy Creek." "A BC Supreme Court judge has refused to extend an injunction that was granted to prevent protestors from impeding logging operations at Fairy Creek on Vancouver Island. Justice John Thompson ruled the reputation of the court outweighed the economic interests of the logging company, Teal Jones. Thompson pointed to the RCMP's enforcement of the court injunction as the main reason for the court's tarnished reputation."

We will sit all together in a peaceful group in the morning, yes? Two of us will be standing and talking. We are stronger when we sit all together. It is Truth and Rec, so they are not working, but they will come tomorrow, early. We don't know what they will do. We must be up early, by 5:30, 6. They will come early. And we need some people on night shift, to watch—who will volunteer?

I volunteer. We will wake at 4 or 4:30 and finish the night.
We will boil water, make coffee. And then we will sit all together
in the middle of the road and wait for them to come.

PREFACE

In the fall of 2021, I began to make intermittent visits to Fairy Creek, near Port Renfrew on Vancouver Island, to participate in what had become the largest civil disobedience campaign in Canadian history. Its purpose was to stop old-growth logging in and around the Fairy Creek watershed, known to the Pacheedaht as Ada'itsx, the last intact watershed of old-growth forest in southern Vancouver Island. The height of the arrests had already occurred in the summer of that year, but the blockades continued as the weather began to turn. On my initial visit, I wanted only to witness what was happening, to bring supplies, and to see if there was any small thing I could do to help for the short time I was there. But this movement—despite its many problems and shortcomings, as with any social movement—with wave after wave of folks who journeyed from across the continent to stand as allies with the trees, offered a beautiful if imperfect model of how we humans might attempt to imagine a different way to be and to live with our more-than-human kin. Along with a good friend, I returned again and again, whenever work and family life would allow.

At this time, I was writing a book of poetry, with a focus on resilience and survival amid crises such as the sixth mass extinction, climate heating, and hypercapitalist resource extraction. This book was later published as *A blueprint for survival* (2024). I was also beginning to write a book in which I thought about the relationship between the lyric poem and ecology. What, if anything, could the lyric ecopoem do in the face of such catastrophe? *Blue thinks itself within me: Lyric poetry, ecology, and lichenous form* traces my thinking as a working poet, inspired by my reading of fellow poets and theorists, ecologists, and activists, along with my experiences at Ada'itsx. As I wrote, I began to glean ideas for a future book-length lyric poem, not yet written, on oldgrowth specklebelly lichen, one of the species at risk that has been threatened at Fairy Creek.

This is not, as such, a manifesto or academic monograph or treatise, although it engages with complex poetic and ecological theories at times. Nor do I offer a history of the lyric poem or a survey of ecopoetry. Instead, this book is in part a document of the creative process at its most nascent, as I begin to imagine how I might experiment in form while staying true to my roots in lyric.

It might be helpful for those who may not know what a lyric poem is, much less a lyric ecopoem, to offer a quick overview here. In Poetry 101 we are often told that a lyric poem is short, in the first person, intimate, of an emotional tenor. I recall my professor at UBC definitively marking up in chalk on the blackboard the three categories of classical Greek poetry: lyric, dramatic, epic. Yet lyric has always been a contested category—whether defined as genre or mode of expression. As the most recent entry in the *Princeton Encyclopedia of Poetry and Poetics* notes, "lyric" is essentially a back-formation of the eighteenth century. The word "lyric" comes from the Greek *lyra*, meaning lyre, the stringed musical instrument that was used to accompany the short songs of ancient Greek poets, who would have called this kind of song *melos*, not *lyric*:

> In the Alexandrian period, when the texts taken from Greek songs were collected in the library, the poems once sung in performance were grouped together and called lyrics. Thus, lyric was from its inception a term used to describe a music that could no longer be heard, an idea of poetry characterized by a lost collective experience.[1]

Lyric has always rejected categorization, is unstable and fluid, "as subject to change as the definition of poetry itself."[2]

1 Greene et al., "Lyric," 826.
2 Greene et al., "Lyric," 834.

If there is no clear idea of what exactly a lyric poem is, then what is a lyric ecopoem? The ecopoem has been described as cousin to nature poetry, yet with an awareness of the destructive role humans have played in the natural world.[3] The theorist Timothy Morton has offered the terms "weak ecomimesis" and "strong ecomimesis" to distinguish between the more traditional nature poem—a poem that "evokes an environment"—and the more recent ecopoem that is situated, self-aware, and linked to "impending and 'threateningly nondiscriminatory' ecological peril."[4] Regarding the nature poem, or weak ecomimetic poem, the British poet Simon Armitage has argued that such poetry can work to make the reader "beguiled" by nature in the tradition of the praise poem.[5] But what more can it do? Morton, in his reading of Coleridge's "Effusion 35," an early version of "The Eolian Harp," argues that even in this example by a first-generation Romantic poet, we find self-awareness and an openness to thinking about human positioning within "the environment." He argues, "with the ecological crisis . . . goes an equally powerful and urgent opening up of our view of who we are and where we are. What, therefore, is environmental art? If what we inadequately call *the environment* entails a radical openness, how does this appear, if at all, in art forms?"[6] He begins with the simple premise that ecological art is not just "about" something but "*is* something, or maybe it *does* something. Art is ecological insofar as it is made from materials and exists in the world."[7]

---

3 Greene et al., "Environment and Poetry," 437.

4 Morton, with reference to David Simpson, *Ecology Without Nature*, 33.

5 Armitage quoted in Hall, "Simon Armitage."

6 Morton, "Of Matter and Meter," 311.

7 Morton, "Of Matter and Meter," 311.

Consider: At its most granular, a poem grows from its environment. The paper on which it is written, paper made from pulp, mulched from the flesh of a fallen tree and stitched into a notebook. Ink with a chemical signature. Letters—the sign, whether concept, breath, a graphite mark, letters joined to form phonemes, words. Neurons firing, to form phrases, music, then transcribed by counterpoint of thumb and fingers that clasp a pen held at a forty-five-degree angle to the page. Later typed: translated from analog to digital, 0s and 1s, and printed by lasers. The energy used to power this: electricity to run the laser printer, to make paper, to farm crops and deliver them to the grocery store, to create meals that feed the poet and fuel the synapses in her brain, pump blood through veins.

To argue that a poem is ecological because it is "made from materials and exists in the world" suggests any poem might be described as an ecopoem; perhaps then it is more precise to say an ecopoem is a poem that has also become aware of these origins and points towards them, like a shirt turned inside out to present the seams. It engages with its own materiality and with our estrangement from this materiality, a materiality within which we are all interconnected.

John Bellamy Foster tells us that Marx described an ecological crisis forced by capitalist modes of production in which humans are severed from the natural world, alienated from the circulation of materials and energy in nature:

> Marx employed the concept of a "rift" in the metabolic relation between human beings and the earth to capture the material estrangement of human beings within capitalist society from the natural conditions which formed the basis for their existence . . . to insist that large-scale capitalist society created such a metabolic rift between

> human beings and the soil was to argue that the nature-imposed conditions of sustainability had been violated.[8]

The ecopoem carries traces of this rift, while also seeking to repair it.

This book also considers at times a more direct political role that an ecopoetry can play: A poem that is sent to the prime minister of Canada and his minister for the Environment, to protest building a second freighter terminal adjacent to Deltaport. A poem that is scribbled on a slip of paper and attached by string to a tree in a forest threatened by clear-cutting; this leads to a constellation of poems documenting a location. A poem written by the young factory worker Xu Lizhi in Shenzhen, China, documenting the supply chains that lead from artisanal cobalt mines to the iPhone I later use to access his poem.

Why lyric poetry and not epic, didactic, experimental poetry, language poetry, Oulipo? My answer is idiosyncratic: Why not lyric poetry? The oldest of literary forms, evolving parallel with song, lyric poetry has an emotional tenor that grounds the reader, grows roots, sends out mycelial tendrils to create slender networks, makes communities. But how might lyric poetry or the lyric mode be joined with these more experimental forms?

---

8 Foster, *Marx's Ecology*, 163. Foster outlines the influences on Marx's thinking here, including concerns regarding soil fertility and degradation in the work of Justus von Liebig, with its focus on chemistry and agriculture, and the popular concept of metabolism or *Stoffwechsel*, as in "material exchange." Marx made use of the concept of metabolism in his thinking on the labour process within capitalism. Metabolism is also a useful analogy—and at times literal description—for the movement of materials and information through the lyric poem.

I circle around key questions: How might the lyric poem—typically a poem perceived to be aligned with subjectivity and emotional content, inward-looking and private[9]—engage with species extinction, clear-cutting, global heating, all the myriad damages and losses, while interrogating elegy, one of the traditional functions of lyric? How might the lyric ecopoem contribute to an imagining of the *Umwelten*[10] of our more-than-human kin, offering a redistribution of sentience, in parallel with legal rights now being extended in some parts of the world to a honeybee, to a watershed, to Pachamama? What are the material conditions—what I will call the poetic ecosystem in this book (economy and ecology)—of the lyric poem, which point towards its own making? How is the lyric poem implicated in the ongoing ravaging of Earth? What expansive forms of attention does the lyric ecopoem tap into, and how might it attune the reader? What openings of consciousness might be offered?

And as oldgrowth specklebelly lichen was constantly in my thoughts for its close association with Fairy Creek, and as there is an abundance of citizen scientist data on this lichen, I ask, What role might data play in the writing of an extended lyric ecopoem? Data is not typically associated with the lyric poem. But I was thinking especially of Nathalie Miebach's meteorological art, in which she incorporates data from hurricanes and atmospheric rivers into beautiful, intricate sculptures where every data point is represented, and where she attempts to "translate" this data, to weave the data into story for the non-scientist.

---

9 Although this is hardly true; look only to the lyric poetry of eastern Europe under dictatorship to see one example of a complex engagement with the political by means of the lyric subject.

10 *Umwelt* (plural *Umwelten*), German for "environment" or "surroundings," is a term coined by Jakob von Uexküll, theorized as "self-centred world," the world that is perceived by a given organism, based upon sensory input yielded by their unique array of senses. Each unique array yields its own somewhat distinct world.

As I hope to write a book-length lyric ecopoem about Fairy Creek, with oldgrowth specklebelly lichen at its heart, I'm also aware that the long poem has not typically been associated with the lyric. Historically, length is aligned with the epic poem, such as Homer's *Iliad*. What is more epic, more world changing, than climate change itself, the breaching of planetary boundaries, mass extinction[11]—phenomena that Morton has referred to as "hyperobjects"—objects so vast in terms of time or space, so abstract, yet at the same time, objects in which we are so completely and materially submersed, that it can be difficult for a human to fathom?

In her *Lyric Trade: Reading the Subject in the Postwar Long Poem* (2024), Julia Bloch considers "how poems both disavow and draw on something they call lyric," in particular, lyric modes as they appear intermittently within the postwar long poem with its "epic ambition."[12] She is interested in the apparent inadequacy of the quiet lyric that poets often invoke and then reject —this "trade" in lyric as mode. She asks, What happens when the long poem "breaks or sweeps into supposedly lyric registers—moments at which the melodic, the personal, the interior, or the private are redeployed to interrogate notions about the subject"?[13] She observes,

---

11 "Planetary Boundaries." While we hear primarily of climate change, as a term it has become shorthand for a raft of crises associated with a damaged ecosphere. The sixth mass extinction refers to human-driven extinction of many forms of life on earth. "Planetary boundaries" is a concept developed by the Stockholm Resilience Centre, a "set of nine planetary boundaries [such as fresh water, ocean acidification, and biogeochemical flows] within which humanity can continue to develop and thrive for generations to come." As of 2023, it is believed we have now crossed six of nine identified boundaries.

12 Bloch, *Lyric Trade*, 3.

13 Bloch, *Lyric Trade*, 5–6.

> When a long poem draws upon the musicality, compression, interiority, or subjective expression associated with something poets and readers call lyric, that poem might appear to reappropriate or reproduce the very kind of lyric it purports to reject. That ambivalent relationship to lyric has implications for how a poem expresses—or does not express—a voice, a self, or a subject. That ambivalence also has implications for the voices, selves, or subjects unaccounted for in language.[14]

I'm curious about this tension, between data and epic length on one hand, and a capacity for the still small voice, the quiet vigilance, of the lyric. How might the lyric mode create spaces or openings for our more-than-human kin, attune our hearing to them, these "voices, selves, or subjects unaccounted for in language"?

I turn also to lichen itself as model for what a long, lyric ecopoem might be, what form it might take. In this, I was deeply inspired by lichenologist Trevor Goward, who offers in his "Twelve Readings on the Lichen Thallus" a beautiful series of essays for thinking sympoiesis, a "making-together" or "making-with." These essays inspired me to think of the lyric poem, as with the lichen thallus, as portal, lens, transcription, emergent; as a conversation, a system "through which matter is continually passing"; as a "community writ small."[15]

Throughout, I consider what a lyric poem can do confronted by the dark ecological crises of our time.

---

14 Bloch, *Lyric Trade*, 5.

15 See Goward, "Twelve Readings of the Lichen Thallus, I–XII."

1. THE DARK MOUNTAIN

An inventory of the current dark-depressing of the planet, an ecological baseline: fire season; the heat dome; the atmospheric river. From the dark-depressing to the dark-sweet. The wild. We mourn; our kin crows and orcas mourn. Ecopoem as seedbank. Ecopoet as interrupter. Urgency and mourning. Elegy and lyric time. Enkidu, offspring of silence. What shining and lichenous form?

> We're fucked. The only questions are how soon and how badly. —ROY SCRANTON, *Learning to Die in the Anthropocene: Reflections on the End of a Civilization* (2015)

> The spectre that many try not to see is a simple vocalisation—the world will not be "saved." Global anarchist revolution is not going to happen. Global climate change is now unstoppable. —ANONYMOUS, *Desert* (2011)

> We do not believe that everything will be fine. We are not even sure, based on current definitions of progress and improvement that we want it to be. Of all humanity's delusions of difference, of its separation from and superiority to the living world which surrounds it, one distinction holds up better than most: we may well be the first species capable of effectively eliminating life on Earth. —PAUL KINGSNORTH AND DOUGALD HINE, *Uncivilization: The Dark Mountain Manifesto* (2009)

> Are we genetically toxic to the wild? I do not know. But I do know that the dominant human culture is increasingly toxic to the wild. —ROBERT BRINGHURST, *Learning to Die: Wisdom in the Age of Climate Change* (2018)

> What is dark ecology? It is ecological awareness, dark-depressing. Yet ecological awareness is also dark-uncanny. And strangely it is dark-sweet. Nihilism is always number one

in the charts these days. We usually don't get past the first darkness, and that's if we even care. —TIMOTHY MORTON, *Dark Ecology: For a Logic of Future Coexistence* (2018)

FIRE SEASON

I began this book in the summer of 2021, just as the heat dome arrived on the West Coast. We were told it was a record heat wave caused by two pressure systems—one from the Aleutians, the other from James Bay and Hudson Bay—which created layers of heated air so high in the atmosphere that the heat couldn't dissipate and remained each night, growing ever more oppressive, untouched by the flow of cooler marine air from the Pacific. My third-floor walk-up apartment in East Vancouver, built in the 1960s, has no AC, no balcony. It can generate a slight cross-breeze with all the windows opened wide. But there was no breeze. The air was deathly still; trapped heat rose from the floors below. As I climbed from the ground floor, I felt the temperature rise by three or four degrees. I can only guess, but I think it was approaching thirty-five degrees Celsius in the apartment.

A heat dome is a rare event, happening perhaps once every two to three decades. I had never experienced one before. We were told it should not be happening at all west of the Cascades. During this event, the hottest temperature ever recorded in Canada was documented in Lytton, BC, on June 29, 2021: 49.6°.

That day I woke to the unrelenting heat in Vancouver and fled my apartment in search of air conditioning on what became a marathon AC crawl: the downtown public library when it opened; the Pacific Centre mall; Canada Place, to receive my second COVID vaccination—Moderna mRNA, to top up a first shot of AstraZeneca—the Generation X cocktail; a restaurant at the train station; a pub by the library. I came home to my apartment at dusk. But the air inside was unbearable, unbreathable, so I went out to the park to lie completely still in the grass, among many others doing the same, immobile. Breathing slowly, trying to glean some small coolness from the earth.

The next morning, I travelled with my friend and colleague Naava to escape the heat dome's edge, taking the ferry from Horseshoe Bay to Nanaimo, driving north through second-growth forests, strips of trees along the Island highway masking clear cuts, to Campbell River. There we caught two more ferries, first to Quadra Island, then Cortes, to the yurt Naava had rented for the summer. We stood at dusk on the deck that surrounds the yurt, built by hand by the two women who rent it out and live here year-round, growing their own food, taking odd jobs, making art. Patchy cell service, as always on Cortes. Three texts from my sister managed to slip through around 9 pm:

> *Lytton in flames—whole town evacuated. Everything burning.*
>
> *Live on TV.*
>
> *Everyone in world now knows about Lytton.*

Later, I read there was hardly time for an evacuation order: "Residents saw the thick black smoke filling the valley, grabbed what they could, and escaped. Within hours, most of the buildings had been consumed by flames."[1] Two people died in the fire. Almost 600 humans died in BC from the heat dome.[2]

---

1 "'Lytton Is Gone.'"

2 Chan, "BC Heat Dome Led to 48 Deaths."

The deck of the yurt, surrounded by cedar and fir, felt cool, shadowed, tempered by sea. We were lucky. At the co-op over the next week, news trickled in, including the heartbreaking report from a UBC marine biologist, Christopher Harley. Based on his fieldwork along the coast in White Rock, BC, he estimated that possibly billions of intertidal sea creatures all along the West Coast—mussels, barnacles, sea stars, clams, crabs, anemones—had been cooked alive in the heat dome, which had unfortunately coincided with a very low tide. These deaths all along the coastline of the Salish Sea were especially notable due to the toughness of intertidal species who are used to a wide range of temperatures, salt water immersion, and daily intermittent exposure to the sun:

> Only an extreme, extreme event could kill them. This massive die-off may result in a radically different shoreline ecology, one without the thick carpet of mussels and rockweed that has lined much of the Salish Sea shore since the last Ice Age. Many land-based species have also died from the heat. I've read numerous reports of flightless nestlings, including hawks and terns, throwing themselves out of nests and off rooftops, risking death and injury to avoid being cooked alive.[3]

This is an extremely rare event. But we are in a climate emergency. Rare events are now common. Creatures are migrating north and south to escape the heat: "Species are shifting towards the poles of the Earth at about 60 kilometres per decade... It often happens in these extreme events, where a large population of something like mussels can die."[4] By mid-July, there were 300 active wildfires in BC, twenty-one fires of note, which meant they threatened human communities.

---

3 Leahy, "If the Hardiest Species Are Boiled Alive, What Happens to Humans?"

4 Malin Pinsky quoted in Shivaram, "Heat Wave Killed an Estimated 1 Billion Sea Creatures."

The interior was tinder, waiting to be ignited by a cigarette spark or a lightning strike. Rain evaporated before it hit the ground.

I don't remember when we began to expect wildfire smoke each summer in Vancouver—2015? 2016?—warnings on hot summer days to close the windows and stay indoors. The eerie, soft pink sci-fi light at noon in Penticton, in Edmonton. Something in the ancient ash-filtered quality of light in Vancouver, most noticeable at sunrise and at dusk, would tell me there were fires inland, or south of us, that Oregon, or California, was burning.

The Intergovernmental Panel on Climate Change (IPCC) Working Group 1 released its report in October 2021 ahead of the COP26 in Scotland and proclaimed a code red for humanity. It outlined twelve tipping points that would

> amplify the impacts of climate change, challenging the ability of species—including humans—to adapt. We will lose current shorelines to rising seas, agricultural land will become barren in extreme heat, and permafrost will melt releasing millennia worth of carbon dioxide into the atmosphere … 'The worst is yet to come, affecting our children's and grandchildren's lives much more than our own,' the 4,000-page report states. 'Life on Earth can recover … Humans cannot.'[5]

In Ada'itsx / Fairy Creek, which lies northeast of Port Renfrew on Vancouver Island, the largest civil disobedience action in Canadian history was happening on the traditional unceded lands

5 Ratcliffe, "The Leaked IPCC Report Spells Disaster."

of the Pacheedaht First Nation, in protest of the logging of old-growth forests by Teal-Jones in tree farm licence 46, so-called Crown lands. In response to the prolonged protests, a two-year deferral on old-growth logging had been announced by the NDP government at the request of the Pacheedaht and Ditidaht First Nations, but the Rainforest Flying Squad, at the invitation of Pacheedaht Elder Bill Jones, were determined to continue their action to protect nearby watersheds.

Later, in the fall, I would travel seven times to Fairy Creek, once driving in a car convoy led by Bill Jones to attempt to access Waterfall camp, destroyed earlier that summer by the RCMP. We would drive in pouring rain along forest service roads through desolate clear cuts and slash piles canted on the steep mountain side, only to arrive at a yellow-painted metal gate and an idling white Domcor jeep, the security firm hired by Teal-Jones. Behind dark-tinted windows, the employee inside denied the Pacheedaht Elder access to the land, telling defenders that any access would be "at the pleasure of Teal-Jones."

But for now, I stood on the deck of the yurt in the Cortes dusk, summer of 2021, as darkness fell.

THE DARK-DEPRESSING

We're fucked. The only questions are how soon and how badly.

I've heard my sixteen-year-old son echo this sentiment, with an almost cheerful cynicism. In *Learning to Die in the Anthropocene: Reflections on the End of a Civilization* (2015), Roy Scranton characterizes our current world order, fuelled by millennia of ancient sunlight, as a "zombie system, voracious but sterile... astoundingly virulent but also toxic, cannibalistic, and self-destructive."[6] (Morton: "We notice that we are collectively a zombie just executing an algorithm."[7]) It cannot be sustained. There is a tinge of misanthropy in Scranton's assessment—humans as swarming *Homo lux*—jacked into a hive mind—Facebook or Meta, Twitter, Flickr, Discord, *Fortnite,* TikTok, Snapchat, Signal, Slack. "We have become vibrations, channelers, tweeters and followers... biologically reactive, easily panicked, all too quickly stirred to hatred."[8] This is partially true—the speed and anonymity of X can lead to online mobbing, instantaneous verdicts, deplatforming. We have an ancient, 300,000-year lineage as a species and seem to need the synchronizing of biorhythms, of the patterns of intake and outflow of breath, of heartbeat and flicker of eye, the pheromones and minute corporeal gestures that speak just beneath the sounding of words. These biological cues signal empathy and temper anger. Online, we lose ourselves and become entangled in a darknet of emails and Instagrams, images of wildfires, clear cuts, plastic gyres, the rising Keeling Curve, melting permafrost, the drunken trees of the boreal.

In my Instagram feed, I see yet another call to come to Fairy Creek:

> **This is an SOS.**
> **RCMP have fully cleared the road to Heli Camp.**
> **They are now patrolling 24/7 and will be allowing industry up in the coming days.**
> **We need you more than we ever have.**
> **COME TO CAMP.**[9]

---

6 Scranton, *Learning to Die,* 23.

7 Morton, *Dark Ecology,* 117.

8 Morton, *Dark Ecology,* 107.

9 @fairycreekblockade, Instagram post, October 21, 2021.

I press "like" and the little empty heart fills with blood.

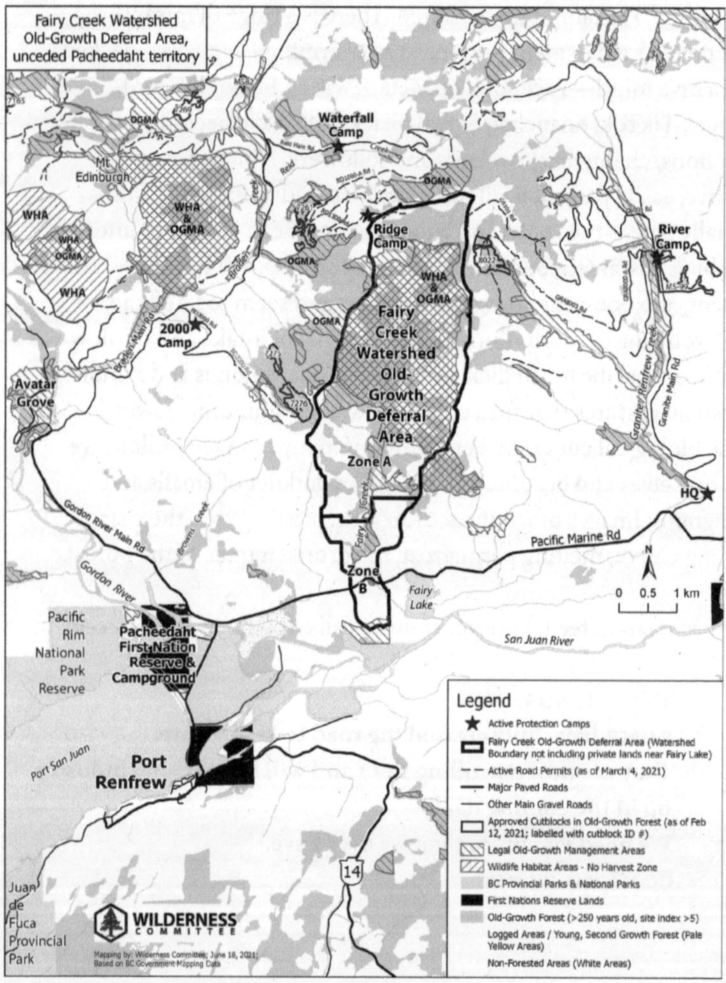

Fairy Creek watershed old-growth deferral area, unceded Pacheedaht territory. *Credit: Wilderness Committee.*

In our hearts we all know the world will not be saved.

The anonymous author of the *Desert* manifesto (2011) cites three alarms from three historical periods, each one increasingly urgent, which I summarize here:

1. Barry Commoner, writing in 1970, the year I was born: "We are in a period of grace, we have time—perhaps a generation—in which to save the environment from the final effects of the violence we have already done to it."

2. *The Ecologist* editors in Edward Goldsmith's *5000 Days to Save the Planet* (1990): "Today we are told that our planet is in crisis, that we are destroying and polluting our way to global catastrophe. We may have as little as fifteen years, perhaps as short a time as 5000 days to save the planet."

3. James Lovelock in 2005—the 5,000-day mark set by *The Ecologist*—in *The Revenge of Gaia*: "we have to understand that the Earth System is now in positive feedback and is moving ineluctably towards the stable hot state of past climates."[10]

I add to this catalogue of alarms the IPCC's Special Report on 1.5 degrees of warming in 2018—"we have 12 years to limit climate change catastrophes, warns UN"[11]—and the IPCC's Sixth Assessment Report, *Climate Change 2021*: "a code red for humanity: the alarm bells are deafening, and the evidence is irrefutable."[12]

---

10 Quoted in Anon., *Desert*.

11 Watts, "We Have Twelve Years."

12 UN Secretary-General António Guterres quoted in United Nations, "Secretary-General Calls Latest IPCC Climate Report 'Code Red for Humanity.'"

Anonymous recounts a familiar litany: tipping points and an irrevocable turn to a hot state characterized by the spread of hot, uninhabitable deserts in the global South and cold deserts retreating in the North; mass migrations of species to the remaining refugia; mass human die-off; rising sea levels; a sixth mass extinction; the end of our period of grace. All of this we have managed to accomplish in thirteen generations.[13] The Earth's current human population is being fed by ghost acreage: "Industrial civilization has managed to push up food supply by both colonising ever-more wild land and developing fossil-fuel reliant green revolution agro-technologies and transportation."[14] They observe, "Most of us are eating oil and illness is largely controlled with energy-intensive technologies."[15]

As an anarchist tract, *Desert* acknowledges that the utopian anarchist visions of past generations have not borne fruit. It takes a bleak and unrelenting look: *The world will not be saved*. Yet the author sees some hope in a world wide system upheaval that may give rise to local, small-scale anarchist experiments—seeds scattered in the scorched hollows. That is, the best we can hope for are dispersed refugia.

We may well be the first species capable of effectively eliminating life on Earth.

The Dark Mountain manifesto tells us we are born in the age of ecocide, an existential crisis the authors link to our underlying myths that set humans over and apart from Sitka spruce, Southern Resident killer whale, paper birch, hemlock looper, oldgrowth

---

13 Anon., *Desert*. Thirteen generations: i.e. since the beginning of the industrial era.

14 Anon, *Desert*.

15 Anon, *Desert*.

specklebelly lichen, Ada'itsx / Fairy Creek, the Salish Sea. We are caught in a progress trap, driven by the myths of civilization and growth, each new carbon-fuelled development a ratchet that locks us into a new and more rapacious gear. We do not see ourselves as part of "nature": We are not "wild." Yet we are wild, and symbionts, carrying within our bodies communities of virions and flora; entangled without, so very much of our genetic code shared by all other species on Earth. They say, our myths betray us. The litany:

> The fallout from this imaginative error is all around us: a quarter of the world's mammals are threatened with imminent extinction; an acre and a half of rainforest is felled every second; 75% of the world's fish stocks are on the verge of collapse; humanity consumes 25% more of the world's actual "products" than the Earth can replace—a figure predicted to rise to 80% by mid-century. Even through the deadening lens of statistics, we can glimpse the violence to which our myths have driven us. And over it all looms runaway climate change, which threatens to render all human projects irrelevant.[16]

Their assessment, as with Anonymous, is bleak. For Anonymous, anarchism will not save the world; for the Dark Mountain authors Kingsnorth and Hine, the green movements have been absorbed and co-opted by neoliberal hypercapitalism. Sustainability is an opportunity for growth and profit. The economy must *always* be nurtured and fed. There is truth to this, if the desire is to sustain the current incarnation of globalization and capitalism. The arguments provided to justify cutting the last 3 percent of old-growth forests in British Columbia include the need to preserve jobs, to keep mills open, to fuel the economy.

---

16 Kingsnorth and Hine, *Uncivilization.*

Industry argues there can be no successful transition to second-growth forests until the last of the old-growth forests are cut down.[17]

My grandfather, Frederik Janke, was a logger—a faller—in the camps around Port Alberni on Vancouver Island, in the 1930s. I have photographs of him in caulk boots and suspenders, in the forest, handsaw slung across his shoulder, axe propped beside him. He met my grandmother in a dance hall in Vancouver, proposed within six months, travelled back and forth from a boarding house to the camps until he'd earned enough money cutting trees, shearing the dense mountainsides, to pay for their first house in East Vancouver, cash down. Bill Jones, the Pacheedaht Elder at Ada'itsx who has challenged the decisions of the elected band council, was a logger of a later era, in the '80s. I've heard him recount that he was told when he began that he'd have a job for life; less than a decade later, he had been laid off, as there was less and less forest, less work. In British Columbia, "we have had a policy of liquidating our forests. For several generations in coastal BC, we demolished good forests, clear-cut countless valleys,

---

17 Parfitt, "Leaked Data Reveals New Threat to BC's Old Growth Forests." In March 2024 Ben Parfitt of the Canadian Centre for Policy Alternatives revealed the BC government has continued, as always, to "talk and log": "For months, officials in the Ministry of Forests have been working on a map that radically departs from the recommendations of a panel appointed by the provincial government to advise it on how to protect British Columbia's imperiled old growth forests. The map suggests that behind the scenes bureaucrats in the ministry, which is often accused of having a deeply embedded logging bias, are intent on undoing the work of the panel and freeing up as much old growth forests as possible to be cut down... 'What's happening behind the scenes is sabotage. The science clearly states we need to protect what little old growth is left, yet our timber friendly forests ministry wants to scuttle those plans,' says Michelle Connolly, director of Conservation North."

and watched giant corporations come through and liquidate this great natural asset and then move on."[18] This legacy continues at Fairy Creek: outrageously, half of the ancient trees cut down by Teal-Jones in tree farm licence (TFL) 46 turn up as wood chips or sawdust, "on its way to a pulp mill or a bag of garden mulch or some other low value product."[19]

@FairyCreekBlockade posts to Instagram:

> X HELI IS FALLING X despite the recent prospective deferral announcement that would affect parts of the Heli camp cut block logging is continuing there at a breakneck speed. It's critical that @johnhorgan4bc put an interim pause on logging while nations have an opportunity to review the deferrals @bcndp is overseeing the destruction of critical habitat to the endangered Old Growth Specklebelly Lichen—we are now finding fallen trees covered in the endangered species. There are too few people at camp to stop the logging from taking place and the contractors for Teal-Jones are pushing into increasingly dangerous conditions as they seek to get all of the trees on the ground before the snows come. Willing to brave a few days in the bush? Come to camp.[20]

I call out to my friends—come to camp. They say they are there in spirit. Some donate money, always welcome. Some don't respond at all. My friend and I plan our next trip around work and family schedules, buy needed supplies, book a 7 am mid-week ferry reservation for the *Spirit of British Columbia,* and pack our bags.

---

18 Williams, "Restoring Forestry in BC," 5.

19 Broadland, "Teal Cedar's Big, Dirty Secret."

20 @fairycreekblockade, Instagram post, November 6, 2021.

❦

Are we genetically toxic to the wild?

This is not a question, so much as a statement. It comes from a little book with a line drawing of two skulls on the cover, also called, as with Scranton's book, *Learning to Die* (2018). It combines an essay apiece by two established Canadian poets, Robert Bringhurst and Jan Zwicky. The observation above is made by Bringhurst. I have puzzled through this book several times, frustrated by the almost cheerful tone of Bringhurst, an elder settler who has had the best of the twentieth century, offering wisdom to a younger crowd who will inherit the worst of it, its grim cascade of emergencies and tipping points in the twenty-first century and beyond, on how to die with grace. His argument seems to be that humans won't survive—look at all the previous mass extinctions—but the wild surely will, he insists, such as the *Vespa orientalis*, which has learned to harvest energy directly from sunlight. The world does not need to be saved—it will continue, as it always has, but in a new form.

Much of his critique focuses on the human species as living adjacent to, or oblivious of, the wild. As he notes, there were

> settler-colonialists arriving on the North American continent in little ships: carracks, caravels, and galleons. Like people who fly in airplanes today, they travelled too fast ever to get where they were going. So they stepped ashore and walked right by the wild. When they noticed it at all, they routinely misconstrued it as a barrier and a challenge.[21]

---

21 Bringhurst and Zwicky, *Learning to Die*, 12.

Yet Bringhurst does this also in his essay, reifying with such generalizations an arbitrary distinction between humans and the wild by building theoretical walls: The wild is that which does not require management by humans, that may suffer from human interference, that is "sufficient to itself" so that "we never know the wild completely"; we are possibly "genetically toxic to the wild," and "the dominant human culture is increasingly toxic to the wild."[22] Even as he writes that the wild is "here inside us too," the walls stand—we contain the wild, but we are not *it*. Recently, I came across an observation by Gisele Maria Martin, a Tribal Park guardian on Wah-nah-jus Hilth-hoo-is (Meares Island), in which she counters such a frame: "We don't have a word for 'wilderness' in Nuu-chah-nulth languages… The closest translation is 'home.'"[23]

Elder ecopoet Gary Snyder's more expansive definition of the wild encompasses this idea of sufficiency, animals as free agents, plants as self-propagating and flourishing, land which has intact indigenous vegetation and fauna "entirely the result of nonhuman forces."[24] Yet he also extends this definition to human individuals: Our bodies are "wild" in their instincts; the unconscious is an "inner wilderness." Human societies are wild when "in a close and sustainable relation to the local ecosystem."[25] Language is a meandering river, or "like some kind of infinitely interfertile family of species spreading or mysteriously declining over time, shamelessly and endlessly hybridizing, changing its own rules as it goes."[26] Snyder quotes Lévi-Strauss as observing that the "arts are the wilderness areas of the imagination surviving… in the midst of civilized minds."[27]

---

22 Bringhurst and Zwicky, *Learning to Die*, 20.

23 Renner, "The Deep Roots of BC's Old Growth Defenders."

24 Snyder, *The Practice of the Wild*, 10.

25 Snyder, *The Practice of the Wild*, 10.

26 Snyder, *The Practice of the Wild*, 7.

27 Snyder, *The Practice of the Wild*, xi.

I like the idea of the ecolyric poem as the wildest of such areas, employing language at its most prolific, shape-shifting, and free.

Both the Dark Mountain manifesto and this little book, *Learning to Die,* seem to counsel withdrawal from all human society and even, at times, admit they look forward to its demise. Here is the most misanthropic, the most dark, of depressing.

Nihilism is always number one in the charts these days. We usually don't get past the first darkness, and that's if we even care.

As I write here on Morton's version of the dark-depressing, it is in the golden, oblique light of a mid-November afternoon, 2021, listening to a press conference assessing the damage done to southern British Columbia yesterday by an atmospheric river event—once in a century, yet the fourth such event this year, following the heat dome, a bomb cyclone, and a tornado near the University of British Columbia. Vancouver has been cut off from the rest of the country as portions of the Coquihalla and the Trans-Canada were wiped out by flash floods and mudslides. Some travellers are still stranded on highways, waiting to be airlifted out. These are the same communities that suffered from the heat dome and the wildfires three months ago. The rivers are rising. This is climate change. COP26 has just closed and been declared largely a failure. (Greta Thunberg: *blah blah blah.*) I recall a video clip I saw on Instagram, posted by Extinction Rebellion Australia, of an uncanny animatronic kangaroo held aloft, crying, smoke rising from its burned body as the lower half is revealed to have been rent of all flesh by the fires, nothing left but seared bone.

Morton charts a conceptual progression through what he calls dark ecology: "It is ecological awareness, dark-depressing. Yet ecological awareness is also dark-uncanny. And strangely it is dark-sweet."[28] He writes that we must move from the dark-depressing through the uncanny to the dark-sweet. The depressing is clear. We know this dark-depressing. We speak now of climate despair and solastalgia; to those most impacted by climate change, people experience this darkness not only as ecological grief but in material and damaging ways—loss of arable land, villages sliding into the ocean, destruction of homes and of ways of life and of lives. This litany is most dire in the global South, as in many Indigenous territories in the North; the Canadian Arctic is heating at four times the rate of the rest of the globe, with severe impacts on Inuit communities.[29] Drought. Starvation. War. Migration. Death. Morton links the uncanny to our 12,000-year history as Mesopotamian farmers, caught in a positive feedback loop, or what Kingsnorth calls a progress trap that progressively ratchets us into destruction of the planet. We are symbionts, hosting worlds within us—gut flora, mitochondria, bacteria, and virions. We are "strange strangers": We are ourselves, yet uncannily not ourselves. We hold worlds within us and are also dispersed across the planet as a massive hyperobject[30] unable to truly comprehend our own widespread distribution. To use Morton's example, I turn over the car ignition and I drive to work; I turn over the car ignition and the planet burns. No single human is responsible for global heating, yet we all are—a sudden awareness of self as criminal. We can't deal with shifts in scale:

> Our sense of planet is not a cosmopolitan rush but rather the uncanny feeling that there are all kinds of places at all kinds of scale: dinner table, house, street, neighbourhood, Earth, biosphere, ecosystem, city,

---

28 Morton, *Dark Ecology*, 5.

29 Rantanen et al., "The Arctic Has Warmed."

30 Morton, *Hyperobjects*.

> bioregion, country, tectonic plate. Moreover, and perhaps more significantly: bird's nest, beaver's dam, spider web, whale migration, wolf territory, bacterial microbiome.[31]

We awaken from a Mesopotamian dream into the uncanny dark.

The dark-sweet is less clearly articulated in Morton; it appears to be a placeholder, like Wainwright and Mann's "Climate X,"[32] for an as-yet-unknown sweet, possibly unattainable future, one which Morton implies might be reached through poetry and play:

> [L]et's go from happy nihilism ["We're fucked!"] to dark nihilism. At first dark nihilism is depressing. Then it's mysteriously dark. Then it's dark and sweet like chocolate. You find the sweetness inside the depression. Don't fight it. Find a way to tunnel down. Find a way to see how things sparkle all by themselves. How they play despite intentions.[33]

I like Morton's categories of darkness, his charting of a path from dark-depressing through dark-sweet—let's call it a placeholder for now, and a space for beauty, negative capability, art, the lyric poem (although always accompanied by many forms of action and community building). And I like his constant attention to, and inclusion of, more-than-human

---

31 Morton, *Being Ecological*, 10.

32 In *Climate Leviathan: A Political Theory of Our Planetary Future* (2018), geographers Joel Wainwright and Geoff Mann from Simon Fraser University posit a "Climate X" as a placeholder for a future planetary government that might avoid the perils of a "Climate Mao" or "Climate Leviathan"—two systems they speculate might evolve out of either communist China or Western democracies. In either instance, the state is monolithic, and climate solutions are dictated by a centralized governing body.

33 Morton, *Dark Ecology*, 116–17.

kin in his writing—bird, spider, whale, wolf. But for now, I will stay a while in the dark-depressing, turning to grief and the role of elegy.

KIAW, KIAW, KIAW

Grief wells up from loss. Energy directed towards a loved one is no longer received. Songs and lamentations allow us to formally channel and ground this energy when the original recipient has been taken from us: a parent, a lover, a child, a newly born orca, an ancient western red cedar. Mourning is hard, necessary work that negotiates our relationships—kinship, friendship, more-than-human kinship—with those who remain and those who are lost. Tears, screams, caoins, rent flesh, ripped cloth, numb extremities, black ashes, dark veils. We dream that the lost one still lives. We hold a wake. We sit shiva. We attend a ceremony, speak ritual words. The mourner's Kaddish. The committal of the dead. A psalm. An elegy. A canticle. *Man that is born of woman hath but a short time to live, and is full of misery. He cometh up, and is cut down, like a flower; he fleeth as it were a shadow, and never continueth in one stay.*[34]

Thom van Dooren observes that our human relationship with death—our knowledge of it and the work of mourning—has historically been included with other characteristics felt to be distinctively, exclusively, human, as with language, rationality, and moral agency, to draw a boundary between humans and all other life on Earth. He then collects many examples of animal behaviour that most humans would interpret as forms of mourning. Elephants are known sometimes to cover the bones of their dead "with leaves or branches and at other times slowly and silently [touch] them with their trunks and feet."[35]

---

34 "The Order of the Burial of the Dead."

35 Van Dooren, *Flight Ways*, 132.

Marc Bekoff described a similar act by magpies, in which one by one they approached the corpse of a companion magpie, "gently pecked at it," then flew off to collect grasses to lay beside the corpse.[36] Konrad Lorenz documented the grieving call of the last remaining jackdaw in his aviary: "It was not how she sang, but what she sang. Her whole song was suffused with the emotion which obsessed her, with the sole desire of bringing back her lost ones by means of the 'Kiaw' call, 'Kiaw' and again 'Kiaw' in all tones and cadences, from the gentlest piano to the most desperate fortissimo."[37] It was noted, of a Ho'okena bird—a Hawaiian crow—after the loss of her mate that she "cried out for weeks... a terribly high-pitched sound, like an inconsolable moaning."[38]

I think of the southern resident orca, J35, known as Tahlequah, whose calf died almost immediately after birth in the summer of 2018. She then carried her calf for seventeen more days over 1,600 kilometres through the Salish Sea, around the San Juan Islands, and along the BC coast. She grew emaciated. Other members of her pod took turns carrying the calf so that Tahlequah could rest. Orca biologist Deborah Giles wrote, "You cannot interpret it in any other way. This is an animal that is grieving for its dead baby, and she doesn't want to let it go. She's not ready."[39] On the seventeenth day, Tahlequah dropped the calf and resumed social interactions with her pod.

Similarly, the West Coast biologist Alexandra Morton describes an orca called Tsitika losing a calf and speculates it was buried by another orca called Blackney in a cleft in the rocks in Tribune Channel, noting that to this day Tsitika has never returned to the waters off

---

36 Bekoff quoted in Van Dooren, *Flight Ways*, 134.

37 Lorenz quoted in Van Dooren, *Flight Ways*, 134.

38 Van Dooren, *Flight Ways*, 134.

39 Giles quoted in Chiu, "An Orca Calf Died Shortly After Being Born."

the Broughton Archipelago, as if remembering her loss. Morton documents another moment when two male orcas, Top Notch and Foster, following the death of their matriarch, Eve, circled Hanson Island, "calling and calling and calling. For the first time in thirty-three years, Top Notch heard no response from his mother."[40]

Crows mourn. Elephants gently touch the bones of their dead. Orcas grieve. Grief, Van Dooren tells us, signals a shared world; we are entangled with our kin, living and dead, as with our more-than-human kin. We search for words and rituals to express our grief in the midst of the sixth mass extinction. Amy, an artist friend, wrote to me in the summer of the heat dome, mourning the loss of all the sea creatures, the mussels, anemones, cooked to death, of the stench of rotting flesh as she walked along the shore at Halfmoon Bay. We live and work with and through our ecological grief, seeking to give it material form.

TOWARDS THE DARK SWEET

In his preface to *Dark Ecology* (2018), Timothy Morton concludes with a poem, in which he describes art as thinking that comes from the future, that which cannot yet be thought explicitly. He concludes that we must "veer toward art" as a result:

> Art is thought
> How thought longs to twist and turn like the serpent poetry![41]

Does this place too much burden on poetry—what really can poetry do? Morton's own poem somewhat heavy-handedly fails to do

40 Morton, *Listening to Whales*, 239.

41 Morton, *Dark Ecology*, 1.

what he praises poetry for—twisting beyond the grasp of certain meaning, embracing polysemy, offering new imaginings, probing along the edges of thought—by placing a straitjacket on the poem: Poetry does this, not that. He is more convincing in the discussion of object-oriented ontology (OOO) in relation to (not) approaching the thing in itself, and I will return to his treatment of the thing in itself, especially in relation to aesthetic concerns, in chapter 7. But I agree with him that there is something poetry can offer when it comes to approaching the radical alterity of the other. The role of art in our approach to the world outside our own selves is important, as is his observation that, inevitably, in artistic registers, as in plain speech, we are "entangled" with the sense data that we study.

In Bringhurst's contribution to *Learning to Die*, as in his poetic sequence "The Ridge," a poetic translation of his essay, there is less beauty and hope, more resignation. He aligns this with "*letting something happen*"[42]—his description for writing a poem, somehow linked to a practice of "thinking like an ecosystem." This is unclear to me beyond a general agreement—I do agree that drift is an important aspect of writing a poem, what Keats called "idleness." Yet Bringhurst's implication is that this practice of letting things happen in poetry is analogous to letting the world go, of learning to die, quite literally. This advice seems unhelpful if you still have half of your life to live, or more; if you have children; if you think not simply as ecosystem but for the next seven generations of kin and more-than-human kin, as you find yourself living through the sixth mass extinction. However, I draw from Bringhurst's essay one shining detail, the evolution of *Vespa orientalis*, oriental hornet, which has an ornate girded band of the pigment xanthopterin that allows it to harvest sunlight, a testament to the resilient adaptation of species on Earth to changing conditions.

42 Bringhurst and Zwicky, *Learning to Die*, 31.

Kingsnorth and Hine's Dark Mountain manifesto lies within earshot of Bringhurst and Zwicky; they express largely grief and resignation, including relief in being able to embrace this grief, and a darkly ironic satisfaction, as former environmental campaigners, in predicting the inevitable destruction of human civilization: "We do not believe everything will be fine. We are not even sure, based on current definitions of progress and improvement, that we want it to be."[43] Where they do show more hopefulness than Bringhurst and Zwicky is in their call for a new kind of art—by artists, writers, musicians, who can unpick and rework narratives that serve as supports for the current hypercapitalistic global regime:

> Ecocide demands a response. That response is too important to be left to politicians, economists, conceptual thinkers, number crunchers; too all-pervasive to be left to activists or campaigners. Artists are needed... Where are the poems that have adjusted their scope to the scale of this challenge? Where are the novels that probe beyond the country house or the city centre? What new form of writing has emerged to challenge civilisation itself? What gallery mounts an exhibition equal to this challenge? Which musician has discovered the secret chord?[44]

I worry that this emphasis on the role of art to confront ecocide—as with Morton's emphasis on poetry as the serpent thought—places too much expectation and burden on the arts, unless it is accompanied by a multitude of other responses, from large policy and legal interventions through energy transition, collective living arrangements, conscious degrowth, and changes in lifestyles. In

---

43 Kingsnorth and Hine, *Uncivilization.*

44 Kingsnorth and Hine, *Uncivilization.*

the face of ecological catastrophe, a lyric poet can feel quite useless. Kingsnorth has written of the accusations he has received of withdrawal and quietism. In his essay "Dark Ecology"—written around the time Morton was drafting his book of the same name, apparently a coincidence—Kingsnorth addresses these concerns by suggesting that civilization as a project has always been about control, intervention, manipulation, and can only ever go forward—progress as ratchet, "every turn forcing us more tightly into the gears of a machine we were forced to create to solve the problems created by progress."[45] He offers five responses an individual can make to this progress trap we find ourselves in, which I summarize here:

1. Withdrawal from the trap: refusal to participate.

2. Preservation of non-human life: for example, by rewilding a patch of land that you have bought: "how can you give something that isn't us a chance to survive our appetites?"

3. Rooting of self in the dirt: get digging, at human scale.

4. Acknowledgement of nature's innate worth, beyond utility.

5. Building of a refuge: "Can you think or act, like the librarian of a monastery through the Dark Ages, guarding the old books as empires rise and fall outside?"[46]

But is there an "outside"? He seems to fall into the same trap as Bringhurst, denying human exceptionalism while simultaneously averring our existence outside of the "wild." Do we hope for nothing

---

45 Kingsnorth, "Dark Ecology."
46 Kingsnorth, "Dark Ecology."

more than the creation of refugia to weather the coming storm? Kingsnorth concludes by suggesting that the world cannot be saved, and that those who believe it can be saved are the ones we need to save it from. There's a strong misanthropic, defeatist, cynical darkness, not at all sweet, shot through the Dark Mountain manifesto.

The *Desert* manifesto, by contrast, is more optimistic. Although here the anonymous author also asserts that the world cannot be saved, they see possibilities to seed wildness and liberty, and that there are "feral possibilities in the cities as almost everywhere." This sounds consolatory, but again, as with refugia, is this all that we can hope for? Possibly. What feral poetry might emerge? Anna Tsing, in *The Mushroom at the End of the World* (2015), cites the *Desert* manifesto when she speaks of the necessity of looking for hope in the disturbed forests and scorched hollows of the earth. Gerard Manley Hopkins, via Anonymous: "Long live the weeds and the wilderness yet." They note that the Chernobyl Exclusion Zone, now lush and overgrown with wildlife, is an example of nature's resilience, with seeds and weeds acting as a form of ecological resistance: "Nature's incredible power to re-grow and flourish following disaster is evident, both from previous mass extinctions and from its ability to heal many lands scarred by civilization."[47] There may still be the same adherence to human as special category, but Anonymous's celebration of the exclusion zones suggests resistance to human exceptionalism.

I began with an epigraph pulled from Scranton's *Learning to Die in the Anthropocene*: "We're fucked. The only questions are how soon and how badly."[48] And while this felt most bleak and dire when I first read it, his book embodies the most hopeful sentiments that

47 Anon., *Desert*.

48 Scranton, *Learning to Die*, 16.

can be gleaned in Morton, Bringhurst and Zwicky, Kingsnorth and Hine, and Anonymous. Scranton uses "die" metaphorically—we as a civilization, a zombie system fuelled by carbon capitalism, must learn to die, in order to live: "Humanity's survival . . . will hinge on our ability to let our old way of life die while protecting, sustaining, and reworking our collective stores of cultural technology."[49] As with Kingsnorth's idea of a monastery or refugia, Scranton specifies the need for biological and cultural arks "to carry forward endangered genetic data . . . endangered seed stock."[50] This is being carried out literally in the form of the Svalbard Global Seed Vault, which collects seeds from seedbanks around the world, in anticipation of a local or global catastrophic event. Similarly, attempts to preserve a vast library of human texts in many languages, including an entire snapshot of the English-language Wikipedia (along with some human DNA and a pinch of tardigrades), has been attempted by Arch Mission Foundation via the Israeli Beresheet rocket that crash-landed on the moon in April 2019.[51] I feel uneasy about this salvage paradigm, but possibly it is simply realistic, and we have no choice.[52]

In my fourth collection of poems, *A blueprint for survival*, the "seed" became an organizing unit for the book as a whole; the first section, "Wildfire," describes in short lyric poems the wildfire seasons we increasingly experience in western Canada; the second section, "Seeds," attempts to describe a range of organisms, ideas, and human-made artifacts that carry useful

---

49 Scranton, *Learning to Die*, 23.

50 Scranton, *Learning to Die*, 109.

51 Rabie, "Why Tardigrades Spilled."

52 The Svalbard Global Seed Vault and Arch Mission Foundation are only two of the more spectacular examples of such archives. I find most hopeful the small seedbanks that carry local landraces. Svalbard essentially functions as a backup to the backup and is global in scale.

knowledge and ways of being in a constantly changing and ravaged world. The two sections are joined by the idea of serotiny—some seeds require fire, heat, burning to germinate and thrive.

Equally compelling to me is Scranton's adaptation of Peter Sloterdijk's conception of the philosopher as an interrupter; instead of resonating with contemporary culture that is amplified through social media channels—the "hive mind"—the philosopher seeks to resist viral waves of thought and emotion. Sloterdijk conceives of interruption, says Scranton, as suspending "continuous processes. It's not smashing, but sitting with. Not blockage, but reflection."[53] Becoming a conductor simply thickens "the reflexive connective tissues of mass society" while interrupting such channels is "anarchic and ... helps us stop and see our world in new ways."[54] I see this concept of interruption as a variant of Simone Weil's conception of waiting, attention, and the void (*l'attente, l'attention, le vide*). I will discuss this in chapter 4. The poet can also be an interruptor, resistant to standard narrative channels, working obliquely, telling the truth slant, drifting always at the edges of the circulation of commodities within a capitalist system, working in lyric time.

In addition to refugia and interruption, Scranton insists on the need to work and rework our "cultural technologies,"[55] the "roots and heirloom varietals of human symbolic life," that "[i]t is not enough for the archive to be stored, mapped, or digitized. It must be *worked*."[56] Writing, as it became more sophisticated, from the earliest preserved scraps of Sappho to the epic *Gilgamesh*, absorbed

---

53 Scranton, *Learning to Die*, 87.

54 Scranton, *Learning to Die*, 87.

55 Scranton, *Learning to Die*, 94.

56 Scranton, *Learning to Die*, 99.

"[r]itual song, image-making, mythology, religion, rhymed speech, memorization, metonymic association, metaphoric abstraction—technologies of social attunement, information storage, ideological mapping, emotional regulation, and political organization."[57]

What Scranton is missing in his discussion, which emphasizes the important role of the humanities in making and remaking our cultures—our books and our cultivated seeds—is a consideration of our entanglement with all other living beings on Earth. His focus is on human culture; this is evident in his discussion of the epic of *Gilgamesh*. Enkidu, "a hair-covered man-beast... the 'off-spring of silence'"[58] who runs with gazelles and sabotages hunters' traps is presented by Scranton, in the battle with Gilgamesh, as a staging of the shift from hunter-gatherer to agriculturalist, and in their union, as a warning against the joining of "civilization and wildness" that leads to "an all-consuming war machine that disrupts the sacred order."[59] More simply, we might read *Gilgamesh* not as a story of Enkidu becoming human but of losing that which is wild: "His friends / Had left him to a vast aloneness / He had never felt before."[60] It is Gilgamesh who insists on journeying to the forest of Humbaba and who, by cutting the giant cedars, brings down upon them Humbaba's rage and Enkidu's fatal wound:

> Everything had life to me, he heard Enkidu murmur,
> The sky, the storm, the earth, water, wandering,
> The moon and its three children, salt, even my hand
> Had life. It's gone. It's gone.[61]

---

57 Scranton, *Learning to Die*, 106.

58 Scranton, *Learning to Die*, 101.

59 Scranton, *Learning to Die*, 103.

60 Mason, *Gilgamesh*, 18.

61 Mason, *Gilgamesh*, 48.

Enkidu is the wild that encompasses the human, the timekeeper who watches over the flocks through the long night, the offspring of silence.

It is mid-December 2021. I'm parked at the side of Pacific Marine at Ada'itsx / Fairy Creek. It's approaching 4 pm as dusk gathers. Shreds of mist drift through dark conifers. Every so often a logging truck rolls past, lights blazing. Roadside is quiet. Landback Bridge, which I helped to retake the last time I was here, and which was held for a week or so, has been lost. More of Heli has been logged.[62] There are not many people left—everyone hopes for the snow to fall so that the road-building and logging might stop until more defenders can come in the spring, when the students are free and weather improves. We are maybe ten or twelve at Roadside, twelve on the mountain, in hiding, on recce. A meeting is called. We stand in the warm tarpee[63] that hosts the kitchen. We stand in a circle and say our camp names. *I'm Cricket. I'm Maximus. I'm Santa Claus, Marlin, Crow, De-Moon, Foxtrot, Bastard Moss.* Timeless arrives late. There are chores—dishes, night watch, building a platform for Logan Staats's performance tomorrow, erecting a shelter for a second campfire down by the creek, turtling to carry supplies—food and firewood—up to the crew hiding on the mountain who will meet at Grandfather Tree. Foxtrot and I offer to do the dishes, as well as a shift on night watch at Roadside. It's a quiet, sombre mood. *But remember,* someone says, *this began as a way to save the Fairy Creek watershed, and we've done that*

---

62 Heli was a land defenders' camp at Fairy Creek, named after the loggers' use of helicopters to access the remote terrain.

63 Pacheco, "Seattle's Contribution to Standing Rock." A tipi-like structure made of tarps and two-by-fours. Pacheco observes that this structure was created by W̱SÁNEĆ (Saanich, "the emerging people") First Nations inventor Paul Cheyok'ten Wagner for protestors at Standing Rock.

so far—nothing has been touched in the watershed. Now we're fighting to save the neighbouring sections of Grandmother and Grandfather Trees.[64]

The oldgrowth specklebelly lichen. The trees at Heli.
The trees at Ridge. The clear cuts I've walked through.
The constant rain edging towards snow. The year darkening.
I have lost someone, recently, the loss dehiscent and raw.

Elegy does the work of mourning in every language. Its Greek roots are in pastoral, a lineage traced from Theocritus, mourning Daphnis; Bion mourning Adonis; Moschus mourning Bion; Shelley mourning Keats in *Adonais*, which gestures back to Bion:

> I weep for Adonais—he is dead!
> Oh, weep for Adonais! though our tears
> Thaw not the frost which binds so dear a head![65]

---

64 Natasha Lavdovsky reminds me in an email: "Fairy Creek was never saved. And it wasn't just the watershed they were fighting for, it was the old-growth in that whole area (on the mountain sides adjacent to the Fairy Creek watershed) and beyond. 'Fairy Creek' was a misnomer... the watershed was just the starting point from which the blockades expanded. The forest where I found the Oldgrowth Specklebelly lichen (on the outer edge of the Fairy Creek watershed) was mostly all cut down in the winter of 2021. That forest was one of the many proposed cutblocks that the blockades were trying to protect on the East flank of the outer Fairy Creek mountain. Inside the watershed the government 'deferred' the forest from logging which is not protecting it... countless forests have been cut in the past few years that were in these so-called deferral zones. The deferrals were meaningless."

In June 2023, the deferral of "old-growth harvesting" in the Fairy Creek watershed was renewed until February 1, 2025. See "Province Extends Fairy Creek Old-Growth Deferral."

As I make final revisions for this book in May 2025, the deferral has been renewed until September 30, 2026. See Coles, "BC Extends Old Growth Deferral in Fairy Creek."

65 Shelley, *Adonais*, 74.

Elegy can be described as a practice of mourning and a manual or liturgy for navigating personal loss.[66] They are stylized laments with ritualized elements and incantatory refrains: "Nonhuman elements of the pastoral world are enlisted in the mourning: nymphs, satyrs, the landscape itself."[67] Now we human elements have been enlisted in mourning the land we have destroyed and the creatures we do not equitably share it with nor recognize as kin.

I don't know what form this expression of grief will take in my own practice. Rage may be a more effective aesthetic from an ethical perspective, and rage has long been an element of elegy, which moods "are sorrow, shock, rage, longing, melancholy, and resolution—often in quick succession."[68] But I am reluctant to move quickly towards resolution; we face urgency and outrageous destruction yet at the same time must learn to see anew, to slow down, to inhabit lyric time, which I feel most acutely, sensuously, in the raincoast forests, often at dusk, as rain begins to fall. How to combine this sorrow with urgency, rage with contemplation? I'm thinking of the oldgrowth specklebelly lichen poem I want to write. I believe a music of ritualized form is necessary, if it is punctured by expression of raw grief coupled with rage—the torn collar, rent skin, gashes like clear cuts or the hoarse caoin of Logan Staats as he sings "Deadman" at dusk, by the chewed-up mouth of Granite Main. He finishes a song and calls out to the two blues who patrol the road, asserting their presence—

> So a couple of weeks ago I was picked up by my braids and slammed on my face by the RCMP, peacefully protesting, singing a water song, protecting an Elder. And you know

---

66 Preminger, "Elegy," 397–99.

67 Preminger, "Elegy," 398.

68 Preminger, "Elegy," 398.

> what the proudest moment for me in the midst of all their fucking colonial violence was? I was able to stand there with a great peace in my heart, and I forgive them and I'll still fight for them and I'll still fight for their children.[69]

There's a tension between elegy—the oldest lyric form, along with lullaby and praise—and this urgent need to resist eulogy, to channel grief into rage, and to fight for the survival of oldgrowth specklebelly lichen and yellow cedar and red sapsucker and marbled murrelet. The sixth mass extinction has begun. We are breaching planetary boundaries. Microplastics and toxic elements saturate our water, our soil, our air. The Earth is heating. A ritual language to do the work of mourning is necessary—we must acknowledge everything we have already lost and will lose, due to rapacious hypercapitalism, neoliberalism, mismanagement, inattention. But this articulation of grief must also act as furious witness to our historical moment, while simultaneously creating a space or clearing for further action. This book considers the form I want my own poetry to take and asks, What tools might lyric poetry bring to a project of co-making of the world with our more-than-human kin, in the face of this slow-burning ecological catastrophe? What furious witness? What shining and lichenous form?

69 I have transcribed his words from my camp journal of December 2021.

2. APERTURE

Fire creates clearings; serotinous beings thrive. Chapter 2 considers the lyric poem as an opening and builds on Heidegger's concept of "clearing" and Timothy Morton's development of "aperture" in relation to an ecological aesthetics of attunement. Cobalt supply chains: What are the material contexts, the poem's ecosystem? I begin to gather materials for the writing of a poem on oldgrowth specklebelly lichen.

OPENINGS

I have been thinking about openings. Writing a poem, when it works, feels as if I have walked into a clearing—all the myriad scraps I've gathered assemble at a subconscious level like underground mycelial threads: cobalt blue, Starlink, oldgrowth specklebelly lichen's translucent *sinuous edges*, chirrups of neodymium, fire watch at Roadside, woodsmoke, Ada'itsx, the tree fairies, *ƛ̓ekoo ƛ̓ekoo.*[1]

APERTURE

In Coleridge's earliest conversation poem, "Effusion 35"—an early draft of what would become "The Eolian Harp"—Timothy Morton identifies an experiment in environmental form, "a way of thinking about relationships between human and nature." The environment, he argues, entails a "radical openness," while the ecologically tuned poem functions as an opening or aperture to receive and sound this openness.[2] He extends this to the critic's work:

---

1 "Thank you" in Ditidaht-Pacheedaht, which I heard as *klecko, klecko,* as we stood around the watchfire listening to Pacheedaht Elder Bill Jones. Spelling is taken from "Ditidaht-Pacheedaht Language Circle."

2 Morton, "Of Matter and Meter," 310.

> A truly ecological reading... would think the environment out of the box—it would include as much as it could of the radical openness of the ecological thought, the profoundest meditation on how everything is interconnected.[3]

Similarly, this interconnectedness is embodied in the poem as artifact—the lined paper in a notebook I bought in a Penticton dollar store during wildfire season, made from second-growth spruce pulp; spruce transported by freighter truck that runs on fossil fuels—compressed remains of carbon-based life, that is, fossilized sunlight; letters of the alphabet formed with black ink made of water, carbon, magenta and cyan pigments; lines drafted at the base of Locomotive Mountain in the Lílwat Nation, sheltering against cool rock as a moth with soot-coloured fur lands on the page.

The Nuu-chah-nulth writer Umeek (E. Richard Atleo) calls this sense of interconnectedness *tsawalk*, a concept—a way of life—which for him is grounded in local traditional ecological knowledge of place. The full phrase is *heshook-ish tsawalk*, "everything is one," where "the universe is regarded as a network of relationships."[4] I see a version of this network in a map of fungal relationships that Merlin Sheldrake reproduces in his *Entangled Life* (2020) of a 30-by-30-metre plot in a BC forest.[5] Each green spiky circle represents a Douglas fir tree; straight lines show links between tree roots and mycorrhizal fungi, with differently coloured lines indicating genetically identical fungal networks: pink for the fungus *Rhizopogon*

---

3 Morton, "Of Matter and Meter," 310.

4 Umeek, *Tsawalk*, 118.

5 Beiler et al., "Architecture of the Wood-Wide-Web," 545. A "dry, cool interior Douglas fir (*Pseudotsuga meziesii* var. *glauca*) forest near Kamloops, Canada (51°51'7"N latitude, 120°31'46"W longitude)."

vinicolor, blue for *Rhizopogon vesiculosus.* Tiny black dots identify sites where samples were taken by the lead researcher, Kevin Beiler, and his team. A small black arrow pointing to a Douglas fir symbol at the bottom right of the diagram identifies the most highly connected of these trees, with links to forty-seven other trees. Here is a beautiful scientific representation of the idea of *tsawalk,* albeit showing only one thin slice of the interconnectedness of the world, like a slide or snapshot of the whole, but still, an opening.

OLDGROWTH SPECKLEBELLY LICHEN

I haven't written a poem for over a year. No, that isn't quite right. I have been gathering words, images, notes for a new "seed"—one of a sequence of poems exploring organisms or human-made artifacts that might offer models of resilience and survival: tiny house, yellow glacier lily, the order Hymenoptera, codex, seed vault, the beautiful cell.[6] Possibly it will become the seed of a new book, on Fairy Creek. The organism I have chosen for this new seed is oldgrowth specklebelly lichen, *Pseudocyphellaria rainierensis,* which has

> curtain-like lobes, a pale greenish blue upper surface, a green algal photobiont (accompanied by a cyanobacterial photobiont in the form of internal cephalodia), ragged, lobulate to isidiate lobe margins, and a pale lower surface bearing scattered small white spots (pseudocyphellae).[7]

---

6 My "Seeds" sequence forms the second half of my fourth poetry collection, *A blueprint for survival* (2024).

7 Committee on the Status of Endangered Wildlife in Canada, "COSEWIC Assessment," iv.

This description in itself is a small, embroidered poem, just as each lichen is a tiny ecosystem, a symbiotic community of photosynthesizing algae and cyanobacteria embedded within a matt of interwoven fungal filaments.[8] It thrives only at the drip zone of ancient yellow cedars and is found growing mostly on conifers (such as amabilis fir) older than 200 or 300 years and which absorb the nutrients their elders transfer from coastal sea fog.[9] Its presence was documented by the artist Natasha Lavdovsky at Fairy Creek, where she found over sixty trees draped in glittering specklebelly. @FairyCreekBlockade:

> X ALL approved cutblocks at Fairy Creek could be clear-cut in the coming weeks. UNLESS @johnhorgan4bc intervenes.
>
> These videos were taken Friday as Teal-Jones workers started to clear-cut the core of the cutblock once defended by Heli Camp. They are now destroying the core habitat of the rare old growth specklebelly lichen. BC Timber Sales' own rules state that these rare lichens require a 200m buffer from logging, and yet @johnhorgan4bc has done nothing to suspend work in this area (which is immediately adjacent to the Fairy Creek watershed—i.e., on the opposite side of the same ridgeline).

---

8 US Forest Service, "About Lichens."

9 Bureau of Land Management, "Management Recommendations." "Oldgrowth specklebelly is nutrient-demanding and establishes exclusively on the bark of conifers with a pH greater than about 5.0. The primary host tree over most of its range is amabilis fir. Yellow-cedar (*Xanthocyparis nootkatensis = Chameacyparis nootkatensis*) enhances the nutrient status of trees growing within its dripzone and thus promotes the establishment of oldgrowth specklebelly in habitats where it would otherwise be unlikely to occur (COSEWIC 2010). Yellow-cedar itself rarely acts as a host tree."

With numbers at camp low we have been unable to stop these trees from falling.

We hope that this footage will be a wake up call.

Drop what you're doing.

Come to camp.[10]

The finding of such a large community of oldgrowth specklebelly was evidence of the age of this forest that Teal-Jones was in the process of cutting down in the summer and fall of 2021. This lichen requires old-growth forests for its nutrients and moves slowly, slowly, in lichen time, dispersing incrementally. The community's size indicates that the forest has been here, untouched by forest fires, long before the lifespans of the current yellow cedars. Lichenologist Trevor Goward observes that when you find such a large population of oldgrowth specklebelly lichen, it suggests the forest has been here for thousands of years: "I'd be astonished if anyone is able to find evidence of charcoal. [Those trees] have been standing in place since glaciation."[11] That is, this population of trees, and their ancestors, have stood in place for the last 10,000 years. We have destroyed many of the oldgrowth specklebelly populations in the last twenty-five.[12]

---

10 @fairycreekblockade, Instagram post, October 24, 2021.

11 Goward quoted in Acker, "Artist Finds New Population."

12 "Species Profile: Oldgrowth Specklebelly Lichen." According to the Canadian Species at Risk Act (SARA), it is listed as Schedule 1, Special Concern, which should prompt an immediate inventory, as well as protection of its habitat. "On northern Vancouver Island, nearly half of the original oldgrowth forest land base within the horizontal and elevational range of Oldgrowth Specklebelly has been harvested, most of it within the last 25 years. In a rainforest region where wildfire…

Lavdovsky translates chemicals found in tiny samples of lichens into sounds. In an image published on her website, entitled "Chemicals of Lichen Species via Thin Layer Chromatography," a purple rectangle is lined at the bottom of the frame by circles of yellow, blue, and pink rings with dots in the middle; tubes of striped colours rise from each circle, each one its own distinct "signature." It is as if looking at a row of test tubes through a violet aquarium.[13]

She notes:

> I processed tiny samples of lichen species from a seaside tree through a chemical analysis called thin layer chromatography. Each column (rising from the circles at the bottom) shows the particular acids present in that lichen, all glowing under UV light. This visual data is now being translated into a soundscape, with the pitch determined by the height of the spot, and the tone generated from lichen micro-sounds or field recordings from the lichens' habitat.[14]

I envy her clear and intriguing process, a poem made of violet circles and streaks of acid glowing in UV light, words run through chromatograph or MIDI board. My own fieldwork began at Fairy Creek in the fall of 2021. I had not come to Fairy Creek with the idea of writing a poem; I had been driven only by an intense sense of urgency to save the old-growth trees. But doing so began to

---

... is rare, industrial-scale forestry thus stands as by far the most important cause of decline in Oldgrowth Specklebelly—both as a result of habitat loss per se, and, in the long term, of on-going fragmentation of the remaining oldgrowth islands" (last updated May 30, 2017). British Columbia, as of November 2024, has yet to legislate a species at risk act.

13 Lavdovsky, "Music for Lichens (In Progress)."

14 Lavdovsky, "Lichen Acid Noise Soundscapes (In Progress)."

seem inevitable over time, as I almost always incorporate my own life into my poetry. For now, I am still at the drifting and gathering stage: an old Instagram post calling defenders to come to camp; rivers of mist threading dark conifers along Pacific Marine; a species profile from the Government of Canada SARA (Species at Risk Act) registry; opalescent specklebelly's glitter within the concave lens of a hand-held scope; two days in pouring rain blockading Landback Bridge; a community of lichen in place since the last glaciation.

ROADSIDE, ADA'ITSX / FAIRY C̓REEK

October 29, 2021, late afternoon. My colleague and I are coming to camp. There's a two-sailing wait at Tsawwassen for Swartz Bay. We arrive in the dark. Drive to Victoria, Sooke, Jordan River, along the coast highway to Port Renfrew on the west side of Vancouver Island, beyond which lies the Pacific. Swathes of sea mist drift over the road. Headlights. Starlight. A graffito on concrete, *#landback*. If this were our first time coming, we'd be lost. At the gas station we turn right, towards Fairy Lake, and arrive at Roadside an hour past midnight. There are two banked fires, and a sleepy, friendly man on watch, camp name Santa. Everyone has a camp name, to avoid easy identification by the RCMP and Domcor, Teal-Jones's hired security force; my friend is Foxtrot, I'm Crow. The sparse crew of land defenders is mostly asleep in their vans or cars. This is our third time here. Every time it is different. We hike down to the creek, pitch our tents under the overpass, and sleep.

We first came to Fairy Creek the day after the injunction[15] was lifted and helped to rebuild HQ—dubbed at the time HQO—as well as to

15 "Judge Grants Temporary Injunction at Fairy Creek." In April 2021 an injunction had been granted to Teal-Jones to stop the protests. It was temporarily lifted by…

fill in the trenches Teal-Jones had gouged out to block public access to Granite Main.[16] The second time we came, the injunction had been reinstated, and we helped to build new barricades. This, our third time, all the camps are down. Land defenders have been forced back to Roadside, now a straggling line of vans, cars, and pop-up tents. There's a kitchen, a woodpile, a warming tent, and a raised platform with the watch fire. Every structure is fortified with heavy-duty tarps to protect against the constant rain. (Arctic Fox, one night at the blockade of Landback Bridge: *Would it just stop raining for one hot minute??*)

The next day we share supplies we've bought from donations made by friends: headlamps, compression sacks, dry bags, whistles, and a body cam for arrestees to wear in order to document their experiences. That night we take the late watch—tend the fire, take notes in a small well-thumbed notebook of any vehicles that pass, keep an eye on

---

...Judge Thompson on September 28, 2021, citing RCMP violence as bringing ill repute on the court, and then reinstated days later by Judge Sunni Stromberg-Stein. Indigenous and ecological protestors argue that injunctions have been weaponized by industry to aggressively pursue energy and resource extraction projects on Indigenous lands. Statistically, injunctions heavily favour industry over Indigenous ancestral territorial rights enshrined in UNDRIP (UN Declaration on the Rights of Indigenous Peoples), to which both Canada and BC pay lip service. The injunction has been transformed "from a tool used by Indigenous people to protect their lands and rights to one which suppresses Indigenous opposition and denies the exercise of Indigenous law" (Gunn, "Injunctions as a Tool of Colonialism").

16 Granite Main is one of the forest service roads (FSRs) that provides access to TFL 46, so-called Crown land—which in theory should be accessible to the public. Teal-Jones used heavy machinery to carve a deep trench across the mouth of the road so that land defenders couldn't access it except on foot. Without a car, it becomes difficult to reach sites and transport supplies higher up the mountain. All defenders now must hike up; tools and supplies similarly must be delivered by "turtles" (hikers laden with heavy packs).

the parked cars and vans that provide shelter for sleeping defenders. Nearby is the carefully guarded Starlink satellite dish, ghostly ear cupped to the sky. At last, we have Wi-Fi and check our phones, hungry for connection. Tending the fire as we watch through the night is an experience familiar to humans going back millennia. We combine the most basic of technologies, fire, and one of the most complex, the smartphone, as we hold vigil with forest and kin.

COBALT / SUPPLY CHAINS

I return to Morton's observation that "Ecological art *is* something. Art is ecological insofar as it is made from materials and exists in the world."[17] This is in keeping with his extended discussion of ecological aesthetics in *Ecology Without Nature* (2007), with reference to the medial, by which he means any reference to the medium in which the art or text is produced. Medial writing "highlights the page on which the words were written, or the graphics out of which they were composed. Medial statements pertain to perception. Usually, we spend our lives ignoring the contact. When the medium of communication becomes impeded or thickened, we become aware of it."[18] He seems to suggest all artworks that reference medial aspects are "environmental in form,"[19] that art by virtue of being made *of* materials, and self-aware as such, is ecological.

If "[a]rt is ecological insofar as it is made from materials and exists in the world," then my iPhone might be considered "ecological" by this definition, and the concept is attenuated, less useful, unless

17 Morton, "Of Matter and Meter," 311.

18 Morton, *Ecology Without Nature*, 37.

19 Morton, "Of Matter and Meter," 38.

I reflect upon it not as opaque, a black box that yet somehow mysteriously opens a window to the world—allows me to talk with someone in Alaska, to view live video of the war in Gaza, to share photographs of a water ceremony I attended recently at the terminal of the Trans Mountain pipeline—but as an amalgam of complex elements sourced through global supply chains.

The iPhone, a smooth, dense lozenge with a pleasant heft, as if an axe head or ritual object, contains miraculous, largely invisible technology brought together through complex supply chains. Briefly, there are sixty-two metals required to make an iPhone, including aerospace-grade aluminum, sapphire glass, lithium, cobalt, graphite, silicon, phosphorous, antimony, gallium, indium, arsenic, boron, copper, gold, silver, tungsten, tantalum, nickel, praseodymium, dysprosium, iron, potassium, and tin. Indium tin oxide, for example, creates the shimmering touchscreen so that I can tap on a hyperlink, open a Gmail, swipe left or right. Sapphire glass creates a lens almost as hard as diamond. A chirrup to notify me of a text is generated from such a tiny space by high-powered neodymium magnets.[20]

At least five of these elements are known as conflict minerals—tin, tantalum, tungsten, cobalt, gold. It has been estimated

---

20 Desjardins, "The Extraordinary Raw Materials in an iPhone 6s"; Avery, "Apple Breaks Ties with 12 Suppliers"; Kara, *Cobalt Red*. Desjardins's article, while informative on the components of an iPhone, is sponsored by Red Cloud Klondike Strike, an equity crowdfunding in mining; they point out that Apple has "managed to guarantee the use of conflict-free tantalum in February 2014." Avery observes that Apple has since had to break ties with twelve suppliers for concerns over conflict minerals, including tantalum. To Apple's credit, it does a yearly "mineral audit," but as Kara observes in his 2023 book, *Cobalt Red*, it is virtually impossible to guarantee that a mineral such as cobalt is mined without the use of child labour, among other human rights and ecological abuses.

that "to obtain the 100 or so grams of minerals found in a single iPhone, miners around the world have to dig, dynamite, chip and process their way through about 75 pounds of rock," in places such as the mines of Cerro Rico ("rich hill") in Bolivia and the mud pit mines of Bangka Island, Indonesia.[21] Clean and ethical supply chains are difficult to monitor:

> Every other year or so, a new "revelation" of terrible mining conditions seems to send [Apple] scrambling. In 2016, the *Washington Post* revealed that "artisanal" mines in Congo, a prime source of cobalt for Apple and other companies, employed children and adults who dig by hand hundreds of feet into the earth for subsistence wages.[22]

While Apple's official mission statement indicates that it seeks to "safeguard the well-being of the millions of people touched by our supply chain, from the mining level to the facilities where products are assembled,"[23] Siddharth Kara, in *Cobalt Red* (2023), has indicated that as of 2022, "there is no such thing as a clean supply chain of cobalt from the Congo."[24] He documents substantial human rights abuses: children taken out of school to work in the mines; deaths from toxic working conditions; injuries, including amputations and wounds that suppurate and lead ultimately to death without the requisite antibiotics; wages of less than one US dollar per day; and "incalculable environmental harm,"[25] obscured by multinational supply chains: "[b]y the time one traces the chain from the child

---

21 Merchant, "Op-Ed."

22 Merchant, "Op-Ed."

23 Quoted in Kara, *Cobalt Red,* 3–4.

24 Kara, *Cobalt Red,* 17.

25 Kara, *Cobalt Red,* 17.

slogging in the cobalt mine to the rechargeable gadgets and cars sold to consumers around the world, the links have been misdirected beyond recognition."[26] They become invisible "externalities."

If the iPhone offers me an aperture into the world—images from the war in Gaza, a Signal to join a water ceremony at Barnet Marine Park on a Sunday morning in June, a phone call from Alaska—a reflection upon the material conditions of its production offers a different kind of aperture into worlds normally concealed by its sleek minimalist shell: "artisanal" mining, child labour, slave labour, deforestation, toxic tailing ponds, an environmental scourge. This list is not exhaustive; the past abuses of the workforce that manufactures iPhones has also been documented, as in the case of the death of twenty-four-year-old poet Xu Lizhi, who, from 2011 through 2014 in the manufacturing town of Shenzhen, wrote poems of his experience as a factory worker for Foxconn Technology Group, known for manufacturing electronic gadgets for Microsoft, Acer, and Apple, among others.[27]

In his poem "I Fall Asleep, Just Standing Like That," Xu documents the assembly line, "machine, work card, overtime, wages . . . / They've trained me to become docile."[28] He describes his body as iron being tooled; his "corners" and "words" are ground away in exchange for a monthly pay slip. In "The Last Graveyard," the workers' iron stomachs are "Full of thick acid, sulfuric and nitric" while "The jig forces the skin to peel / And while it's at it, plates on a layer of aluminum alloy."

---

26 Kara, *Cobalt Red*, 10–11.

27 Rauhala, "The Poet Who Died for Your iPhone."

28 All translations in this section from the poetry of Xu Lizhi are taken from Nao, "The Poetry and Brief Life of a Foxconn Factory Worker: Xu Lizhi (1990–2014)."

The assembly line produces docile bodies and alienated labour:

> Don't know how to shout or rebel
> How to complain or denounce
> Only how to silently suffer exhaustion.[29]

The act of writing—and by extension the lyric poem itself—is also compared to the automated assembly line, which is chiselled with a "steel pen"; this image is elaborated in "Workshop, My Youth Was Stranded Here":

> tens of thousands of workers [*dagongzhe*]
> line up like words on a page. "Faster, hurry up!"
> Standing among them, I hear the supervisor bark.[30]

In poems written towards the end of his life, he describes himself as swallowing "industrial sewage" and "life covered in rust"—all

> now gushing out of my throat
> Unfurling on the land of my ancestors
> Into a disgraceful poem.[31]

Now the analogy between poem and the ingestion of toxic materials is made clear: Young factory worker ingests sewage on the assembly line, piecing together elements sourced in the mines of the Congo and

---

29 From the poem "I Fall Asleep, Just Standing Like That" quoted in Nao, "The Poetry and Brief Life."

30 The image of a "steel pen" is from the poem "I Fall Asleep, Just Standing Like That"; the image of workers lining up like words is found in the poem "Workshop, My Youth Was Stranded Here," both quoted in Nao, "The Poetry and Brief Life."

31 From the poem "I Swallowed a Moon Made of Iron" quoted in Nao, "The Poetry and Brief Life."

vomits a "disgraceful poem." The lyric poem here becomes as much a product of the assembly line and its supply chains as the iPhone.

In one of his last poems, dated January 9, 2014, "A Screw Fell to the Ground," Xu Lizhi draws an analogy between a falling screw and a worker who has chosen to end their life by plunging off the roof of the factory:

> A screw fell to the ground
> In this dark night of overtime
> Plunging vertically, lightly clinking
> It won't attract anyone's attention
> Just like last time
> On a night like this
> when someone plunged to the ground.[32]

With this common trope—worker as cog or screw—he prefigures his own death. He took his own life in similar fashion on September 30, 2014.[33]

Just as the iPhone is an aperture—if we choose to look—into the entwined chains of labour abuses associated with artisanal mining in the Congo and Chinese assembly line production of high-tech gadgets for those most privileged, so are the lyric poems of Xu Lizhi.

By extension, we must consider the complicity of the lyric ecopoem as well, both in general terms and in the specificity of each poem—as a poet I must consider the poem's "ecosystem," by which I mean

32 Quoted in Nao, "The Poetry and Brief Life."

33 Nao, "The Poetry and Brief Life." There were fourteen deaths by suicide reported to have taken place at Foxconn in 2010. The company responded to this spate of suicides by installing nets around the workers' dormitories.

the conditions of its making, which can comprise everything from the trees felled to create the paper on which a first draft is scrawled; the smart minerals mined by abused humans and their alienated labour to produce a laptop on which the poem is typed up, so as to be submitted to publisher or literary journal; even the life of the poet, who has the food and water, energy, time, and other resources to observe, think, travel, and write the poem. I'll return to this idea of the poem's ecosystem in the next chapter, in my discussion of Wordsworth. But I will assert here that to incorporate the ecosystem into the poem does not demand a tone of guilt or atonement or elegy; rather, it requires awareness, engagement, and fury at the abject global system that mindlessly produces such externalities as a suppurating wound, a dearth of antibiotics, a damaged child. The poem's ecosystem can be stitched into its fabric, can reveal its seams and the externalities of its own production.

RADICAL ATTUNEMENT AND THE LYRIC POEM

I return to Coleridge's "Effusion 35," as read by Morton, as an aperture, an opening into other worlds; it is a "good poem for thinking with" that offers a "strange contemplative materialism,"[34] not a shutting down but an opening.

In a draft of "The Eolian Harp"[35] in which Coleridge attempts the section on pantheism, in which all beings and things are described

34 Morton, "Of Matter and Meter," 316.

35 The eolian harp is a harp played by the wind, a popular domestic instrument in the nineteenth century.

as lutes that soul animates, the poem's medial nature is obvious—ink splotches, words scratched out, an attempt at an idea. The draft reads,

> And what if All of animate life
> Be but as Instruments diversly fram'd
> That tremble into thought, while thro' them breathes
> The infinite and intellectual Breeze?

Seven lines are then scored out. Morton's appealing description of an ecological reading would ask us to consider this writing as process, the manuscript itself as transcription of the act of thinking, of writing into an opening—process and trace are elements of the ecological poem, as much so as an awareness of its mediality, such as the supply chains embedded in the materiality of the page—the crushed pulp from a tree that may have taken from a hundred years to a millennium to translate sunlight into carbon; the elemental, molecular contents of the ink—gall nut, iron sulphate, gum arabic—used to scratch letters into paper on August 20, 1795; the metal type that impressed uniform shapes into the page of the 1796 edition of *Poems on Various Subjects* under the title "Effusion XXXV," a poem to which Coleridge returned many times throughout his life, working and reworking it, as if the poem itself were an eolian harp that slumbered, then sounded again when the spirit took him.

Morton reads the eolian harp in Coleridge's poem as a figure of automation, which recalls Xu Lizhi's factory poems where the lyric poem itself is figured as aperture for the documenting of externalities that the poet has of necessity internalized and then expelled. In *Ecology Without Nature,* Morton develops this figure of the eolian harp within a larger framework, naming one of the six modes[36] of the ecological

---

36 Morton, *Ecology Without Nature,* 30. In the first chapter, Morton contrasts weak...

aesthetic the "eolian," which "ensures that ambient poetics establishes a sense of processes continuing without a subject or an author."[37] In the eolian mode, there is no obvious source for the music or voice, as in a voice-over in a film. As with the medial mode, this move not only shifts the production of ecological meaning from poet to critic, who is now the one required to offer a creative, attuned, ecological reading of the materiality of the poem and the method of its production of various categories, such as "nature" and so on (and Morton is a beautifully creative reader). Yet the lyric poet can equally become attuned to the medial, which is adjacent to what I've called the poem's "ecosystem."

A consideration of the poem's ecosystem places emphasis on automation, production, and inevitably supply chains, in relation to place, as in the poetry of Xu Lizhi, who offers a radical attunement of the individual worker/poet to the automated processes that currently govern our lives. These processes are articulated in his poems, which can be accessed via the 8 grams of refined cobalt in a smart phone[38] possibly mined by a seven-year-old child in the Congo, thus enabling our own indentureship within the closed loop of endless self-reflective scrolling guided by tailored zombie algorithms.

... ecomimesis—"whenever writing evokes an environment," and which can be traced back to classical rhetorical strategies—with David Simpson's concept of the modern idea of situatedness, "linked to the urgency of impending and 'threateningly nondiscriminatory' ecological peril." Morton identifies this idea of situatedness with a strong ecomimesis, which he describes as making use of a "poetics of ambience," of which there are six features or modes: rendering, the medial, the timbral, the eolian, tone, and the re-mark.

37 Morton, *Ecology Without Nature*, 41.

38 Kostadinov, "The Cobalt Rush."

Yet the eolian harp, as with the lyric poem, offers openings not only into these convoluted and complicit capitalist networks but also to the bodies and consciousnesses of other beings, and therefore to a different, complementary form of radical attunement. In her brief history of the eolian harp, the stringed instrument that is played by the wind, Shelley Trower outlines how it became a model for various theories of perception in the nineteenth century, a "model for a human/mind/body conceived as a machine for translating sensory vibrations into consciousness."[39] That is, as new theories of the human nervous system arose—for example, David Hartley understood nerves as analogous to strings that vibrate—the eolian harp was seen as modelling this process. The strings receive the wind and, from this reception or openness, form harmonious sounds; there is an entangling of stimulus—both from outside the body and from within, as the nervous system, the nerves, respond. Similarly, then, according to Trower, "such vibration will be at its most intense when the transmission takes place directly between human bodies. Poetry spoken aloud vibrates between the bodies of the poet and the listener."[40] It becomes a shared vibration, enabled by the musical sonority of the poem, and offers a glimpse into the consciousness of another human and their thought processes. Trower limits her observations to intra-human communication, but poetry has many aural and conceptual tools at hand to empathetically imagine the bodies and potentially sentient experiences of more-than-humans, thereby dilating being and time, creating an opening for another being—wind, starfish, yellow cedar, specklebelly. To convey such experiences or *Umwelten*, different senses inaccessible to humans, and different engagements with time, must be imagined, as in Bawaka Country et al.'s discussion of starfish time—"[s]tarfish may seem to be still, but longer attention, through time-lapse photography for example,

---

39 Trower, "Nerves, Vibration, and the Aeolian Harp," para. 2.

40 Trower, "Nerves, Vibration, and the Aeolian Harp," para. 17.

shows them moving, changing."[41] They reference Ada Smailbegović's discussion of the impact of global heating on larval hatching and note that "[l]arval time is the right time for eggs to hatch, a deeply relational and contingent time."[42] Smailbegović observes in her *Poetics of Liveliness* (2021) that the temporal rhythms of geological processes and more-than-human kin may exist beyond the "human sensorium."[43]

Different impressions of time experienced by more-than-human kin—including what Bawaka Country et al. describe as "radically different" impressions—call to humans for the most open and receptive forms of attention and imagining. I love this idea of larval time, starfish time, tree time, as acknowledging and protecting these different ways of being—the long duration of a yellow cedar (*Xanthocyparis nootkatensis*) in Fairy Creek that draws carbon down out of the sky, turns sunlight into energy, stitches hydrogen to carbon, releases oxygen, makes incremental rings of dark wood and light wood, exchanges signals with other trees through subterranean mycorrhizal threads. Bawaka Country et al. argue that this radical alterity is "incomprehensible to humans. We can't know how and what these beings know. But we can be aware that they have knowledges and experiences beyond us."[44] I would argue that awareness is a good beginning, but artistic practice allows for a sympathetic imagining, which can be extended to a yellow cedar as to a red-legged frog, a specklebelly lichen, a western screech owl. This tuning in and being in resonance, in tune, with other beings on this earth is an expression of *guruttu*—"more than human kinship"[45] and is within hearing of *tsawalk*, everything is one.

---

41 Bawaka Country et al, "Gathering of the Clouds," 298.

42 Bawaka Country et al, "Gathering of the Clouds," 298.

43 Smailbegović, *Poetics of Liveliness*, 284.

44 Bawaka Country et al., "Gathering of the Clouds," 298.

45 Bawaka Country et al., "Gathering of the Clouds," 296.

I have been thinking about the lyric ecopoem and its constitutive elements in my own practice as I draft the conclusion to this essay. It is fire season again here on the West Coast, as across the continent. *The Washington Post*'s headline reads "It's Canada's Worst Fire Season in Modern History, as Smoke Fills Skies."[46] The boreal is burning across the country, a dense, particulate smoke caused by the incineration of ground-level flora and peat. Images are posted of New York City; Washington, DC; Montreal; Toronto, all mired in thick haze. North American wildfire smoke has even travelled across the Atlantic on the jet stream and caused brilliant sunsets in the UK.[47] In BC, the Donnie Creek wildfire is the largest BC wildfire on record, burning 5,715 square kilometres as of July 2, 2023, and might continue through the winter, "smouldering in deeper organic layers" only to return again next season.[48] Its smoke is visible from space.

How can a lyric poem respond to this burning? I remind myself that fire creates clearings in which serotinous beings thrive. The poem might represent such a clearing or be one of these serotinous beings that thrive in the scorched hollows.

I open my notebook to a blank page and make a list.

The lyric ecopoem I seek to write:

---

46 Livingston, "It's Canada's Worst Fire Season in Modern History."
47 Russell, "Satellite Images Show Canadian Wildfire Smoke over UK."
48 Kulkarni, "What Happens After the Donnie Creek Wildfire, Now Larger than PEI, Stops Burning?"

- is an aperture, a clearing, and seeks attunement: with the world as it currently exists in its fractured and desolate being, and with other beings.

- is medial and recalls its material being: paper, ink, tent, nest, shell, clay; is a made thing and takes cues from the chickadee nest and the snail shell; is an act of co-making this world; is an ecosystem, self-aware of the externalities that produced it.

- is vigilant; uses the right hemispheric forms of broadband attention; is alert; practises a sustained attention; is open to new possibilities, sights and sounds, in order to participate in a redistribution of sentience.

- is an ecological witness, in the manner of field notes; will test data and materials, like a Miebach sculpture.

- is open to listening and imagining the *Umwelt* of other beings and our more-than-human kin; will carry the music of these *Umwelten.*

- will acknowledge and draw strength from Indigenous models of grounding song in specific place, in the knowledge that "everything is one."

- will respect the darkness of other beings in their withdrawing.

3. CO-MAKING

Paper, ink, nest, shell, clay. A poem is a made thing and takes cues from the chickadee nest and the snail shell. A poem is an eclectic assemblage of clicks and phonemes, silence and sounds, ink strokes, slashes, dots, letters, white spaces, and fibre, tracing the movement of ligament and sinew and bone through time. The poem as extended phenotype for the redistribution of sentience to the more-than-human world.

NESTWORK

My artist friend and sometime collaborator Amy, whose current work involves cloth, lettering, light, and community performance, asks for my help in revising her proposal for an artists' panel she is organizing, in which the artists will be called to work with a common pattern, a *nestwork*. Their context will be "new models for making amidst what is a great unmaking of the world."[1] The unmaking is palpable—the rise in zoonotic viruses as humans penetrate the farthest reaches of the earth—COVID, SARS, MERS, Zika), the greatest release of carbon dioxide into the atmosphere since my birth in 1970. Amy describes her own intimately known site along the Pacific Flyway in Ladner, which she walks and observes each day as part of her artistic practice:

> This year I saw no butterflies at my site. Two years ago, many species of lichens disappeared. The eagles' nest fell in a place where trees grow scarce—I watched the pair attempting to build in inadequate trees for months until they stopped. The swallows, aerial insectivores, the greatest of aviators, disappear here at 7% per year. A widening silence grows, the world emptying.[2]

1 Huestis, "Co-making This World," private draft shared with author.

2 Huestis, "Co-making This World."

I suggest looking at Elaine Scarry on making, Donna Haraway in *Staying with the Trouble* (2016), Anna Tsing in *The Mushroom at the End of the World* (2015), on searching for life in the capitalist ruins. Amy feels intense grief at the losses she perceives all around. Her proposal offers to take this ecological grief and channel it into a creative interweaving with more-than-human partners, a cultural rewilding:

> I propose we entangle our practices with biological systems, and bring science, story telling, and culture together in the same landscape. I propose we build a nest into this academic ecology, and imaginatively increase biodiversity within this online conference format. The nest as place for regeneration, a becoming place, a place for delicate and vulnerable things, for entanglements, a healthy place for common purpose.[3]

Amy chooses as her model the nest of the black-capped chickadee, *Poecile atricapillus. Poikilos,* as in *Poikile*—dappled, pied, many-coloured; and *atricapillus*—black-headed. Its common name "chickadee," or, in Abenaki, *kejegigilhasis,* is onomatopoeic[4] for

---

3 Huestis, "Co-making This World."

4 Cowasuck Band, "Lesson 10—Animal Names"; Schwartz, "How Five Common Birds Got Their Names"; Liebich, "'Tshcick-a-dee-dee': Chickadees." According to the Cowasuck Band, *kejegigilhasis* is Abenaki for "chickadee." There are seven types of chickadees in North America. Schwartz writes, "Anyone who has heard these inquisitive little birds will likely have no trouble imagining where their name comes from. They seem to say 'chicka-dee-dee-dee' as they hop from branch to branch. Turns out this was not lost on the white people that 'officially' named the bird in North America nor the native tribes that were here before. Multiple sources cite the Cherokee word for this little bird 'tsigili'i' as the Cherokee also attempting to ascribe a name to the bird imitative of its sound. While the Cherokee name was recorded in texts before the English term was, it's unknown if the English word was an Anglicization of the native name or if the two words were coined independently to describe the same distinctive sound." Liebich says the Gwich'in call the…

its "astoundingly complex" call: *chick-a-dee-dee-dee, ke-je-gi-gi-gi.*[5] It is a call used to locate food and warn of predators.

This past spring I discovered a pair of black-capped chickadees had nested in the small green birdhouse nailed under the roof of my covered porch. I would see one of the pair fly up to the peephole with food in its mouth and poke half of its body into the dark. There would be the sound of many little bodies peeping. When the parent turned around and flew away, a little head would pop up and peer through the opening, waiting for the next delivery. This carried on for several days, until I forgot to look for them, and suddenly realized one day that they must have all fledged and gone.

Chickadees will build their nests in the cavity of a tree, a nesting box, the empty nest of a woodpecker, or any rotting trunk that can be excavated. The excavation, if required, is carried out by both male and female chickadee, and can take seven to ten days to complete. It is the female chickadee who builds the actual nest, "which is fairly complex, starting with coarse material like moss, pine needles, or strips of bark as a foundation. Then it is lined with softer material such as animal fur/wool/hair (rabbit, deer, dog), downy plant fibres (e.g., cattails), spider webs, insect cocoons or feathers."[6] The nest is tiny, approximately 1 inch deep, as is the clutch of six to eight eggs, each egg ⅔ by ½ inches and streaked with reddish brown lines and spots at the egg's larger end.[7]

... chickadee "Ch'idzigyaak," while the Inupiaq know the birds as "iknisalaq," "misikaagaq," and its voice as "cikepiipiiq," which is the Yupik name for the bird.

5 Proppe et al., "Acoustic Transmission"; Cowasuck Band, "Lesson 10—Animal Names."

6 Zimmerman Smith, "All About Black-Capped Chickadees."

7 Zimmerman Smith, "All About Black-Capped Chickadees."

The bird nest is an example provided by Richard Dawkins of the extended phenotype; he argued that "it attempts to free the selfish gene from the individual organism which has been its conceptual prison. The phenotypic effects of a gene are the tools by which it levers itself into the next generation, and these tools may 'extend' far outside the body in which the gene sits, even reaching deep into the nervous systems of other organisms."[8] That is, the chickadee's genotype not only carries instructions on how to make the body of the chickadee but also an intrinsic knowledge of how to make a nest in order to reproduce itself.

Recently, Amy told me with delight of the materials hummingbirds use to construct their little nests, "tiny archaeological gems."[9] It reminded me of Anna's hummingbird, which stopped the building of the Trans Mountain Expansion (TMX) pipeline along the Brunette River in Burnaby for almost four months in 2021 when workers were found felling a tree with an active nest.[10] These are some of the earliest hummers to nest, beginning with the rains in November. The CNFN (Community Nest Finding Network) reported finding eight active nests at the worksite and noted there were many more.[11] CNFN co-founder Donna Clark said, "in the last 30 years, we've lost 70 per cent of our birds... These beautiful mama Anna hummingbirds, these little birds that have stopped the pipeline, they are... the canaries in the coal mine."[12]

Here is how Anna's hummingbird, *Calypte anna*, builds her nest. She finds a thinner branch on a deciduous tree, preferably at a fork in the branch (never a cavity in a tree) that is sheltered from the elements;

---

8 Dawkins, "Preface," *The Extended Phenotype*, 6.
9 Hummingbirds Plus, "Hummingbird Nest Facts."
10 Logan, "Hummingbirds Put a Temporary Halt."
11 Logan, "Hummingbirds Put a Temporary Halt."
12 Clark quoted in Logan, "Hummingbirds Put a Temporary Halt."

eucalyptus, oak, and sycamore are favoured but sometimes Douglas fir will be used if necessary. She begins with twigs and bits of plants to create a scaffolding—thistle, cattail, willow. Softer materials are used to line the nest, such as leaf fuzz, small feathers, cotton fibre, bark, and insect cocoons. The wind-facing side is thicker than the top, which is thinner for temperature control and air flow. The outside is camouflaged with bits of moss and lichen, and the entire structure is woven together with spider silk. A video I have seen shows an Anna's hummingbird fly to her nest with gossamer strands strewn across her beak and breast; she settles down and extends her neck to rub the gossamer onto the edges of the nest; "[t]he silk, which holds the nest together and anchors it to a foundation, is inserted into nooks and crevices to ensure attachment. Construction requires several hours each day" for a week or so.[13] The completed nest looks like a tiny cup, perhaps the size of a Ping-Pong ball, and resembles a tree knot; it is elastic and spongy, so that the nest can expand as the tiny jelly-bean-sized eggs, a clutch of only two, hatch and the young grow.[14]

These are recent migrants to BC and have only been breeding here since 1986; they are especially resilient in urban environments and thrive near humans. An Anna's hummingbird weighs perhaps 3 to 4 grams (think a nickel). Yet they are strong.

Kukpi7 Judy Wilson of the Neskonlith Indian Band noted, regarding the halt to construction of TMX when Anna's hummingbird nests were found:

---

13 Details on Anna's hummingbird nest construction are drawn from Stonich, "Hummingbird Nests 101."

14 Stonich observes, "Because it is adorned with compacted green lichen, moss, and spider silk, a hummingbird nest can appear like a small knot of wood. Its shape and coloring work as camouflage to keep hummingbird eggs and chicks safe."

It is very symbolic that a tiny hummingbird has stopped local construction of this pipeline. At the same time, it is not entirely surprising, either. Many stories honour the qualities of Hummingbird, and one that stands out, in particular, is Hummingbird's tenacious loyalty to the forest. Even as the forest burned and all the other animals fled, Hummingbird carried drops of water—in their tiny beak—from the river to the forest fire. In response to the other animals, Hummingbird said: "I'm doing what I can."[15]

Anna's hummingbird (*Calypte anna*) nest, California.
Credit: Steve Berardi, Flickr, CC Attribution-Share Alike 2.0 Generic.

15 Kukpi7 Judy Wilson quoted in Logan, "Hummingbirds Put a Temporary Halt."

SNAIL SHELL

Another beautiful kind of making, although not an extended phenotype, is the snail shell, chiralic, logarithmic. The newly hatched snail devours its remaining eggshell as a source of calcium and then moves on to other calcium-rich sources—turnip, spinach, kale, limestone. A shell is slowly secreted at the mouth of the protoconch, spiralling to form the apex—the tip or highest point—of its shell. There are three layers: a thin outer layer, the *periostracum*, made of protein; a middle layer, the *ostracum*, made of hard calcium arranged in prisms and plates; and an inner layer of calcium carbonate or *nacre*—mother of pearl. The colouring of the periostracum is drawn from the food it eats. The shell is chiralic—asymmetrical—they cannot be "superimposed on mirror images of themselves."[16] And they are logarithmic—a *spira mirabilis* or "marvellous spiral": on each revolution of the shell the spiral increases in size but its shape remains the same. *Eadem mutata resurgo*—'Although changed, I shall arise the same.' The logarithmic spiral is found in many natural phenomena: nautilus shell; sunflower head; the approach of a hawk to its prey; of an insect to a source of light; the spiral arms of our galaxy, the Milky Way; the nerves of the cornea; the bands of hurricanes.[17]

In the prose poem "Snails," in Francis Ponge's *Le parti pris des choses (Partisan of Things / Taking the Side of Things)*, first published in 1942, we learn that snails glue their whole bodies to the earth, "they carry it, they eat it, they shit it. They go through it, it goes through them. It's the best kind of interpenetration."[18] Entanglement gives way

---

16 Stein, "How a Snail's Shell Gets Its Twist."

17 Examples of *spira mirabilis* come from Wikipedia, "Logarithmic Spiral," accessed May 20, 2021, https://en.wikipedia.org/wiki/Logarithmic_spiral.

18 Ponge, *Partisan of Things*, 19.

to humour: "their immaculate clamminess. Their sang-froid. Their stretchiness";[19] their existence is refracted through human emotion and human perception. Ponge's translator Joshua Corey, in his introduction to *Partisan of Things*, praises Ponge for discovering "a subversive and quietly Ovidian subjectivity in ordinary things, manmade (a crate, a cigarette) and otherwise (trees, a pebble)—a subjectivity matched by the perversity and wilfulness of words themselves."[20] He reads Ponge's focus on things as a "war" Ponge wages against "the overwhelming subjectivism of language" while taking the side of things also offers "a resistance to the thingification of human beings central to Nazification."[21]

Similarly, in Jane Bennett's *Vibrant Matter* (2010), in which she attempts to "present nonhuman actants on a less vertical plane than is common" and therefore to undermine human exceptionalist positions, she emphasizes "the material agency or effectivity of nonhuman or not-quite-human things."[22] While the phrase "not-quite-human things" undermines her desire (more-than-human, which I use, perhaps does so also by continuing to centre humans in the phrase), she beautifully insists on considering the "shadows" and acts as advocate for the vitality and agency of matter, from earthworm through electrical power plant. She says her instinct is that "the image of dead or thoroughly instrumentalized matter feeds human hubris and our earth-destroying fantasies of conquest and consumption. It does so by preventing us from detecting (seeing, hearing, smelling, tasting, feeling) a fuller range of the nonhuman powers circulating around and within bodies."[23] Anthropomorphization

---

19 Ponge, *Partisan of Things*, 19.

20 Corey, "The Challenge of Francis Ponge," i.

21 Corey, "The Challenge of Francis Ponge," ii.

22 Bennett, *Vibrant Matter*, ix.

23 Bennett, *Vibrant Matter*, ix.

and personification become valuable tools, then; she says that at times she "overasserts" agentic powers typically ascribed only to humans when describing other-than-human beings and materials, to counter human narcissism. Hers is also an ethical project that seeks to generously redistribute the value we place on particular bodies and to underscore the entanglement of such bodies: "in a knotted world of vibrant matter, to harm one section of the web may very well be to harm oneself."[24] She further elaborates on this as directing a "sensory, linguistic, and imaginative attention toward a material vitality."[25]

Lyric ecopoetry participates in such a project[26] and is well served by poetry's tools: *to direct sensory attention* towards other beings in the form of imagery, which draws upon all human senses and can make attempts to translate unfamiliar senses experienced by other animals and organisms, thus translating their unique *Umwelten; to direct linguistic attention,* in its lexical, semantic experimentation that transgresses language barriers and often places emphasis on the sonorous and semiotic over the symbolic; and *to direct imaginative attention* through the use of tools such as metaphor, metonymy, and analogy, drawing comparisons between unlike things, seeking sympathetic yet surprising connections.

To spiral out from these observations, Ponge equates the snail's sticky, "slimy trail" as ephemeral, associated with "everyone who

24 Bennett, *Vibrant Matter*, 13.

25 Bennett, *Vibrant Matter*, 18–19.

26 My Marxist cultural geographer friend Noah jots a note in the margin of my manuscript: *I think you need to make the further point here that the poem is co-making in the sense that there are active agents (e.g., landscapes, ecosystems, branches, papers) that are participating with the poet in making the work (although a real "Actor-network theory" approach to a poem might consider the store where the paper was bought, the rice maker which saved time for the poet to avoid cooking, etc., all steps in the network.)*

speaks in an entirely subjective way, in verses and lines only, without taking care to build their phrases into a solid dwelling with more than two dimensions."[27] But their shell, their existence, is a "work of art" like a dwelling, which remains.[28] The subjective is chided within the tradition of the lyric poem—by which I take Ponge to mean that language in lyric poetry most often attempts to present the thoughts, sensations, qualia, of the poet herself and becomes too self-preoccupied, too human-preoccupied. Lyric poetry, misconstrued in this manner as locus of such subjectivity, has too often been the whipping girl of post-structural theory, when in fact, lyric can and has been subversive, political, capable of speaking in code, sympathetic to other beings, attentive, entangled. And as I just noted, lyric poetry has a role to play in the redistribution of this subjectivity, in sympathy with Bennett's ethical project regarding vital matter. Ponge, in attempting to use this subjective quality to redistribute sentience in prose poems about moss, molluscs, a cigarette, and so on, makes an important intervention in, and modification of, the lyric form.

Despite critical denigration of the lyric poem as subjective and solipsistic, overly preoccupied with the self, with consciousness, with the person, the private life; as unpolitical, apolitical, interior, bourgeois, reactionary, naive, ignorant of post-structuralist or postmodern conceptions of the transhuman; as lacking in experimental or conceptual élan, etc. (the list is endless), the lyric poem has a long history as a subversive genre precisely because it is simultaneously accessible, personal, empathetic, metamorphic, and polysemous, most capable of slipping past censors.[29]

---

27 Ponge, *Partisan of Things*, 22.

28 Ponge, *Partisan of Things*, 22.

29 See my blog post, Trainor, "'the idyllic era of cushions was at an end.'"

More generally, then, the problem in terms of human exceptionalism has not been *too* much lyric subjectivity but its uneven distribution, which Ponge's *Partisan of Things* takes as its central project. Gerald Bruns, in *The Material of Poetry* (2012), reads Ponge's poem "Snails" as a "burlesque" of lyric subjectivity. We might see this in Ponge's exuberant use of personification: the snail's sang-froid; the snail "has few friends. But he needs no friends to be happy. He sticks to Nature, he enjoys his perfect nearness, he is the friend of the soil which he kisses with his whole body"; the snail exudes a "slime of pride."[30] Yet Bruns misses the more important intervention that Ponge makes in redistributing lyric subjectivity, a point obliquely made by Ponge's translator, Joshua Corey. I would like to see more poetic work on imagining what it might be like to *actually be* a snail.

There is value in the lyric subjectivity of the poet as empathetic lever that allows for an imagining of varied perceptions and ways of being, a clearing or even a dwelling or shelter for other beings to inhabit. As Ponge describes in "Snails," making is shared by human and snail: Human language is made or secreted into poem, as clay into hut or calcium into shell, and creates a dwelling—literally, figuratively, language as extended phenotype. Rilke to Orpheus:

> And where there had been
> at most a makeshift hut to receive the music,
> a shelter nailed up out of their darkest longing,
> with an entryway that shuddered in the wind—
> you built a temple deep inside their hearing.[31]

---

30 Bruns, *The Material of Poetry*, 21.

31 Rilke, "Sonnets to Orpheus I," *The Duino Elegies*, 83.

WHAT IS IT LIKE TO BE A TREE?

A small dark green hardcover book called *TreeTalk* (2020) by poet Ariel Gordon represents the culmination of her Symposium Art Consultation residency in Winnipeg. It took place over a hot, humid weekend on July 29 to 30, 2017, at the Tallest Poppy café's patio beneath the shade of a boulevard tree, an American elm. Gordon describes this tree as ranging in age from perhaps seventy to one hundred years; she notes that it has "survived round after round of construction, billows of pollution, drought, and even gig posters stapled to it."[32] The month before her residency had seen three tree infestations—cankerworm, elm spanworm, and tent caterpillar—that had defoliated many trees and made elms more vulnerable to Dutch elm disease. The elm she conducted her residency under was okay, she notes, but not flourishing. However, "by the end of the weekend, the elm had a second, temporary canopy of leaves: 234 poems—111 written by me, 107 written by passersby and 16 from other sources."[33] She gives no indication in the book which poems are hers and which were written by passersby, which further underlines its communal and polyvocal nature, as in the leaves of a tree. Many of the poems are somewhat reminiscent of Ponge, in that they address the tree as a subject, as if a human in tree form. One poem reads,

> You wear a macramé belt of poems you are
> powerless to remove or read.[34]

This suggests a lack of agency in the face of human action. Another suggests the tree's generosity:

---

32 Gordon, *TreeTalk*, 78.
33 Gordon, *TreeTalk*, 77.
34 Gordon, *TreeTalk*, 40.

> Thank you, protector. Thank you for holding
> light, shelter and keeping the whispers of our
> people as we pass you by, day by day.[35]

The poems/leaves are given human qualities:

> It starts to rain. Leaves shed water.
> My poems get pulpy, bleed
> ink & dye.[36]

A few of the poems edge a little closer towards imagining qualia from the perspective of the tree itself, regarding its experience of time:

> I've heard it said that trees move through time
> rather than space, as we do.[37]

and

> A person will walk 300 miles to reach another
> person. A tree will wait 300 years for a person to
> come to her.[38]

While the tree is said not to have agency, in the sense of being able to remove the "macramé belt" of poems, it asserts a different form of agency through its longevity; these last two poems ask us to adjust our framing of agency and movement from that of the human to the arboreal.

---

35 Gordon, *TreeTalk*, 61.

36 Gordon, *TreeTalk*, 51.

37 Gordon, *TreeTalk*, 25.

38 Gordon, *TreeTalk*, 69.

Gordon's project bears some resemblance to the Han Shan Poetry Project of 2012, initiated by Canadian poet Susan McCaslin in an attempt to stop Langley City Council in British Columbia from selling off a small 10 hectare forest known as McLellan Forest Natural Park to developers. Most of the trees were about 140 years old, as much of the old-growth had already been lost to agriculture and urban encroachment, although there existed one elder, a black cottonwood over 240 years old. McCaslin came up with the idea for her project in order to help WOLF (Watchers of Langley Forests) to raise money to try to purchase the forest from the city:

> The thought of it going down or being chain-sawed made me think about poetry and activism... and that's how this project was born. The Han Shan Poetry Project takes its name from a Chinese hermit poet who wandered through the wilderness, leaving his poems on rocks and trees, during the Tang Dynasty, more than 1,000 ago.[39]

Here is a good example of a poet mobilizing poetry for ecological conservation. At her callout, poets began to send poems from across Canada, poems that were strung up in the trees of the McLellan Forest; 140 poems had already been placed at the time the article appeared. Here is an excerpt of one of the poems, "Negative Space" by Lorna Crozier:

> The space where the tree stood
> is bigger than a poem can hold.
> Its death is all the deaths
> you've ever known.[40]

---

39 McCaslin quoted in Hume, "Writers Hang Poems."

40 Crozier quoted in Hume, "Writers Hang Poems."

I have spoken of the poem as an opening, a conceptual clearing to think into the future; Crozier here points out the ecological damage caused through logging creates a gash in the world bigger "than a poem can hold."

Whether or not a result of the publicity garnered by the Han Shan Poetry Project, the forest was saved due to a generous donation by the Blaauw family and is now called the Blaauw Eco Forest. It contains mixed and coniferous forests, ponds, a bog; over 115 animals have been discovered there by student researchers, including species at risk such as northern red-legged frogs and Pacific sideband snails. The forest itself and the many kin it sustains are protected by a "restrictive covenant" for future generations.[41]

POEM AS MADE (OF) THING(S)

When I write a poem, there are neurons, synapses, sparks of light, tendons and veins, fascicles; a pen, a line of black ink, a notebook filling with inked letters, symbols on paper marking breath; a word, words, trace of a resonance of sound in the ribs, chest cavity, spine, their vibrations in the little ear bones—hammer, stirrup, anvil. There is a blank page of blue-lined paper made of pulp fibre made of tree made of carbon plucked out of air and fixed with H_2O by sunlight; a scrawled manuscript; a first draft; a material thing.

Gerald Bruns argues that the poem "appears to have come into the world the way everything has (a stone, a plant, or, for all of that, a word. All words are found objects)."[42] That is, it has a material

---

41 "Blaauw Eco Forest."

42 Bruns, *The Material of Poetry*, 89.

existence, it is a material thing, yet also an assemblage of things. He cites one of Jack Spicer's letters to Federico Garcia Lorca:

> Dear Lorca, I would like to make poems out of real objects. The lemon to be a lemon that the reader could cut or squeeze or taste—a real lemon like a newspaper in a collage is a real newspaper. I would like the moon in my poem to be a real moon [43]

This is charming and asks us to consider the "real," whether found or made, status of language. Object-oriented ontology, as outlined by Graham Harman, would consider a word, a poem, or a fictional character as much an object as a lemon or a moon. Ponge also describes language itself as material, words as having a "semantic thickness," layered with associations and histories of use, "a thing that one can mold precisely because it has the quality, the thickness, of potter's clay. It is a physical object with many dimensions."[44] An acquaintance of mine who trained in clay at art school once told me how hard it is to work with clay because it is a living thing—it requires water to drink and air to breathe; it must be taken care of. We were both young mothers at the time, struggling to look after little children and to practise our art. She had abandoned her studio because she had no time for clay, this fickle living being, absorbed as she was by her twins and their older brother.

Bruns praises Ponge for the attention he gives to everyday things such as a doorknob or snail, "the world beneath notice," and for seeing the poet as "someone who is porous with respect to things, suffering or enjoying them but also, in some way, addressed or

---

43 Lorca quoted in Bruns, *The Material of Poetry*, 89.

44 Ponge quoted in Bruns, *Modern Poetry*, 280.

observed by them."[45] This form of careful attention is similar to Keats's conception of negative capability—the capacity to create space within the self for the other: "if a Sparrow come before my Window I take part in its existence and pick about the Gravel."[46] In *The Body in Pain* (1985), Elaine Scarry presents a heartbreaking version of this with reference not to a poet but to a boy on the battlefield, who must involuntarily cede his own sense of identity:

> He will learn to perceive himself as he will be perceived by others... as he is also inextricably bound up with the qualities and conditions—berry laden or snow laden—of the ground over which he walks or runs or crawls and with which he craves and courts identification... he is the elms and the mud, he is the one hundred and sixth, he is a small piece of German terrain broken off and floating dangerously through the woods of France. He is a fragment of American earth wedged into an open hillside in Korea and reworked by its unbearable sun and rain. He is dark blue like the sea. He is light grey like the air through which he flies. He is sodden in the green shadows of earth. He is a light brown vessel of red Australian blood that will soon be opened and emptied across the rocks and ridges of Gallipoli from which he can never again become distinguishable.[47]

Scarry presents the boy here as permeable to the environment in which he finds himself, just as Keats describes his work as a poet as not simply paying attention to the sparrow, nor simply presenting a human frame to translate the sparrow's existence, but as becoming

---

45 Bruns, *The Material of Poetry*, 81–82.

46 Keats, "To Benjamin Bailey."

47 Scarry, *The Body in Pain*, 83.

porous to the sparrow, allowing it to inhabit his own body—or for him to inhabit its body—through an act of imaginative empathy, to pick about the gravel. Observer and observed, subject and object, are if not dissolved, then intimately enmeshed, one within the other.

CHAPBOOK

While a potter or sculptor works with a more obviously physical medium, poets also encounter the physicality of their own practice—those who write first drafts in a paper notebook, those who create and sew their own chapbooks, which remind us of the materiality of language: shaped letters, ink soaking into fibres of paper, laser printed or letterpress, pages folded and trimmed, stapled or glued or stitched into a small booklet. In English, the chapbook (from *chapman*, itinerant salesman, from Old English *ceap*, cheap) appears in 1553 in Cambridgeshire, with the account of a pedlar selling "lytle books." The French term is *bibliothèque bleue*, "blue library," because such books were "often wrapped in cheap blue paper that was usually reserved as a wrapping for sugar."[48] Wrapping paper used for sugar becomes the covering for a little book.

In my early twenties I took a chapbook-making seminar with BC poet Tim Lander.[49] He showed us a basic model for a chapbook, made by folding 8-½-by-11-inch sheets into quarters, and offered tips on how to crease and cut the sheets—*use a penknife dulled from pruning*

48 Wikipedia, "Chapbook," accessed May 20, 2021, https://en.wikipedia.org/wiki/Chapbook.

49 Noah notes in the margins of my manuscript: *So the handmade chapbook is the poet's version of pottery or handmade bicycles—appropriate technology,* DIY *versus capitalist-industrial processes, getting in touch with materials—this is all part of standard roster of green movements, and sustainable production and consumption.*

raspberry canes or tomato vines; how to do a pamphlet stitch to sew a signature, a kettle stitch to bind them together; how to remove accidental drops of blood, a side effect of stitching—*let it dry on the page and then erase it.* He walked us through the counterintuitive ordering of pages prior to folding and interleaving. Gave us advice on where to make them—*while riding BC ferries*—and how to make them—*do not reproduce without love.* I have since taken other workshops, on Japanese stab binding and Coptic stitch; I have made my own hardcover books and collected a variety of tools: Japanese hole punch, bone folder, white glue, paintbrushes of varying thicknesses, wax paper, metal cork-lined ruler, clips and pincers, awls, needles, beeswax, book cloth, book board, cotton thread. I have made a chapbook for every sequence and collection that has later been published by small Canadian presses. With each iteration, each removal from the first scrawled and scored handwritten manuscript, the poems recede, seem less my own, less real, less alive, just as Ted Hughes describes with reference to his writing of *Moortown Diary*. The poems cannot be entirely detached or disarticulated from the material conditions of their making, from their poetic ecology, without loss of being, loss of meaning.

FASCICULES

Emily Dickinson knew the importance of the material circumstances of the poem.[50] For a time in her writing life, from the years 1858

---

50 Noah nudges me again in the margins: *I would say making a handmade booklet is not the same as coming clean on her society's entanglement with colonial expansion (including ecological imperialism), slavery, deforestation, etc., etc.* I agree; I focus now here, now there—the supply chains of an iPhone and the poetry of Xu Lizhi; the material production of a fascicule, hand-stitched by the poet.

through 1864, she made little booklets, which her friend Mabel Loomis Todd later called "little fascicules." The word is derived from the Latin *fasciculus*, "a diminutive of *fascis* ('bundle')":

> 1. a small or slender bundle (as of pine needles or nerve fibers). 2. one of the divisions of a book published in parts.[51]

Fascicle is also a botanical term used "to describe gatherings like those of pine needles into clumps," as well as gatherings of leaves and so on.[52]

Dickinson makes oblique reference to these booklets (perhaps) in poem 675 (No. 772 in Franklin's *Reading Edition* of 1999):

Essential Oils - are wrung -
The Attar from the Rose
Be not expressed by Suns - alone -
It is the gift of Screws -

The General Rose - decay -
But this - in Lady's Drawer
Make Summer - When the Lady lie
In Ceaseless Rosemary -[53]

I love the word "Attar" here, and the sudden shock of "Screws"—as if torture methods are applied to the rose petal flesh to produce the essential oil. I also hear an allusion to Shakespeare's Sonnet 5:

---

51 *Merriam-Webster*, "fascicle," accessed April 18, 2025, https://www.merriam-webster.com/dictionary/fascicle.

52 Loeffelholz, "What Is a Fascicle?"

53 Franklin, *The Poems of Emily Dickinson: Reading Edition*. Note the handwritten fascicle version ends "In ceaseless Sepulchre."

Then were not summers distillation left
A liquid prisoner pent in walls of glasse,
Beauties effect with beauty were bereft,
Nor it nor noe remembrance what it was.

The connection is strong between these two poems. The fair youth is being encouraged to reproduce in order to preserve his beauty in, and for, the next generation—a distillation or preservation of his essence. But in Shakespeare's sonnets the flesh is soon abandoned for the poems themselves, which can offer a textual preservation.

Similarly, the fascicles—the poems in the poet's drawer—will "Make Summer" when the poet is dead ("In Ceaseless Rosemary," when she lies only in memory, when only the words remember her—rosemary for remembrance). There's the same kind of allusion as well to the treatment of prisoners: screws, pent in walls of glass. The words of a poem imprison but also preserve. This speaks to the question of whether art treats "nature" as standing reserve. I don't think so, if the poet inscribes the poem's ecosystem into the poem itself—an acknowledgement or trace of the materials and conditions of its making, as seen here, in Dickinson's writing practice.

My idea of a poem's ecosystem comprises both a poetic ecology and a poetic economy. Ponge's translator Joshua Corey references the term "poetic economy" in his introduction to *Partisan of Things*. Corey observes that contemporary ecopoetics has transformed our understanding of nature by "critiquing the pastoral Romanticism of poets such as Wordsworth, whose poems tend to reinforce a vision of nature as *for* the human, a kind of sublime vacancy to be filled by the poet's imagination."[54] As with other critics, he contrasts William

---

54 Corey, "The Challenge of Francis Ponge," v.

Wordsworth's rapturous treatment of daffodils—"I wandered lonely as a cloud"—with the diary entry of Wordsworth's sister, Dorothy, on April 15, 1802. Her observations are precise, in situ, self-reflective—"Her active mode of observation scrupulously includes observations of the observer"—and include notes on the cost of their food and board—"We paid 7/ when we came away"—as well as to the starving deer in Gowbarrow park—"like skeletons."[55] It is somewhat unfair to compare lyric poem and prose diary entry, yet a poem that seeks to inscribe the ecological might consider these practical economic elements.

As is often pointed out in ecological studies, the term "ecology," coined by Ernst Haeckel in 1866, is a joining of ancient Greek *oikos* (*oikos*)—"house," and *logia* (logia) or "study of," and has come to reference the study of the interaction of living organisms within their physical environment.[56] The word "economy" shares the same root, *oikos,* joined with *nemein* (*nemein*), meaning "to manage,"[57] and while it is commonly understood to reference the circulation of goods and services within human populations, ecologists well understand that the economy is inseparable from the ecology of the planet, as we live within planetary boundaries, the economy resting on a material and finite foundation, even while the cost of externalities, such as pollution, extinctions, global heating, system collapse, are almost always ignored in economic calculations. So when I speak of a poem's "ecosystem," I reference the local ecology *and* economy out of which a poem emerges. Corey captures some of this in his discussion of the "poetic economy," tracing contemporary ecopoetry as a critique of the "romantic" gesture

55 Quoted in Corey, "The Challenge of Francis Ponge," v–vi.

56 Wikipedia, "Ecology," accessed October 21, 2023, https://en.wikipedia.org/wiki/Ecology.

57 Wikipedia, "Economy," accessed October 21, 2023, https://en.wikipedia.org/wiki/Economy.

of the nineteenth-century poets' inscriptions of a "sublime" nature. The twenty-first-century philosopher and biologist Andreas Weber, however, offers a rehabilitation of the romantics (as does Morton in his reading of them) in his use of the term "poetic ecology," within the context of biology; with the term "poetic ecology," Weber recentres the importance of subjectivity and meaning within a "living reality." He defines "poetic ecology" as ecological relations considered

> from the perspective of subjectivity and meaning. So it's not about cause and effect; instead, it's about the expressiveness of a living reality whose creative process is constantly bringing forth a multitude of fertile relationships. In my view, any thinking in terms of relationship can only come about as a poetics. Any practice of aliveness can only be a poetic practice. A poetic ecology understands nature less as an economy of checks and balances than as the creative interpenetration of sentient beings, so it is animistic in that way. If we wander through a flowering meadow in May, we become enmeshed in this tactile exchange. When we look closely, we may recognise that our nervous system mirrors the infinite mycorrhizal networks beneath our feet. We are intertwined across this threshold through sensation, perception, and organic memory, kind of like an umbilical cord, or what the mythologist Martin Shaw calls "bone memory." That's why we find it enlivening; it rouses our own creaturehood. It reminds us of our place in the natural world and of our intimate belonging to the Earth; we realise we are not so alien after all.[58]

For Weber, ecological relationships are necessarily governed by "interbeing," an enmeshment of organisms who are porous

58 Weber quoted in Close, "The Poetics of Ecology."

and composed of communities of micro-organisms as much as by networks of reciprocity: "the creative interpenetration of sentient beings."[59] I think of the poem's ecosystem as linked both to Weber's conception of a poetic ecology and to the poetic economy referenced by Corey, which is more contingent upon human economic systems, to the supply chains that distribute paper, ink, cobalt, and to the trade book of poetry, also a product of labour that circulates as commodity within a system of exchange.

Dickinson, in poem 675, is certainly acknowledging her refusal of this system of exchange by referencing the homemade quality of her poetry, analogous to the distillation of attar, made from rose petals gathered in her garden; there is self-reflection on the poetic ecology *and* economy of her practice, as one who never appeared under an incorporated imprint in her lifetime.

Dickinson gestures towards the poetic ecosystem of her poem, especially to Weber's conception of the interpenetration of lives and materials, within the second verse with its allusion to the cycle of life and death, the recirculation of nutrients—the rose decays, the lady will lie "in Ceaseless Rosemary." Attar is "an essential oil wrung from flowers, especially the damask rose, used pure or as a base for perfume (from Persian ʿ*atir*, 'perfumed,' from ʿ*itr*, 'perfume,' from Arabic.)"[60] The poem develops the extended analogy of the wringing of essential oils from the rose—oils expressed by suns *and* screws, natural sunlight and human innovation, technology—which is applied to the poem itself as essence wrung from life, reliant on both "natural" and "cultural" forms of production. The

59 Weber quoted in Close, "The Poetics of Ecology."

60 *Collins Dictionary*, "attar," accessed April 18, 2025, https://www.collinsdictionary.com/dictionary/english/attar.

term "fascicules," botanical and anatomical, applied by Dickinson's friend Mabel Loomis Todd to the little stitched booklets made by Dickinson, adds an interesting etymological layering: gathering of roses, of leaves of paper, of fibres drawn from a tree, of the sinews in her hand, drawn together to write the letters on the page.

Similarly, the nature of the production of her fascicles is medial in Morton's conception, self-aware of its materiality, while also deliberately refusing the traditional circulation of texts within a capitalist system.

I return to the ghostly "Sepulchre" found in the final "ceaseless Rosemary" of her poem. Dickinson is famous for her indeterminacy; she welcomed into her poetic ecosystem a proliferation of semantic possibilities: Why choose only one word or one version of a poem when they can exist simultaneously on the page, an unruly genealogy, just as every word carries a diachronic memory of its past? This is appealing and points towards Ponge's observation that "All words should be written to allow their complete semantic thickness."[61] Not only does each word carry levels of semantic thickness, but Dickinson, by including synonyms and substitutes, allows for burgeoning possibilities in every line and echoes the proliferation of the natural, teeming world to which she opens her poems. There is a wildness of language here, as Gary Snyder has observed: "like some kind of infinitely interfertile family of species spreading or mysteriously declining over time, shamelessly and endlessly hybridizing, changing its own rules as it goes."[62]

---

61 Ponge quoted in Bruns, *Modern Poetry*, 280.

62 Snyder, *The Practice of the Wild*, 8.

Ferris Jabr details the proliferation of commonplace fauna and flora to be found in Dickinson's poems: robin, bumblebee, dandelion, wren, clover, spider, oriole, bobolink, crow, lilac, violet, burdock, chanticleer, gentian, leech, hyacinth, wheat, anemone, crocus, hearts ease, angleworm, firefly, and so many more. Jabr argues that Dickinson's backyard, and the patchwork of forest and pasture in nineteenth-century Amherst, Massachusetts, formed a crucial part of her poems' ecosystem. While attending Amherst Academy as a teenager, she "studied botany and began assembling an herbarium of dried and pressed plants that eventually included 424 diverse specimens, such as wild cucumber, passionflower, pigweed, pennyroyal, turtle head, and Grass of Parnassus."[63] In her correspondence, she "sometimes mailed poems about living creatures along with the creature itself—a plucked blossom, or a dead cricket or bee, slipped into the envelope... she deliberately surrounded herself with a diverse and diverting nonhuman society: the creatures in her garden and nearby woods, which she called 'Nature's people.'" Within 1,789 poems, there are approximately 700 references to animals, 600 references to plants, and four to fungi.[64]

By choosing to bind her poems in fascicles, Dickinson chose never to seek publication beyond this kind of private self-publication. Her poems were not sent to a publisher to be produced on a printing press, bound, circulated to bookstores, assigned a monetary price—as such,

---

63 Jabr, "How Emily Dickinson Grew Her Genius."

64 Jabr, "How Emily Dickinson Grew Her Genius." There is some irony in mailing a poem "about living creatures" along with the now dead creature, to a reader; this practice offers a concrete, most literal example of "nature" treated as standing reserve. In this case, in relation to poetry, nature as "subject" has been harvested for the sake of the poem. I don't suggest Dickinson's intention was to harvest the natural world or to frame it as resource, although the effect may be such; this is a concern that all ecopoets engage in, and which an awareness, however oblique, of the poem's ecosystem, might complicate in an interesting manner.

they resist the capitalist system of exchange. There must have been pleasure in creating these distinct bundles, like jars of preserves or rose attar in glass vials. For Emily Dickinson, her riddling poems and fascicles were a refuge—a dwelling; not only does she attend closely to more-than-human kin in the poems, but the poems themselves become their own species. Like the circulation of blood within our bodies, she let her poems exist for themselves in their own dark life.

MAKING

By transcribing her poems on "brown paper bags, magazine clippings, discarded envelopes and letters, the backs of recipes" as well as in her stitched fascicles, Dickinson preserved her poems for the future; once printed in multiple copies, they could be transmitted to others, including future generations. Elaine Scarry has observed, regarding the nature of human language, that we have in this way learned to do just this, to "objectify" our thoughts, our experience of sentience, in language:

> What differentiates men and women from other creatures is neither the natural acuity of our sentience nor the natural frailty of the organic tissue in which it resides but instead the fact that ours is, to a vastly greater degree than that of any other animal, objectified in language and material objects and is thus fundamentally transformed to be communicable and endlessly sharable. The socialization of sentience—which is itself as profound a change as if one were to open the body physically and redirect the path of neuronal flower, rearrange the small bones into a new pattern, remodel the ear drum—is one of Marx's major emphases.[65]

65 Scarry, *The Body in Pain*, 255.

The artifact remembers the labour which made it—the cloth "soaked" in labour, bearing the pattern of threads that remember the complex movements of the hands that wove it. The artifact is a projection and extension of the human body's needs into the world; a bandage anticipates the human's "bodily capacities and needs" to the extent that it seems almost sentient in itself, capable of anticipating and being responsive to the body's needs.[66] Marx, according to Scarry, understands humans as engaged in an ongoing project of making the world; and by working and reworking the materials of these worlds, of making tools to anticipate, extend, and redistribute our sentience, we are likewise transformed or remade:

> freestanding objects remake the live body itself. Such objects, by eliminating the limitations of sentience or, as it can with equal accuracy be phrased, magnifying its powers (the ear trumpet, hearing aid, sign language, telephone, songs, poetry, telegraph, victrola, stereo system, radio, tape recorder, sonar, acoustically precise symphony hall and so forth all extend the range and activity of the air), make sentience itself an artifact.[67]

To briefly recount her argument: A coat stitched by "Mildred Keats" anticipates the needs of a human body for protection and warmth from the winter cold, acts as a second skin, responds to the frailty of the human body. The coat also acknowledges a moral obligation in its redistribution or dispersion of sentience, from the haves to the

---

66 Scarry, *The Body in Pain*, 284. "What is expressed in terms of body part is more accurately formulated as the endowing of interior sensory events with a metaphysical referent: The making of what is originally interior and private into something exterior and sharable and, conversely, the reabsorption of what is now exterior and sharable into the intimate recesses of individual consciousness."

67 Scarry, *The Body in Pain*, 255.

have-nots, where what is "had and had not is the known body";[68] that is, the coat lifts from the worker the harsh realities of the body, the wearer of the coat is no longer required to shiver from the cold, no longer bound by the exigencies of the flesh. The seamstress Mildred Keats anticipates those needs and projects them into the artifact; over the course of ten or twelve hours, she cuts and stitches the cloth to the dimensions of the human body. The coat acts as a lever or fulcrum, Scarry writes, where what it reciprocates (warmth provided to the worker over many years, each time the coat is slipped on) far exceeds the initial labour that goes into its making.

John Keats writes "Ode to a Nightingale," scribbles some lines about the Nightingale's song on sheets of paper—"Perhaps the self-same song that found a path / Through the sad heart of Ruth, when, sick for home, / She stood in tears amid the alien corn"[69]—a series of lines that are typeset and printed in a book of poems, which is mass produced and read one morning by a girl on the West Coast of Canada in 1979, who hears this nightingale, breathes life once more into this artifact made of words, shares in Keats's expansive vision of the music of language. Sentience itself is communal and endlessly sharable.

Both coat and poem rework and acknowledge *human* sentience, in Scarry's formulation, which embraces the artifacts humans make:

> human beings project their bodily powers and facilities into external objects such as telephones, chairs, gods, poems, and political forms, and then those objects in turn become the object of perceptions that are taken

---

68 Scarry, *The Body in Pain*, 343.

69 Keats, "Ode to a Nightingale."

> back into the interior of human consciousness where they now reside as part of the mind or soul.[70]

This making sentient—projecting a sense of aliveness into the found and made artifacts of the world—comes with it a moral obligation; mass-produced objects in particular help to redistribute sentience, to relieve the body's demands for the have-nots, to amplify their voices.

Yet Scarry does not consider the making practices of more-than-human kin: the snail's chiralic, logarithmic shell; the mycorrhizal network that links paper birch tree and Douglas fir; the engineering work of the grizzly bear who digs the soil and helps to cultivate the avalanche lily; the nest of the chickadee. There are many ways of making and being in the world. The work of the poem can be to function as ecological lever that works to amplify the voices of other beings and to participate in the imagining of other ways of being, other *Umwelten*. How might the lyric poem perform imaginative extensions of sentience to more-than-human kin as a way of sympathetically, empathetically, engaging with other organisms? The effects of such redistribution of sentience might range from attuning an individual reader to the integrity of an old-growth forest, to a campaign to stopping its clear-cutting as part of a larger campaign for the extension of legal protections we should accord to all sentient beings.

I refer to protections such as those enforced by Ecuador's decision in December 2021 that mining activities pursued in Los Cedros protected area were threatening the rainforest's right to exist and flourish, a decision made possible by Ecuador's 2008 constitution, which recognizes the rights of Pachamama—Mother Earth—to exist, to "maintain and regenerate its cycles, structure, functions and evolutionary

70 Scarry, *The Body in Pain*, 256.

processes."[71] Another example would be the decision by Curridabat or *Ciudad Dulce* ("Sweet City"), a suburb of the Costa Rican capital San José, to extend citizenship to all native plants, trees, and pollinators, including bats, bees, butterflies, and hummingbirds.[72] The mayor of Curridabat, Edgar Mora, observed, "Pollinators are the consultants of the natural world, supreme reproducers and they don't charge for it. The plan to convert every street into a biocorridor and every neighbourhood into an ecosystem required a relationship with them."[73]

In British Columbia, the Raincoast Conservation Foundation has presented a persuasive report on pathways for legal personhood for the Fraser River estuary,[74] which is currently under threat due to the proposed Roberts Bank Terminal 2 project. I sent broadsides of my poem "Pacific Salmon (*Oncorhynchus*)" to Canadian Prime Minister Justin Trudeau and Minister of Environment and Climate Change Steven Guilbeault, along with an artist statement, as part of my intervention into the environmental assessment approval process. This is a project that, it has been estimated, will have significant, adverse, cumulative effects on species such as western sandpipers, Southern Resident killer whales, and Chinook salmon, effects that would be "regional in extent, permanent in duration, irreversible, and continuous."[75]

---

71 Quoted in Surma, "Ecuador's High Court."

72 Greenfield, "'Sweet City.'"

73 Greenfield, "'Sweet City.'"

74 Pasternak and Walters, *Rights of Nature*. The Raincoast Conservation Foundation observes that "The estuary, and all the living things it supports, are not viewed as having intrinsic worth. Economic imperatives consistently override the need for ecological protection, and as a result, threaten the very existence of one of the most ecologically important regions in the province."

75 Review Panel, "Summary of Key Findings"; Vancouver Fraser Port Authority, "Roberts Bank Terminal 2 Receives Approval." In addition to Prime Minister Justin Trudeau and Minister of Environment and Climate Change of Canada...

A major concern is the impact that a second massive port will have on the delicate mudflats that produce biofilm, a crucial source of nourishment for the western sandpiper, the dunlin, and other shore birds. Without this biofilm, it is feared the western sandpiper will go extinct, no longer able to fuel up at this important stopover along the Western Pacific Flyway, en route to the Copper River estuary in Alaska, before arriving at their final destination, Arctic nesting grounds.

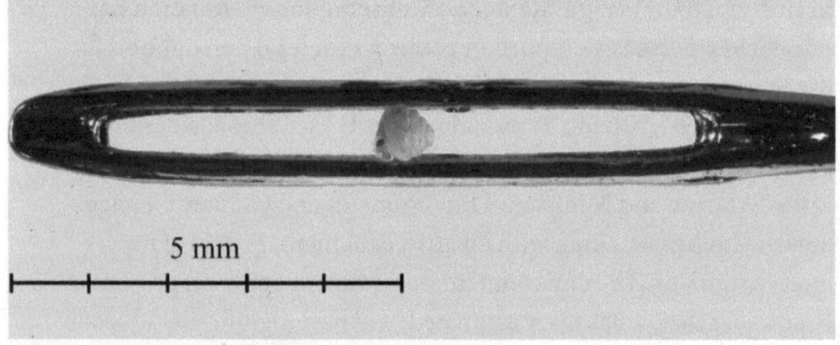

Shell of the tiny land snail *Angustopila dominikae*.
Credit: Dr. Barna Páll-Gergely & Nikolett Szpisjak.

The lyric poem can aid in this reimagining of our extended kin by approaching, again and again, if obliquely and tentatively, the thing in itself, on its own terms with the aim to acknowledge and extend sentience to more-than-human kin; to inspire humans to extend all

---

... Steven Guilbeault, I sent my artist statement and broadside of "Pacific Salmon (*Onchyrinchus*)" to Carla Qaultrough and Joyce Murray. Despite the serious objections by scientists, artists, and local conservation groups, the Roberts Bank Terminal 2 project was approved on April 20, 2023; a legal challenge to this decision began in July 2023.

possible legal protections to these kin from our own ravages of past centuries and to make reparations as best we can; to glimpse the dark interiority of the Sitka spruce as it draws calcium and magnesium from the shreds of fog that drift in off the Pacific Ocean;[76] the tiny, luminous snail *Angustopila dominikae*, wedged into the limestone rocks of Guangxi Province in southern China, its circumference so tiny it can fit in the eye of a needle;[77] the Chinook salmon, its dark reddening flesh guided by stone otoliths in its ears to return to the Fraser to spawn; the sounds the common raven makes, *quoork, quuoork*, ring of a bell, droplets of water into a stone reservoir.

What might it mean to extend sentience to a Sitka spruce? And how do I differentiate the experience of being a Sitka spruce from my experience of human sentience? How do we avoid the heavy-handedness of anthropomorphization, while acknowledging its usefulness in helping us to translate different experiences of *Umwelten*? This is an ongoing experiment that individual poets will consider in their own practice, just as we will need to reconsider the primacy of our role as humans in the ongoing practice of co-making this world.

INSTRUCTIONS FOR CO-MAKING THIS WORLD

Instructions for co-making the world:
Give space to listen to what guides you.
Notice the river flowing around you.
See how it makes your world.

---

76 "Sitka Spruce," BC Government.

77 Irwin, "World's Tiniest Snail."

Examine your ways of making.
Give up your only-human territory.
See what places you wish to rewild.
Put nest-works in them.

Instructions for creating a nest-work (or virtual nesting):
Take as example the nest of a bird.
Create a human form in this structure.
Build this common space from what is disparate and varied.
Consider safety and softness in co-making.
Make a place for things coming into being.[78]

78 Huestis, "Co-making This World."

4. VIGILANCE

Attention is crucial for both scientist and poet. Robin Wall Kimmerer on the secret names of mosses. Iain McGilchrist on the bilateral structure of the mammalian brain: the cultural, historical implications of a privileging of left hemispheric forms of pinpoint attention that yield static articulations of the world, contrasted with right hemispheric forms of a more broadband attention. McGilchrist: "without vigilance, we cannot become aware of anything we do not already know."[1] *McGilchrist's observations long anticipated by Indigenous ways of knowing. Attention and care grounded in place. Nuu-chah-nulth concept of* heshook-ish tsawalk, *"everything is one."* Etuaptmumk, *or "two-eyed seeing." Simone Weil's concept of attention as a form of waiting and an expression of love.*

In the preface to her lesser-known collection of essays, *Gathering Moss* (2003), the botanist and poet Robin Wall Kimmerer observes,

> Learning to see mosses mingles with my first memory of a snowflake. Just at the limits of ordinary perception lies another level in the hierarchy of beauty, of leaves as tiny and perfectly ordered as a snowflake, of unseen lives complex and beautiful. All it takes is attention and knowing how to look. I've found mosses to be a vehicle for intimacy with the landscape, like a secret knowledge of the forest.[2]

Attention, as she describes it, is a form of intimacy; it is receptiveness to learning the stories and perspectives of our more-than-human kin; it is a kind of listening to the secret voices of moss; it is awareness of the interconnectedness of things—past and present, relationships, intersections; it is an openness to mystery. While she writes of the value

---

1 McGilchrist, *The Master and His Emissary*, 39.

2 Kimmerer, *Gathering Moss*, v–vi.

of scientific forms of attention, symbolized by the jeweller's loupe she wears around her neck to peer at the complex, miniature structures of mosses and articulated by her knowledge of Linnaean classification of organisms, she observes that the "scientific way of knowing relies only on empirical information from the world, gathered by body and interpreted by mind. In order to tell the mosses' story I need both approaches, objective and subjective."[3] She observes we can say that we understand a thing only once it is known by "mind, body, emotion, and spirit."[4]

What has been long acknowledged and embodied in Indigenous ways of knowing is explored by Iain McGilchrist, who draws upon both scientific studies of brain disorders and creative works such as music, sculpture, and poetry to consider how these quite different forms of attention—subjective, objective—have been siloed in much of contemporary Western society, to our peril.

GROUND OF OUR BEING IN THE WORLD

In *The Master and His Emissary* (2012), Iain McGilchrist argues that the left and right hemispheres of the brain have evolved to process the world in different styles based on different forms of attention.[5] The right hemisphere allows for sustained attention and vigilance, an openness to the new, to the other who is not yet known, is not *me*. The left

---

3 Kimmerer, *Gathering Moss*, vii.

4 Kimmerer, *Gathering Moss*, vii.

5 McGilchrist lists five kinds of attention: divided attention, focused attention, alertness, sustained attention, vigilance. These are placed on a spectrum, from broadband to pinpoint attention; vigilance, alertness, and sustained attention are all broadband, associated with the "intensity" axis and with the right hemisphere. Divided and focused attention he associates with the left hemispheric ways of attending ("pinpoint"), which exclude reception to what is new or unknown.

hemisphere is focused, pinpoint, selective, recirculating and categorizing information, typological: It takes what has been learned by the right hemisphere, what is not already known, what is newly perceived, and sorts and analyzes it. The right allows us to play with metaphor and puns; the left is more strictly literal. The right responds to living beings; the left prefers complex machinery and tends to see the parts of all things but not the gestalt, the whole. The left hemisphere's ability to

> represent the world artificially—to map it conceptually, substituting tokens for things, like the general's map at HQ—enables us to have an overall strategy; and this is what language achieves. But it inhibits us from being *there*, in the experimental world. It places us at one remove from things.[6]

The left hemisphere in primates, McGilchrist argues, is functional—we form concepts, we abstract and remove ourselves, typologize and make distant, reduce to parts, as with apes, "in order the better to anticipate the world."[7]

Right hemispheric expansion, he argues, is more prominent in humans and is associated with empathy, with "imagination, creativity, the capacity for religious awe, music, dance, poetry, art, love of nature, a moral sense, a sense of humour, and the ability to change our minds."[8] That which allows for nuance, polysemy, figurative language, lateral connections, flexibility, holding two or more interpretations simultaneously in mind—this style of thought is associated with the right hemisphere.[9] Even more significantly, each hemisphere's

---

6 McGilchrist, *Ways of Attending*, 14.

7 McGilchrist, *Ways of Attending*, 15.

8 McGilchrist, *Ways of Attending*, 15.

9 In general. McGilchrist cautions that those who are neurodivergent, left-handed, ...

different style of interacting with the world to some extent constrains or determines our world: "the type of attention we pay determines *what it is we see*."[10] This is not to discount the value of the left hemisphere's role in our survival as a species; it is a style of attention that allows McGilchrist to articulate the different styles, and me to create this abstract list:

LEFT HEMISPHERE	**RIGHT HEMISPHERE**
Known	***Unknown***
processes the already familiar into parts and abstractions	receptive to newness, to that which presences itself to us
that which is already known	receptive to new experience; the unknown
creates schematizations, taxonomies	makes connections between things
creates generalizations that allow for categories	sees things as they are, unique as they exist in themselves
makes things explicit	receptive to implicit, artistic, + spiritual experience
Machinic	***Organic***
attuned to tools, to the inanimate, to the mechanical + machine-like	attuned to living things, which are organic + always in flux (everything flows)
attuned to what it has itself made	attuned to things already existing, not made

…or who have experienced head trauma might have differently wired brains. There is also duplication of functions across both hemispheres in all humans.

10 McGilchrist, *Ways of Attending*, 16.

Segemented	*Flow*
time/space as a series of discrete points	the wholeness of an emergent property, organic and in situ
static moments, still lives, frames, bits	change, over time, fluidity
simple rhythm—sound chopped up into fragments	music, melody, timbre, harmony, complex rhythm, syncopation, betweenness
Flatness	*Depth*
flatness of perspective, detached perception, projected as if on a screen	depth of field
Anger	*Sadness*
attuned to anger	emotional life; attuned to compassion, empathy, sadness
Parts	*Whole*
"assemblage of parts"; objects arranged in space	whole body image
living in / having a body (detached parts)	self-aware, existing / living the body
Certainty	*Doubt*
lacking in self-awareness	sudden insight into a complex problem
overly positive in self-appraisal	intuitive moral sense
morally certain	self-doubt
vocal	without a voice

Detached	Attuned
representation of the world	reception of the world
attention to "the virtual world it has created"	attention to a world it has not created
detached from the Other	attuned to the Other

According to McGilchrist's theory, the asymmetrical, divided hemispheres of the human brain tend towards either attunement to or detachment from the Other and the world all around:

> I believe the essential difference between the right hemisphere and the left hemisphere is that the right hemisphere pays attention to the Other: to whatever it is that exists apart from ourselves, with which it sees itself in profound relation. It is deeply attracted to, and given life by, the relationship, the betweenness, that exists with this Other. By contrast, the left hemisphere pays attention to the virtual world that it has created, which is self-consistent but self-contained, ultimately disconnected from the Other, making it powerful—but also curiously impotent, because it is ultimately only able to operate on, and to know, itself.[11]

Both approaches or styles of interacting with the world are necessary for survival, but he argues that the left hemispheric style has taken over. By contrast, the right hemispheric forms of broadband attention—alert, vigilant, sustained, open to new possibilities, sights, and sounds—are crucial to our long-term survival:

---

11 McGilchrist, *Ways of Attending*, 23.

> [Right hemispheric forms of attention] are the ground of our being in the world, not only at the lowest, vegetative level, but at the highest, spiritual levels ("Brethren, be sober, be vigilant, *O Mensch gib acht!*") Without alertness, we are as if asleep, unresponsive to the world around us; without sustained attention, the world fragments; without vigilance, we cannot become aware of anything we do not already know.[12]

Not only does this form of attention provide a model for the poet, but the elements associated with right hemisphere styles of attention provide the key tools a poet works with. Read the elements of right hemispheric style in the column above and you could be describing the various elements of an ecolyric poem: the formation of new and unexpected connections that happens with analogy and metaphor; attunement to emotional response; the music and complex rhythm of words; insight; and very often, although not always, significant attention to and empathy for the Other.

How does the poem create an opening that simultaneously helps to gather our sustained attention, allowing the world to enter in, that which is new or other or unknown, while still respecting the inherent darkness of the other within its own rich interior life?

GRANDMOTHER TREE, GRANDFATHER TREE

Last weekend, my friend Foxtrot and I returned to Fairy Creek—mid-January 2022. We were lucky—a free weekend happened

12 McGilchrist, *The Master and His Emissary*, 38–39.

to coincide with three beautiful days of sunlight, a drop of temperature to only 0°C overnight, crystalline stars. I woke the last morning to find my tent's fly stiff with a thin coat of ice.

Roadside has been closed for the winter; the snow has finally arrived higher up the mountain and logging has temporarily ceased. The RCMP have abandoned their critical response post at the base of Granite Main, where we first helped to set up the white tarp in October, one day after the injunction had been lifted; the RCMP have left behind only a tangled metal frame detached from its canvas pop-up shelter.

One camp remains—R+R, and it lies outside of the injunction zone. There are possibly others, hidden deep in the mountain—we wouldn't know. Elder Bill Jones has encouraged all land defenders to rest, to reflect, to come and spend time with the trees. We camped alone, not at R+R, but at the edge of Renfrew Creek, arriving in pitch-black our first night. We had come to hike back up to the old River camp, which we never saw when it was up and running but knew later as Landback Bridge. It lies about 7 kilometres up Granite Main, and we helped to retake it on our fourth visit to Fairy Creek, in what I believe was the last action of the 2021 season.[13]

That day in mid-November we had waited around until 5:30 pm—for the dark to fall, for a shift change by the RCMP—before the hike up Granite Main, ostensibly to "see the old-growth forest," but in fact to reoccupy the bridge at the former River camp. It was a slow

---

13 My account here of Landback Bridge is adapted from my article, "We Will Feed the Seeds of Tomorrow," and my camp journal. Filmmaker Jessey Dearing was also at Landback Bridge and presents the blockade from Indigenous land defender Strawberry's perspective (Shy-Anne Gunville) in a 14-minute video: Dearing, "At War for the Forest."

hike of stops and starts, accumulating more people as we climbed through the dark and the steady rain. At a certain point we reached a juncture where two patrol cars were idling, lights on. We clumped together and slipped between them silently—they made no attempt to stop us. Tremendous rushing of water as we climbed up and up Granite Main, until at last, several hours later, we arrived at a bridge.

Immediately out came "utensils"—crowbar, pickaxe, shovel. Immediately, people digging at either side of the bridge. Arctic Fox making a fire, splitting wood. (Arctic Fox: *If it would just stop raining for one hot minute!*) Pitch-black. Pouring. No hope of staying dry or of keeping our gear dry. Others looking for wood and stringing rope to set up tarps. We helped find firewood, damp mostly. But at last, being too cold and wet and tired, Foxtrot and I set up our tents side by side, our doors facing each other. I draped my blue and green tarps over the opening between the tents and covered the head of my tent with my rain poncho for extra protection. We scrunched in and boiled water for a bag of vegetarian pad Thai; it quickly became like a sauna beneath the small tarp. We hardly knew where to begin, between taking off our boots, undoing sleeping bags, trying to avoid the wettest parts of our packs. Ate bowls of pad Thai. Bliss. I kept on all my clothes: long-sleeved merino wool shirt, T-shirt, long johns, rain pants, two buffs, tuque, requisition Helly Hansen waterproof jacket, moss green like the forest, and crawled into the slightly damp bag. I folded my sleeping pad down to form a pillow as mine was soaked; I had to sleep on my left side, curling myself around a bulge in the earth beneath my tent. It was 1:37 am.

And woke to a clanging on metal and the cry, *Time to wake up, Fairy Creek defenders!* We got up, pulled on our boots, emerged to pouring rain. Boiled water for tea. 7:30 am. Overnight two hard blocks[14] in the

14 A "hard block" is a blockade that includes an embedded human being—for...

form of sleeping dragons had been built, one at either end of the bridge. A sleeping dragon consists of a hole in the ground with a piece of PVC tubing cemented in place, so that those in the hard block extend one arm into the tube in the earth and use a carabiner to clip into a metal ring secured at its base; they lie flat on the ground, supported by pillow, sleeping pad, sleeping bag. We offer constant assistance to those in the hard blocks: heat, tea, food. A tarp overhead keeps the rain off.

A meeting was called: how to form as a blob to defend the bridge.[15] We practised linking arms—the tallest and strongest of us in front, the smaller in the second row, towards the centre. A cop car came and went, came and went. Each time we ran to the bridge and stood and sang.

The RCMP came on foot, observing, taking photos across the bridge and up the hill. Back down. Took off. Then back again—one green, two blues.[16] The green was brusque—insisted we would have to move back to the middle of the bridge as they began the first extraction. A paddy wagon arrived, two or three cars, an excavator, three blues who stood and watched us from beyond the yellow caution tape they'd set up. Five or six blues and a green carried out the excavation with pickaxe, drills, chainsaw—chewing out pieces of wood from the support structure of the bridge. It was difficult to watch—imagining

---

... example, locked into a sleeping dragon. A "soft block" is a blockade consisting of solely material objects, such as rocks and boulders strewn across a road to slow down access by the RCMP, who must stop their vehicles and remove the debris.

15 As there were so few of us, this version of a blob consisted only of two rows of protestors with interlocking arms; the larger the numbers and rows, as suggested by its name, the more effective a strategy of resisting the RCMP, hence the RCMP's resort during the summer of 2021 to pepper spray.

16 "Blues" are regular RCMP officers; "greys" are liaison officers; "greens" are the officers with paramilitary training and associated with C-IRG, the Community-Industry Response Group.

the young woman in the hard block, fragile flesh contra sharp metal and electric tools. It took them two hours and forty-five minutes to excavate her. Intermittently, we stood on the bridge at the caution tape, singing, and called encouragement to the girl.

The same green came through again, brusque and irritated, insisting we had twenty-five minutes to clear everything from the road—all of our tarps, tents, packs—or he would take them. *If I see a tarp, I'll take it. If I see a rope, I'll cut it.* Raven warned, *Everything important to you, carry on your back.* We took our emptied tents and placed them in the ditch. Stacked the wet tarps along the road's edge. Raced back to the bridge. The angry green was back. He ripped the tarp off the second hard block, said he was taking it as we hadn't moved it quickly enough; pulled the cover and sleeping bag off the girl inside. Raven and Matihi challenged him. As soon as the first extraction had finished and the girl in the hard block had been taken down off the mountain, two blues walked up to a location just beyond all our stashed gear and tents and strung another caution tape line—a new warning, to move even farther back, past the tape. We had five minutes. A pause—some talk of a forming a blob, but not coordinated in time. At the last minute we rushed up the hill, grabbing tarps and pots. I helped drag a tarp filled with firewood. Arctic Fox carried the embers of the fire on a metal tray. Immediately he began to build a new fire.

They began the second extraction at dusk, bringing out an excavator and drill. Three blues watched us as they patrolled just beyond the caution tape. It grew dark. Raven began to play some music off her phone and shouted, *Dance party! Whoever wins the dance party wins the mountain!* A group of seven or eight women danced with her—along with Butterfly, who came up the mountain with an umbrella, tall, skinny, punning, and eccentric, like a character out of Dr. Seuss. People warmed up by the fire. We cooked another pad Thai and ate. This second extraction took less time and was conducted under blinding police lights as mist rose off the trees. The dance party continued—gyrating, twisting defenders. Sparks from the fire. Crashing of the river below. When officers extracted the second arrestee and had taken her away in a paddy wagon to the sound of our calls of encouragement, the excavator filled in the trench; the RCMP left. We hadn't been sure what might happen—if they might try to make us leave, in which case, the plan was to move slowly off the mountain, for individuals to then slip off into the forest and rendezvous later at Grandfather Tree. But the cops simply left. Probably exhausted and pissed off after spending eight hours on the mountain in a cold rain, digging two defenders out of the trenches. They've been doing variations of this for a year now.

Everyone grab a tent and take it to the other side of the bridge. We grabbed tents and set them up on the far side of the bridge, so that we could defend the entire span once again in the morning, pushing our front back down the mountain. Began to build another soft block—logs, rocks, anything to slow them down, to make them get out of their cars to remove the obstacle. This time we filled two barrels with rocks, brought in large logs, pieces of wood. Lightning Bolt insists on making it beautiful—before, there had been a smiley face made of cedar branches, with yellow caution tape eyes. This new soft block is meant to be a dragon, decorated with cedar. In the dark, off the side of the forest service road, I found a carefully built path with stepped roots and handrails formed out of branches, which meandered past the most magnificent yellow cedars up to a space called the Medicine Wheel. Rocks, in a spiral pattern, a lantern. A sign, asking for respect of this place. Truly ancient in feeling, as if finding a door into a secret room. As we slept, a new hard block was dug, and two women locked themselves in, side by side.

The second day began as the first, a clanging on tin and a voice: *Wake up, everyone. Wake up, Fairy Creek!* Got up and dressed: rain pants, merino wool, work jacket. Blissfully waterproof, if cold. Boiled water, made tea. Shoved an apple, trail mix, headlamp, phone, Kleenex, handwarmers into my pockets. Boots on. I'd packed up everything—sleeping bag, sleeping pad, all my gear, everything shoved into the backpack, all my wet tarps lashed to the outside of my pack, everything but the tent. Suddenly the cry went out: *Two cars—blues!!* Strawberry, one of the Indigenous land defenders, appeared: *Quick—get everything out! Quick—or they'll get the tents. Everyone grab the tents.* Butterfly grabbed mine, even the rock I'd secured to the fly, and lifted it over the hard block to the line of defenders already there. We climbed over the tarp strung across the bridge on a thigh-high rope. Several larger tents still to come down. Someone, not having heard the warning call, continued making a pot of porridge. As the blues got out of their car, Raven called out, *Who has a camera?* I did, so she asked me to go with her as witness to film her talk with Commander Raj.

She told him someone had stolen her hammock and her pack, her dry socks. She needed it back. He insisted no one took her stuff. She protested that it had been in the forest. *They've done this before. The green guy yesterday took it—he said he'd take my stuff.* Raj: *No one took it.* Raven: *Look, please ask for it.* Raj tried to change the subject: *We need you to move back on the bridge.* She argued, *How can we build a relationship if you keep changing the topic on me?* He said, *We need you to move back to the middle of the bridge.* He said, *Why did you do this—are those more hard blocks you put in? Both sides?* She said, *Yes.* But in fact there were two girls locked in only by the near side of the bridge, where we had slept. The side higher up on the mountain, the builders had felt, had been compromised the day before when officers had cut into large sections of the wood to dig out the girl in the hard block. Raj insisted, *Why did you do this? Why not wait for the 15th, for your day in court?* She countered, *You know why, Raj. The minute we leave, the loggers come in and the trees come down.*

We moved back behind the hard block. Everyone there now. One of the blues tore away the tarp at some point and cut the rope, so that the two girls—Bombadil and Salal—were exposed to the rain. Consultation. Raven, Strawberry. The discussion was on how to form a blob behind the hard block with so few of us: tallest, strongest people in the front row, especially at the sides of the bridge. Everyone else behind ready to grab onto a front-row defender from behind. In the front, you stand with your arms locked to either side with the person next to you, then your hands locked together behind your back—an excruciating position, especially impossible if wearing a backpack. We were quickly in formation. More trucks arrived. A paddy wagon. More blues. They set up two white pop-up tarps, brought out stacks of wood, made an impromptu table and stacked about four dozen bottles of Gatorade on it, which no one ever touched. Some wag put a cedar branch in a bottle, in parody of our soft block. One of the tarps protected the firewood; another was positioned up front by the hard block.

At any given time, there were three to six blues—five men and one woman with a red cross on her uniform, who rolled her eyes whenever someone chirped from the blob. The older men were either placid or, in Raj's case, angry. *Another fucking day in the rain. (Would it just let up for one hot minute?!)* They were clearly trying to figure out what to do—they couldn't extract with all of us within a foot of the hard block. They couldn't use pepper spray because of the court's condemnation and scrutiny of their brutal tactics earlier that summer. They couldn't charge us because of the girls locked into the trench below us and the river to either side. It was a brilliant tactical position on our part. But people would get tired—it was so cold and so wet; we were soaked. Standing still with your arms locked behind you, your heavy pack on your back, is torture of a kind.

Now and then someone in front would ask to be spelled out, then another. This is how I ended up in the very front—surely the smallest one in line—all the others were mostly young Amazons, who sang song after song. Arctic Fox stood next to me, at the very end as an anchor, and I felt completely secure, ready to be arrested if necessary to save the trees. Strawberry, also small, who walks with a cane, came out past the front line to help Salal under the tarp, and as she did, a blue snuck up towards her and sprang to grab her. But those in the front row grabbed her arms and pulled her back to safety behind our line. I think the blue had said to her, before lunging for her, *You're the instigator of this?* and she'd said, *I'm helping this girl in the ground.* Arctic Fox shouted about our civil liberties and Judge Thompson's report.

Kelly Tatham, who had posted a YouTube video of an earlier arrest of Strawberry (Shy-Anne Gunville), observes in an essay in *Rabble* that Strawberry was often the target of RCMP violence at Fairy Creek. Here Tatham describes an action she witnessed on August 20, 2021, at River camp:

> As soon as the forest defenders sat on the ground, RCMP began pulling people out of the crowd, pushing them to the ground, and binding their hands with zip ties. Defenders sobbed and cried out as RCMP officers pushed bodies and faces into the gravel, pinned down legs and arms, and twisted wrists. During this altercation they singled out an Afro-Indigenous land defender named Strawberry. After the RCMP ripped her away from the friend she was clinging onto, pinned her down, and zip tied her, officers were shouting at one another: "take her right now" and "she's first." I spoke with Strawberry after and she told me that they target her every time she's on the front line and that after they carried her out of sight, they dropped her feet and dragged them along the gravel until her shoes came off.[17]

---

17 Tatham, "The Human Cost." The video of Strawberry's arrest at that time is available on YouTube: "Strawberry's Arrest Police Brutality."

We soon saw a similar tactic directed at Raven, another racialized woman and organizer at Fairy Creek. At some point earlier, I'd run to grab new tarps to place on the ground over each girl; they were secured in place with rocks, but as they were virtually flat, they pooled with rainwater—Bombadil's trench became perilously swamped every time she wriggled and squirmed like a puppy, as water poured into her trench or into Salal's next to her. The blues under the campfire tarp tried to start a fire, one chopping wood, another trying to start some kindling, with no luck at all. Arctic Fox kept chirping at them, goading: *Let me help you! I'll do it for you—I've got all my tools right here! I'll do a workshop for you.* One of the cops joked with him: *Well, you know, that guy, he needs some practice with his survival skills.* A blue brought a cup of propane and poured it on the fire, which flared up, then died. Another cup of fuel, now with little sticks of tinder dipped into it. Another little fire that also fizzled out. It took them at least an hour, to everyone's amusement on the front line, to build a fire that caught. Now Raven came out to help Salal, who needed to pee—especially hard to do with one arm locked into a pipe in the ground and a girl's anatomy. Raven passed Salal a bottle with a wide rim and began to tell her how to do it, just as a cop lunged, grabbed Raven, and dragged her away. She is only 5 feet tall, maybe less, with long black dreadlocks. She sat with her legs splayed in a V like a little kid looking nonplussed, like, "wtf." They dragged her to the truck, searched her for her radio, weapons—none—put the radio in an evidence bag. Put her in the truck. Drove away. Everyone called out to her and howled like wolves.

I was still standing next to Arctic Fox in the front line. Five or six blues, circling. I don't know what signal triggered them, but suddenly several blues lunged towards our side. I think I was the target because I was the smallest by far in the front row. A blue gouged his thumb under my chin, then slipped his hand down to my neck and pressed so hard I couldn't breathe, his other thumb screwed into my right shoulder at a painful pressure point. I felt myself being pushed back, but almost instantly a counter pressure came from Arctic Fox and all the defenders behind me and to my other side. Foxtrot, in the second row, was pushed back so hard by the force of the initial lunge that she almost fell over the side of the bridge. She screamed—someone grabbed her as she heard a cop say, *Oh fuck.* Their attempt made it clear they had no way to breach our line without a potential for serious injury to the girls in the trenches and to the defenders at the bridge's edge.

The day progressed. We stood in formation. There was a rhythm to it. Someone from our side would come forward from the fire Arctic Fox had built, still burning steadily, with a hot drink and everyone would take a sip as it was held gingerly to our mouths. Or another would approach with sticks of pepperoni, or pieces of a Clif Bar to share. Those in the front had to be fed by hand, as our arms were twisted behind our backs. Strawberry called out to us, from the front line, to say how very grateful she was that we were there to help her defend Indigenous land—that it was easy to do in the summer when it was beautiful and warm, but this was hard in the cold and pouring rain. And we were taking back the bridge with only twenty-four people. We could wait them out.

Raj the Commander told us we'd be pushed back no matter what, but we didn't budge. Late afternoon, we sang the same song over and over, swaying faintly as a hypnotic calm came over us.

> Here we stand by the river
> through the wind, the rain, and snow.
> In the wind our branches may quiver
> we may sway but we will stay.
> And one day, when we fall
> we will rot and we will crumble.

But we know that we have given our all
and we will feed the seeds of tomorrow.[18]

Late afternoon, as dusk drew down, the RCMP folded up one of the tarps, leaving one over the fire. They set up a yellow caution tape attached to orange cones in front of the hard block and left two younger officers in charge in a pickup truck. More experienced protestors said they wouldn't come back in force until the morning, but for now they formed a sparse watch. Those of us who needed to leave—a handful of us—and everyone else stood in a row in front of the police tape to create a distraction. Arctic Fox talked with the officers, haggling over how many could hike down, telling them that the girls in the hard blocks were okay. The cops insisted only four at a time, every half hour. But how to enforce this? There's no law to say only four people can leave at a time on Crown land.

Foxtrot and I had to leave, needing to catch the last ferry. While the squabbling ensued, Strawberry helped two new people slip into the hard blocks. Salal and Bombadil were freed. We got word that the switch

---

18 "Here We Stand—Frontline Song Circle." A recording of this song can be heard in a video posted to Facebook, where land defenders sing at the base of a flying dragon. Having been told by a fellow defender that this song was composed by Ayden Catry-Bauer, I reached out to him through FaceBook and he shared with me the story of this song coming from the trees in the Walbran: "[I] was leading a group of kids on a camping trip at Bridge Camp (the WOLF kids program from Salt Spring Island). Early in the morning, I was sitting against a big old cedar right by the river and just started humming the melody to this song. Parts of the lyrics started falling into place right then and the rest of the lyrics got added in the following days as I walked through the old growth. If you share this song, please share where it came along with it. I think the river and the trees would be happy knowing that people are thinking of them as they sing." He notes that the song was "caught a year or two before the Fairy Creek protests" and friends of his taught it to the protestors. (Private communication with author.)

had been completed; Foxtrot and I slipped out along with Copper. Red Cedar and her dogs caught up with us. We began the hike down the mountain as light faded, snapping on our headlamps as a guide.

Now and then an RCMP truck cruised slowly behind us or drove up in the opposite direction. Retrospectively, I realized they were looking for Strawberry, who had planned also to hike down; we learned when we got to the bottom of the mountain that she'd been arrested on her descent. There was a scramble to find out which truck she was in—possibly the one we passed as we hiked out along the Teal-Jones turn-off. An officer barked at us to move on. The RCMP truck sped off towards Lake Cowichan. Almost immediately some defenders followed in a car. But we saw all this later, at HQ.

During the hike down, I could barely keep going at times. In the blue dusk, images of desolate clear cut softened and faded from view. We met two defenders hiking up; we stopped a moment to let them know the bridge was still ours. Farther down, we ran into a dozen or so more defenders heading up, including Matihi and Raven, whose arrest that day had been her first time ever; it had been done illegally as correct process had not been followed. They were already heading back up. I hiked quickly, as I couldn't bear a minute longer carrying the pack—my right shoulder and arm were incredibly painful—partly from carrying it almost all day on my back, partly from having my shoulder wrenched by the officer. At last, I spotted the old clear cut that defenders had planted as a healing garden last summer, then the blur of spotlights and smoke at Roadside.

A woman ran up to us to ask how the two girls in hard blocks had done—Bombadil, Salal. It turned out Salal was her daughter. I said Bombadil had been squirming, maybe struggling, popping up a lot to look around, while Salal hadn't moved—was fine, but stoic. The woman said yes, she would be. Then the cries went up about Strawberry. We hiked over to Foxtrot's car. We had left the lights on by accident, but miraculously the engine turned over. Used the porta toilet, stripped off our wet gear, turned on the heat full blast, and left, hoping to catch the ferry as we drove along the dark, drenched roads, thinking always of the kids still up on the mountain at Landback Bridge, especially the ones in the hard blocks. Those who remained held the bridge for a week.

Over a month had passed and now we had come to hike Granite Main in the daylight, to spend time with the trees. That last time at Landback Bridge, we had been too overwhelmed, too wet, too cold to the bone, too busy building soft blocks and holding the line. I recalled our second night there, after we'd held off the RCMP for another day and moved our own line forward, when I'd wandered into the trees and discovered a small path that led to a Medicine Wheel, a healing garden, which I'd had to use my headlamp to see. The trees were a massive, dark, sentient presence, all around.

Galvanized by that last action, Foxtrot has begun to participate in Save Old Growth (SOG) actions in Vancouver, in which protestors gather before the sun rises and occupy the Trans-Canada, bearing green and yellow signs with one message: SAVE OLD GROWTH. She has been arrested twice now; the second time she crazy-glued her hand to the pavement.[19] One of the girls we met at Roadside, Cricket, now with SOG, has drawn Foxtrot a map with pencil crayon: blue for the river, green to show the locations of Grandmother Tree and Grandfather Tree. We had been told at

---

19 For a description of my own arrest experience with Save Old Growth, listen to the podcast *Arrest Stories*, "Lyric Crow—A Deep Dive into the BC 'Justice' System."

Landback Bridge, *If we are overrun by the RCMP, if we must separate, we'll reassemble at Grandfather Tree.* But we didn't know where Grandfather Tree was and, in the end, didn't need to, as we hiked back down to Roadside in darkness, while the line still held.

Now we hiked up Granite Main, in sunlight, at a steady pace, seeing the traces of our earlier visits, and the remains of earlier camps and conflicts before our time, these battle scars on the mountain's broad shoulders. We saw the mound of debris that we had helped to gather, used to create a barricade days after the injunction had been reinstated, decorated at the time with a cheeky hand-painted sign that read in bright pink letters, *Welcome Back Boys*. We hiked past the clear cuts higher up, barely visible in the dark when we'd first climbed but sensed as an opening, an absence. At one of these clear cuts, rising high above us along a steep slope to the skyline, red dresses had been carefully placed on huge stumps and piles of slash, dozens and dozens of red dresses, rising high above us, accusatory, blood red: *You kill our trees, you kill our sisters, our mothers, our daughters. You take everything that you want, with violence, as you have always done. No more.*

We climbed higher, passing markers indicating the distance we'd come along the FSR, 6.5 km, 7 km, 7.5 km. The air grew colder; up ahead, a distinct line appeared where the snow had fallen and remained. Some days earlier a Teal-Jones truck had come through, leaving two deep tire tracks—I took one, Foxtrot the other. The snow grew thicker the higher we climbed. We came to the fork in the road that led to the bridge. To the right—thick snow, no tracks; the Teal Jones truck had turned left, towards the bridge.

It looked smaller than I remembered. Peaceful now, except for the two black tracks that crossed the bridge and continued up the steep hill beyond until they curved out of view. I found the path easily that I'd taken our first time here, which led to Grandmother Tree; we wandered past giant cedars, windfall, patches of forest floor, patches of snow, everything green, cloaked in moss and lichen, beads of glittering water, steam rising in sunlight, breathing and veridian. Grandmother Tree was listening, sensing our presence, transmitting signals underground, linked by slender threads of mycorrhizae like nerves, rooted, dispersed, alert, vigilant.

Later we used Cricket's map to find Grandfather Tree, back along the road we'd come and then into the forest, along a slender track, Foxtrot leading the way. She called back to me, *I don't think this is right,* or *Maybe we won't find it*—something like that, yet she was looking straight at him—so large and wide and tall her eyes had skipped over, while he observed our approach, had heard us coming. Massive and sentinel. He had been watching our approach for hundreds of years.

We sat at his feet, as close as we could, as he stands on a precipitous slope, his flared base massive—I think it would take fifteen or twenty people, arms outstretched, to circle him. Maybe more. More. Two cyclists passed on the road far below, completely unaware of us, as we sat quietly and watched, and felt blessed to have found him, and to do our part to defend the old-growth.

A few days after this hike, on January 26, 2022, the BC Court of Appeal extended the injunction at Fairy Creek through September 26, 2022. It ruled unanimously in favour of Teal-Jones, a private logging company, to continue to cut down thousand-year-old trees for profit. RCMP would be directed, as in the summer before, to protect the economic interests of profit over people. "The conduct of police does not tarnish the reputation of the court; the court and police are constitutionally independent. The public interest in upholding the rule of law continues to be the dominant public interest in cases involving civil disobedience against a private entity," the judge wrote.[20]

TSAWALK

Our contemporary world order is an expression of an emergent left hemispheric dominance, with its connection to "handedness" or manipulation, and its emphasis on the mechanical, the part over the organic whole; it has been linked to reason and scientific method, which necessarily relies, to some extent, on abstraction, taxonomy, a breakdown into parts. Indigenous theories of knowledge have sought not to reject or excoriate such methods, but to offer a frame shift and to emphasize the interconnectedness and entangledness of all things—just as the scientist Lynn Margulis argued for a theory of endosymbiosis to explain the emergence of multicellular life on Earth, a theory which the scientific establishment resisted for decades.

Two theories adjacent to the practice of an ecological poetics are the theory of *tsawalk* and the concept of *etuaptmumk*. These two theories are grounded in the concept of traditional ecological knowledge (TEK), which is necessarily a local knowledge, specific to a particular place, its terrain, fauna and flora, seasons, migrations, and harvesting patterns, through time. TEK is the accumulated knowledge of place in all its interconnections, learned through time by a people who live in situ and transmit this knowledge from one generation to the next, over many generations.

20 Quoted in Egan-Elliott, "Teal-Jones Wins Appeal."

The theory of *tsawalk* is introduced by Nuu-chah-nulth writer Umeek (E. Richard Atleo), and comes from the phrase *heshook-ish tsawalk*, "everything is one." This is "a Nuu-chah-nulth perspective that is inclusive of all reality, both physical and metaphysical"[21] where "the universe is regarded as a network of relationships."[22] I am reminded again of the Beiler et al. map charting the links made between tree roots and mycorrhizal fungi, a thin cross-section of this entangledness.[23]

As with McGilchrist, on the emerging primacy of the left hemispheric style of seeing—and therefore instantiating that vision of the world, Umeek also expresses concern for what scientific methodology and its attendant reason, although valuable, obscure or filter out from our understanding of the world, dismissing what might be most crucial. The result, Umeek argues, is a notable imbalance—ecological, material, emotional, mental, spiritual.

I see this imbalance when the BC government spends almost $9 million to fund the RCMP, and more specifically C-IRG,[24] to protect

21 Umeek, *Tsawalk*, xi.

22 Umeek, *Tsawalk*, 118.

23 Beiler et al., "Architecture of the Wood-Wide-Web."

24 BC RCMP, "Critical Response Unit—British Columbia (CRU-BC)"; Morin, "'We're Not Going Anywhere.'" According to the RCMP's own description, C-IRG, or Community-Industry Response Group, was created in 2017 "to provide strategic oversight in addressing energy industry (gas and oil pipeline) incidents and related public order, national security and crime issues. Its mandate was to ensure a consistent, standardized and impartially administered police response across the province, using a measured approach in facilitating the peaceful resolution of public disorder issues." Renamed the Critical Response Unit—British Columbia (CRU-BC) on January 1, 2024, it claims to support "the measured approach to public order enforcement through relationship building, impartiality, interoperability…

the rights of a private logging company at Fairy Creek to cut down thousand-year-old trees for profit. The RCMP, as of the end of 2021, was reported to have spent almost $9 million to enforce the injunction at Fairy Creek: "At $6.22 million, personnel accounts for the majority of the total costs, with transportation and telecommunications in second at $1.68 million. The RCMP spent $826,525 on rentals and leases and $108,823 on utilities, materials and supplies."[25] This figure was as of November 30, 2021, calculated from the beginning of the protests. I saw some of these resources being spent in my six visits in the fall of 2021, and most significantly in my time at Landback Bridge, as we stood in two rows, arms linked, behind the two girls locked into hard blocks. C-IRG presence consisted of: between eight and twelve RCMP officers at any one time; two canvas pop-up shelters; firewood; propane, to start the fire; meals; many police cars and paddy wagons; the cost of the extractions—the backhoe,

---

... and education throughout all the stages of conflict" and continues "to engage partners at all levels in any critical incident to find strategies and solutions that minimize police enforcement."

Here is a description of C-IRG by Brandi Morin ("'We're Not Going Anywhere'"): "As the name suggests, the unit is responsible for managing conflicts between industry and communities. Unfortunately for those (overwhelmingly Indigenous) communities, conflicts have more often been managed by militarized commando raids than good faith negotiation. The unit exists to flatten opposition to natural 'resource' projects and has sought to do so, with mixed results, in places like Wet'suwet'en territory and Fairy Creek. Wherever Indigenous Peoples are halting the flow of profits, the C-IRG will show up, lock down the area, exclude journalists and then arrest everyone—far from the prying eyes of the public."

According to Morin, an investigation into C-IRG's conduct began in early 2023 as a result of almost "500 formal complaints over violence and violations of Charter and Indigenous rights" reported to the RCMP's civilian oversight body, the Civilian Review and Complaints Commission (CRCC). A CBC *Fifth Estate* investigation has also covered the C-IRG (see "Whose Police?").

25 Egan-Elliott, "RCMP Has Spent Nearly $9 Million."

the angle-grinders, the drills and generators, the wire cutters; the wages, the overtime, the salaries and pensions and benefits. All to protect the "right" of Teal-Jones to cut down Grandmother and Grandfather Trees, and the "social contract" that allows them to do so.

I think of this imbalance when I see the iconic, heartbreaking photograph that appeared in the summer of 2021 of the cross-section of a Sitka spruce grandfather, 2 metres (7 feet) in diameter, being driven down Nanaimo Parkway en route to a Port Alberni mill to be made into acoustic guitar soundboards—or so Teal-Jones would like us to believe:

> About one-half of the ancient forest Teal cuts in TFL 46, trucks to its log sort at Duke Point, and then booms across the Salish Sea and up the Fraser River to its mill in Surrey, spends time as a pile of sawdust and wood chips on its way to a pulp mill or a bag of garden mulch or some other low value product. About half.[26]

Or more recently, in the summer of 2023, when I read of the planned logging of Bugaboo Creek:

> Cut block 4733 in Bugaboo Creek is the most spectacular ancient forest currently scheduled for logging—likely in 2023—across TFL 46. Teal-Jones has constructed a massive and sprawling system of roads into the 75-acre cut block proposal, which has yet to be submitted to the government for approval.[27]

26 Broadland, "Teal Cedar's Big, Dirty Secret."

27 @fairycreekblockade, Instagram post, June 10, 2023.

They point out that oldgrowth specklebelly lichen has been documented at Bugaboo Creek, one of only fifty or so locations in British Columbia. Other species at risk here are the marbled murrelets, a seabird that nests only in old-growth trees and which has declined by over 40 percent in TFL 46 since 2002, and, of course, the yellow cedar trees that can be turned into easy profit, ancient giants "up to 9 feet thick, and approaching 2000 years old."[28]

I think of this imbalance when I hear Inuit hunters in the documentary *Qapirangajuq: Inuit Knowledge and Climate Change* insist that "the Earth has tilted on its axis."[29] Umeek quotes John Ralston Saul on the "Dictatorship of Reason," in which he describes

---

28 Omstead, "Environmental Groups Celebrate Court Ruling." In February 2024, the federal court sided with the marbled murrelet, contra Minister of Environment and Climate Change Steven Guilbeault's interpretation of federal protections for at-risk migratory birds. Several environmental groups alleged that "Minister Steven Guilbeault took a position in 2022 that the federal government had no obligation to protect anything other than nests on provincial lands, and not the wider habitat at-risk migratory birds need to survive. Chief Justice Paul Crampton's ruling last week found the minister's interpretation was unreasonably narrow, sending the minister's protection statement back to the government for reconsideration. 'It was not reasonable or tenable for the Minister to limit that critical habitat to "nests" alone,' the decision said."

29 Observed by an Inuit hunter in Zacharias Kunuk's *Qapirangajuq*. NASA scientists confirm that according to their calculations, the Earth has *not* tilted on its axis; yet the Inuit hunters confirm that the angle at which the sun rises is different, hence their assertion that the "Earth has tilted on its axis." Both can be said to be correct, in that it was later discovered that increased particulate matter in the atmosphere refracted the light of the rising and setting sun, thus giving the appearance that it was setting in different places, that the Earth had tilted; more importantly, the Inuit explanation for how this happened is metaphorically true, something has tilted or shifted, something is wrong, or out of tune.

reason as "outdistancing" so many important human characteristics, including "spirit, appetite, faith and emotion," as well as intuition and experience, to the extent that "the mythological importance of reason obscures all else."[30] In our current instantiation of the developed world, we have failed to see the entanglement of all things, how everything is one—connected, irreducible to distinct components. Umeek also introduces the concept of *isaak*, or "respect," which he notes is not a term of human origin, "but is understood in terms of creation and its meaning. It creates a climate or environment for the practitioner in which communication with other life forms is possible."[31] This, he says, is a Nuu-chah-nulth term not used in daily life, in terms of inter-human relations; *isaak* is more broadly linked to creation and "made effective communication between the Nuu-chah-nulth and animals like the salmon and wolf a reality."[32] Yet he feels it can be applied (he is speaking in terms of educators and researchers) to human practices:

> What does *isaak* mean in practice? It means that life forms of every kind are held in equal esteem. All life forms have intrinsic value. Humans of every race have equal value, as do the deer, the wolf, the whale, the eagle, the cedar tree. Holding life forms in equal esteem demands that balance and harmony be maintained among them by the development of protocols.[33]

I have already pried these two concepts—*isaak* and *tsawalk*—out of their very specific context. Umeek presents them in his book,

---

30 Ralston Saul quoted in Umeek, *Tsawalk*, xii.

31 Umeek, *Tsawalk*, 16.

32 Umeek, *Tsawalk*, 16.

33 Umeek, *Tsawalk*, 16.

Tsawalk: A Nuu-chah-nulth Worldview (2004), through a series of stories, beginning with the story of how Raven steals the light for the people who live in darkness. He contextualizes the telling of such a story—a longhouse with families gathered around a fire, the darkness beyond. This is not my own story to tell in its particulars; I refer you to his book for his telling of the story. Variations appear among First Nations all along the West Coast.[34]

Another Indigenous reframing of a twenty-first-century Western lens[35]—scientific method, reason, left hemispheric privileging of manipulation, the mechanical, abstraction, typology, the part over the whole—has been offered by Mi'kmaq Elder Albert Marshall, in the concept of *etuaptmumk*, or "two-eyed seeing," a "gift of multiple perspective" that he says is held by many First Nations and Inuit cultures. *Etuaptmumk* "refers to learning to see from one eye with the strengths of Indigenous knowledges and ways of knowing, and from the other eye with the strengths of Western knowledge and knowledges and ways of knowing, and to using both these ideas together, for the benefit of all."[36]

This practice is necessarily grounded in a particular land base and the traditional ecological and phenomenological knowledge that a community has acquired of this land over generations. As with the terms *tsawalk, heshook-ish tsawalk,* and *isaak, etuaptmumk* is rooted in place, and I am hesitant to suggest these terms might be directly used to describe the ways of attending and listening that I associate

---

34 Umeek, *Tsawalk*, 16.

35 "Western" is not a truly accurate term—WEIRD (Western, educated, industrialized, rich, developed) might be more accurate, referencing the most wealthy nations that have benefitted from making use of such tools. I do not mean to suggest they are not valuable tools for humans, but at what cost, if not used with care?

36 Marshall as relayed in Bartlett et al., "Two-Eyed Seeing," 335.

with ecologically oriented poetry, just as *heshook-ish tsawalk* is adjacent to, but not equivalent to, the Gaia principle, just as *isaak* resonates with a safeguarding of biodiversity by respecting all forms of life. In particular, the spiritual element is often downplayed in scientific terms such as endosymbiosis or mycorrhizal networks. Yet, while not equivalent, they are adjacent and resonant.

Poetry as a method of approach to the Other, as a practice of vigilance, is kin to *isaak, heshook-ish tsawalk*, and *etuaptmumk*, in its openness to perceiving and tracing entanglements in situ, instantiated. Poetry might be understood as a cousin to *etuaptmumk*, a sounding that can supplement and enrich our scientific ways of knowing. Both are a form of vigilance. Marshall observes, "The advantage of two-eyed seeing is that you are always fine tuning your mind into different places at once, you are always looking for another perspective and better way of doing things."[37]

This description accords well with my own experience of writing a poem, which also begins with a fine-tuning of the mind into different places at the same time, often happening just below the level of consciousness, humming along.

I can't remember the moment it occurred to me that I would write a long poem about (or more hopefully, with) oldgrowth specklebelly lichen, within the context of the complex relationships and networks drawn at Fairy Creek, only that it began surely with a form of vigilance. As a newcomer, I came to observe, quietly, to see how others carried out necessary tasks in the camps, to learn

37 Quoted in Bartlett et al., "Two-Eyed Seeing," 336.

how to interact appropriately with the RCMP and the C-IRG unit, just as at night, exhausted from running supplies, washing dishes, participating in circle gatherings, I fell asleep feeling the layers of rich humus contour itself around my body, hearing the shush of wind through cedar branches. I learned of protocols regarding stories; offerings of cedar, food, and tobacco; songs; these are not mine to share, and so I do not recount them here. I listened to Elder Bill Jones speak of the importance of Ada'itsx to his family, of his work life as a logger. From Grandma Losah, I learned how to build a fire in the drying tarpee, and how to use fierce humour and care when allies crossed boundaries and disrespected traditions.

And beyond these lessons, I was gathering such an eclectic assortment of physical and digital ephemera—the scent of woodsmoke suffusing my hair and my rain jacket for days after leaving camp; an Instagram post on the discovery by Natasha Lavdovsky of oldgrowth specklebelly lichen on already fallen trees; a newspaper report on the brutality of C-IRG; a night spent turtling supplies up to Waterfall camp; scouring textbooks and scientific articles that describe the morphology and distribution of oldgrowth specklebelly lichen on Vancouver Island.

And this gathering continues, a constant sense of awareness or alertness, and of waiting for what might come. This need to wait, to attend, is in tension with urgency as well, as in seeing a post on more oldgrowth specklebelly being found in a scheduled cut block at Bugaboo Creek, an urgency that I know a lyric poem cannot address in the same way as a blockade or an arrest.

I first encountered the idea of two-eyed seeing in a blog post by the Mi'kmaw poet and speculative writer Tiffany Morris, when we were both invited to be part of a series on ecopoetics curated by

Jesse Holth in *The Ex-Puritan*'s blog, *The Town Crier* in 2020. After noting that ecopoetry is an important form of witness, Morris observes that speculative or apocalyptic ecopoetry—perhaps all ecopoetry has become apocalyptic and speculative, to a large extent, due to our current circumstances—is able to see both what is present now and to imagine a better future:

> Apocalypse ecopoetics deals with this crisis of world-ending and collapse, and the urgency of climate crisis is central to that mode. But there is, if nothing else, room to imagine a new world where an old one ends: one of healing, decolonization, and futurity.[38]

Etuaptmumk is placed in opposition by Morris to "the ecofascist ideology that centres humans as a parasitic or aberrant presence in nature. *Etuaptmumk* can be, in short, a method of decolonizing our thinking about the apocalypse. Holding these dualities in mind is important."[39] I think this is a crucial rejection of the viral idea of humans as parasitic or super predator—yet another form of human exceptionalism.

Another key idea she introduces is the necropastoral, which she defines as "holding sacred the fungal importance of decay."[40] The necropastoral expands the concept of natural processes, embracing the full cycle from first bloom or birth through decomposition.

While *etuaptmumk* favours sight as its central metaphor, Seamus Heaney, in his Nobel Prize speech, describes his own experience of

---

38 Morris, "Decolonizing the Apocalypse."
39 Morris, "Decolonizing the Apocalypse."
40 Morris, "Decolonizing the Apocalypse."

attending in aural terms while growing up in a three-room thatched farmstead in County Derry, absorbing as a young child the adult murmurs in the kitchen, the scurry of mice on the ceiling, horse whinnies, rumbling of a railway line, and signals picked up by an

> aerial wire attached to the topmost branch of the chestnut tree. Down it swept, in through a hole bored in the corner of the kitchen window... transmitting from beyond... and beyond every voice, the frantic, piercing signaling of Morse code.[41]

He presents this attunement as analogous to the work of poetry, a "re-tuning of the world... transitive like the impatient thump which unexpectedly restores the picture to the television set, or the electric shock which sets the fibrillating heart back to its proper rhythm."[42] The young child, attuned to the world, is aerial receptor, open and vigilant to all that comes to him, as is the poet.

The Vancouver poet Pat Lowther, writing in the 1970s, also comes close to describing this fine-tuning that Marshall and Heaney describe, in "Hotline to the Gulf":

> Only a hot vein
> wires me
> to the perimeter
> straining
> to hear syllables
> in the hiss of blood.[43]

---

41 Heaney, *Crediting Poetry*.

42 Heaney, *Crediting Poetry*.

43 Lowther, "Hotline to the Gulf," 86.

Radio and poetry are analogues. The poet is in the abyss, embryonic and wired, tuning in the static of angels, of loved ones, of those who are lost. The poet is embodied, grounded in the body—the embryo tethered to its mother and so to the outside world through the umbilicus—and cybernetic, linked to the world through modern communication technologies: radio, hotlines. The poet is in the gulf but receives and seeks communication with the outside world, material and ethereal, spiritual. Poetry, like radio, this most intimate medium, channels through the body the ecological news of the day. The poet is in the gulf, transmitting and receiving signals to and from the perimeter, receptive to scientific and cultural knowledge, an open receptivity, and transmuting it in the process of writing a poem, which becomes a transmitter, as much as a receiver.

LE VIDE / EMPTYING

Simone Weil defined attention in this way:

> Attention consists of suspending our thought, leaving it detached [*disponible*], empty [*vide*], and ready to be penetrated by the object; it means holding in our minds, within the reach of this thought, but on a lower level and not in contact with it, the diverse knowledge we have acquired which we are forced to make use of... Above all our thought should be empty [*vide*], waiting [*en attente*], not seeking anything [*ne rien chercher*], but ready to receive in its naked truth the object that is to penetrate it.[44]

44 Weil, quoted in Rozelle-Stone and Davis, "Simone Weil."

This could be a description of the writing of a poem, in which any foundational knowledge or research that has been conducted is left below the level of consciousness; a space or clearing is made within thought to receive the other. Weil describes this as "negative attention," an ethical practice that requires the ability to perceive the suffering of another, including the conditions or climate that caused such suffering, and to simultaneously be aware that one could also suffer in a similar way.[45] In French, the word *attention* (attention) is closely linked to the word for waiting, *attente*; one pays attention through patient waiting, opening the self to the other. Weil also uses the word "penetration"; the other enters within; attention is a form of vigilance, of remaining watchful, or awake, receptive to the coming of the other. This waiting/attending should not be a searching or "muscular attempt" at thought that attempts to fill the emptiness; it should instead be a "negative effort";[46] "[t]he soul empties itself of all its own contents in order to receive into itself the being it is looking at, just as he is, in all his truth."[47] She frames this in the context of science and poetry:

> Active searching is prejudicial, not only to love, but also to the intelligence, whose laws are the same as those of love. We just have to wait for the solution of a geometrical problem or the meaning of a Latin or Greek sentence to come into our mind. Still more must we wait for any new scientific truth or for a beautiful line of poetry.[48]

45 Rozelle-Stone and Davis, "Simone Weil."

46 Weil, *Waiting for God*, 109, 111.

47 Weil, *Waiting for God*, 115.

48 Weil, *Waiting for God*, 196.

The "I" is stripped away (*dépouillement*), which "allows for an impersonal but intersubjective ethic,"[49] a form of negative attention. Instead of forcing knowledge, one must wait; this is akin to grace, within Weil's Christian framework. As Rozelle-Stone and Davis observe,

> attention is openness to what cannot be predicted and to what often takes us by surprise. In this way, attention resists the natural tendency of humans to seek control and dominance over others. At stake in this ethical mode, then, is the prevention of injustices that result from projects of self-expansion, including the French colonialism Weil criticized in her time.[50]

Attention as an ethical act that resists force, particularly within the context of the ongoing impacts of colonialization and resource extraction at Ada'itsx / Fairy Creek, are on my mind here.[51]

Just as Weil describes attention as a kind of decreation in which the self must be withdrawn, my experience of writing poetry has always been that of simply waiting and being open to what might come. Whenever I have tried to force a poem, it has never worked out. Keats speaks to this need for patience (and empathy with another's suffering) in the concept of "negative capability," as noted in previous chapters:

---

49 Rozelle-Stone and Davis, "Simone Weil."

50 Rozelle-Stone and Davis, "Simone Weil."

51 I am aware of the contentious divisions within Indigenous Nations over resource extraction projects and the complex legacy of the colonial system and the Indian Act; this includes divisions within the Pacheedaht Nation over logging in Fairy Creek. The protestors at Ada'itsx proceeded with actions to preserve the old-growth forest with support from Elder Bill Jones and other members of the Pacheedaht Nation, conscious of the fact the elected tribal council held a different position. Fairy Creek is a complex ethical space.

emptying of the self, the ego, the muscular need to be, to produce, to be active, to make—all must be resisted and replaced with the need to empty oneself out, to be patient, calm, and open, to clear space within oneself—this need expressed by Keats is embodied in his image of becoming the sparrow pecking about the gravel. This is Weil's stripping away of the self, emptying of the I, *dépouillement*, and decreation. The experience Weil describes as grace I have experienced in writing a poem—a sense of energy that comes through me.

I recently wrote a very early version of a poem on oldgrowth specklebelly lichen, but before this I waited for over a year. Now and then, there was gathering of some scraps and fragments, as I have earlier noted—an Instagram post, a tiny embroidered description of the lichen's sparkling underbelly drawn from a Government of Canada monograph, an image posted in a Fairy Creek Signal channel. But this was not an active or muscular searching or researching as one might think of research when writing a book, as here, or when writing a dissertation or article.

In 2016 I was asked by Anita Lahey to participate in the *Malahat Review*'s annual poetry gathering, Words on Ice, in a panel discussion called "The Investigative Poet: Observer, Researcher, Analyst," with poets Arleen Paré and Kyeren Regehr; this was moderated by Anita. I recall that I was resistant at the time of the panel to the suggestion that what I do is research; searching, yes. I will often do Google searches, keyword searches in library catalogues and archives, image searches, and what I call for the sake of convenience field "research." But even in the case of going into the field—that is, into the world, into the forest—I go without a preconceived hypothesis to test, without a specific degree requirement to fulfill or article to submit that meets certain criteria. The articles, images, documents, and "data" that I access I might read in part or in full, annotate, or not, but I don't know what I'm looking for; I have no preconceived plan; I'm not searching for pieces to click together to form a larger argument as a poem is not an argument. Often all of this "research" or searching might be distilled to a single phrase or image, or even simply a word—*sinuous edges,* poikilos, *poikilos,* specklebelly. I am still waiting to hear what oldgrowth specklebelly lichen might say to me, to see what it might reveal to me, if I can make space within myself to receive it.

The time I've spent at Fairy Creek—intermittently, of necessity, as family and work schedule allow—has been a form of attending, as a counter to force. The land defenders I have encountered at Fairy Creek have largely sought such grace: resisting force in the form of pepper spray; forming blobs that inch forward incrementally to retake lost ground; going limp or sitting down as a manner of passive resistance when confronted by C-IRG and the RCMP; creating art out of hard and soft blockades; using humour to counter violence. This is not to say that all defenders were entirely passive or peaceful—this is an anarchic movement—but this was always the vibe I experienced, a seeking of secular grace as distilled through the trees and the mist. And being in Fairy Creek, in the forest, among the yellow cedar and the Douglas fir, the hemlock, the salal and sword fern—this has always felt to me like an opening, my entire body opening up and breathing in the matter of the rainforest all around and sensing the often invisible intertwined connections, such as the mycelial threads in the soil beneath us when we lay in our tents, the trees' roots drawing moisture and nutrients up into the branches far overhead that sheltered us. At Ada'itsx I have sensed this entwined matter and enmeshed lives that offer responsibility, care, and careful attention to one another, countering force with grace.

5. POEMS LIKE MIEBACH SCULPTURES

New experiments with data. Miebach sculptures and scores. The lyric ecopoem as ecological witness; the poem as a series of field notes. Why this matters. Sympoiesis. What might constitute an ecopoetic lichenous form? Lichen / poem as portal, prosthetic, transcription, archive.

THE BURDEN OF EVERY DROP

Circles of blues, like umbrellas or the tops of wildflowers, viewed from a drone: blue daisies, cornflowers, flax, chicory, globe thistle, Himalayan poppies, blue-eyed grass. These give way to a patchwork of tiny squares, also in shades of blue but with pops of mustard and mint; some squares are hatched black and white; little cocktail umbrellas in shades of green and blue are punctuated by triangles of coral. As a whole, it is beautiful and chaotic, a metal and glass mobile strung with blue beads, a complicated child's toy, a gear, a circuit board.

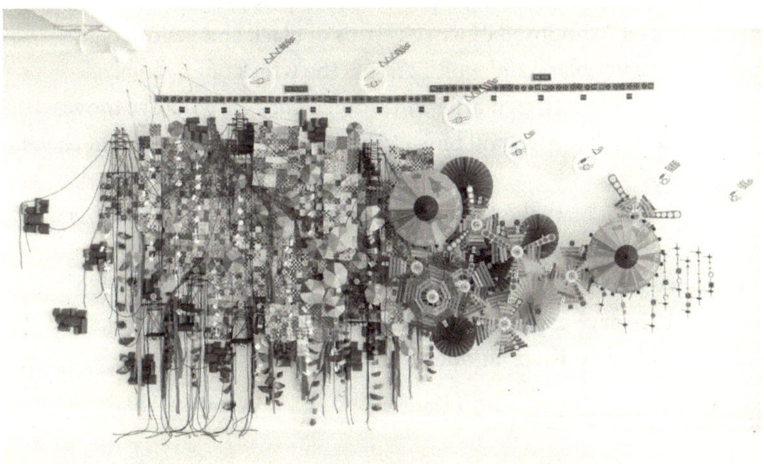

The Burden of Every Drop / 2018 / Wood, paper, rope, data / 17' x 10' x 1'. *Credit: Nathalie Miebach.*

My eye is first drawn to the blue circles, and as I move from right to left, there is an impression of disintegration, as the blue circles yield to the patchwork, and to an increasing tangle of severed black cords that dangle onto the gallery's white floor. Two long measuring tapes frame the upper portion of the sculpture; across these tapes passes a diagonal path of white circles reminiscent of satellite dishes.

It is not immediately apparent from the photograph that this installation spans more than 17 feet and therefore contains much more detail than the gestalt suggests.[1] A close-up image yields numerical data: The blue tapes contain numbers that drop roughly by intervals of five or ten, from right to left—165, 160, 155, 145, 140, 115; above the tape measure on the right are the words "THE SILENCE"; above the left tape measure, "THE RISE." There's a spectrum of blues—cerulean, sun-faded mauve, grey blue, pastel blue, indigo; beneath both tapes, at intervals, what seem to be hourly time-stamps are written in by hand—01:00 through 20:00. The largest blue umbrella is also inscribed with numbers, while the tiny squares appear pixelated: Each little square is itself composed of woven strips of black and yellow, pale blue and cream, black and white. Across the wreck of frayed black electrical wires are strewn little white doll chairs. As your eye moves from right to left, order, and blue circles, give way to damage and chaos.

I am describing Nathalie Miebach's *The Burden of Every Drop* (2018), an artist's interpretation of the data generated by Hurricane Maria, a category 5 hurricane believed to be the "worst natural disaster in recorded history" experienced by the islands of Dominica, Saint Croix, and Puerto Rico.[2] Suddenly the installation clicks into

---

1 Houston Center for Contemporary Craft, "Nathalie Miebach: The Water Line."

2 Wikipedia, "Hurricane Maria," accessed April 22, 2025, https://en.wikipedia.org/wiki/Hurricane_Maria.

focus for me—how did I miss it? I am reading it backwards. The blue flowers are the storm, having just crossed the island of Puerto Rico, causing the tangle of strewn white chairs and downed power lines, and is about to move offshore. The rise of the storm is followed by the silence wrought by the hurricane's impact.

The Burden of Every Drop (detail). *Credit: Nathalie Miebach.*

The catalogue for the exhibit observes:

> Spanning close to 17 feet long, *The Burden of Every Drop* (2018) tells the fraught story of the effects of Hurricane Maria on Puerto Rico by combining weather and other numerical data with anecdotal information from news reports about the storm's aftermath. Miebach juxtaposes the fierceness of the wind and rain with the stark silence of communication caused by the breakdown of electrical

> systems on the island. The piece begins with wind data that crescendos, as the storm reaches landfall. Miebach creates a sort of unraveling quilt to represent the chaos of information, including the underestimated death toll, the fleeing population, and the slow reconstruction of the U.S. territory.[3]

Miebach has described her process as one that begins with data. She often uses data observations she has made herself, using "basic measuring tools like thermometers purchased at the hardware store" and meteorological data gathered online, from "water stations, satellites, and anchored buoys bobbing up and down in open water";[4] data takes the form of temperature, rainfall, barometric pressure, humidity, wind speed, even tidal schedules and krills' migratory patterns. Lovelace even notes that Miebach documents "how sound travels differently on a humid day."[5] This data then guides the shape of each sculpture, which uses the techniques of basket weaving. Miebach describes her work as staying true to the data, so that any given piece is held together by a "numerical logic."[6] "[E]verything in the sculpture, whether it's a colourful bead, whether it's a string, whether it's a dowel, or whether it's a reed, represents some sort of data point so nothing is put on there for purely aesthetic reasons."[7] In one of her Instagram posts, she writes:

> What is data? I've worked with data over 20 years now and I still don't quite know how to answer this. Something happens when you lift numbers off a spreadsheet and turn

---

3 Houston Center for Contemporary Craft, "Nathalie Miebach: The Water Line."

4 Koren, "Transforming Raw Scientific Data into Sculpture and Song."

5 Lovelace, "Composing Chaos."

6 Miebach, "Keynote."

7 "The Weather Artist."

> it into something tactile, visual or audible. Something also happens when you allow data to build its own metaphor, driven by the human experiences it is connected to.[8]

She notes that she wants her sculptures "to live in the science world as much as in the sculpture or in the craft world. I want you to still be able to read the weather off of these sculptures."[9] She seeks to lure the viewer, to evoke a visceral response, and so she also introduces human-generated data, such as tweets, as she sifts through data for the stories it tells. For example, her installation *Harvey's Twitter SOS*, on the category 4 hurricane that caused massive flooding in Houston,[10] is studded with small white squares of messages printed in all caps: TWO DAYS WITH NO FOOD; STUCK IN ATTIC; CAN'T WALK OUT CURRENT TOO STRONG; WATER QUICKLY RISING; THREE KIDS TRAPPED; RUNNING OUT OF TIME.[11] There were over 2,000 tweets signalling distress during Hurricane Harvey; Miebach maps these against the socio-economic status of neighbourhoods in Houston, bayou failure points, and the highway system.[12]

When I talked with Nathalie about her process, she confirmed, as in her Instagram post, that "part of the problem of working with data is that data to me is sort of meaningless unless you start tying it with some human experience, some metaphor that links to human experience, and that search is not an easy one."[13] This sense of meaningless data

---

8 Nathalie Miebach (@miebachsculpture), "What Is Data?," Instagram post, February 4, 2024.

9 "The Weather Artist."

10 Wikipedia, "Hurricane Harvey," accessed April 22, 2025, https://en.wikipedia.org/wiki/Hurricane_Harvey.

11 Houston Center for Contemporary Craft, "Nathalie Miebach: The Water Line."

12 Houston Center for Contemporary Craft, "Nathalie Miebach: The Water Line."

13 Private conversation with author, April 10, 2024.

is true for many of us who are not trained in quantitative research practices; the role of the artist then is to find a way into the data in order to shape it in a meaningful way. For *Harvey Twitter SOS*, she searched for some time for the story the data wanted to tell, describing to me how she felt that data is "very poetic" and "subtle" once you begin to see how the data is linked to human experience:

> Part of the intent of a lot of the work is to try to understand the more complicated responses that we as a species are having to what's going on right now to the planet. And with Harvey, it took me several months of research and with that I mean, first of all gathering numerical data. Looking at buoys, looking at weather stations. Looking at river gauges. So looking for numbers. And then paying attention to how the media was talking about the storm. What kind of data were they bringing up, where were the shelters, what kind of assistance was available? Where were people getting rejections of FEMA [Federal Emergency Management Agency] applications, that kind of more social data? And economic data. And sort of going back to the story month after month. So the storm took place, and I would come back two or three months later.[14]

She also noted, regarding the ecological disasters she interprets through art, that they aren't simply stories; they "reveal underlying weaknesses within that community, whether it's infrastructure weakness, whether that's inequities that are bubbling up."[15] The ecological disaster functions as if an X-ray or an ultrasound, which her art further explores.

---

14 Private conversation with author, April 10, 2024.

15 Private conversation with author, April 10, 2024.

Her process is very much one that I experience in writing a poem—a long process of gathering that is messy and complicated. Although I'm a lyric poet, I am also sometimes looking for a story to tell and searching for a metaphor that might power the conceptual insight of the poem. For Nathalie, the key moment in her search to create "Harvey Twitter SOS" was seeing a *New York Times* animated infographic, "Thousands Cried for Help as Houston Flooded."[16] The online video shows in sped-up time the storm tracking across Houston as Twitter messages begin to pop up, superimposed on the map. The key moment for her was viewing this animation, a "nice mix between very analytical stuff showing you exactly what was going on with the storm but also having these incredibly emotional SOSs. And it's really finding that moment." She also described this as the moment in which the artist "finds traction."[17]

As I've been revising this chapter, recalling our discussion and thinking about her description of searching sometimes for months through the data until she finds traction, I have such a moment myself with regards to the oldgrowth specklebelly long poem. The data accumulated on the citizen scientist app iNaturalist regarding sightings of this lichen include a wealth of information: coordinates, photographs, written descriptions, and confirmations of the ID; maps that show every given sighting of a particular species. Using the Gaia app, it is possible to type in coordinates and see satellite photographs of the area, topographical lines, road maps, layer upon layer of information. In addition, there have been Instagram posts since the beginning of the protests at Fairy Creek from individuals and groups such as @rainforestflyingsquad, @aunty_rainboweyez, @fairycreekblockade, @tjwatt, @virtual.tasha, @joshuawrightfilm, @drsuzannesimard, @ancientforestalliance, and so on.

---

16 Aisch et al., "Thousands Cried for Help as Houston Flooded."

17 Private conversation with author, April 10, 2024.

It occurs to me that I will write a data score for the oldgrowth specklebelly lichen, as Nathalie does prior to creating her sculptures, a score that she then reads as guide to the sculpture that emerges from the materials she works with, often a combination of buttons, dowels, tiny flags, pins, and woven materials, each one corresponding to a data point. My score will map the data collected by citizen scientists on the iNaturalist app, upon which I can superimpose the Instagram posts, Signal chats, and other electronic ephemera that emanate from specific sites throughout the forest. The subsequent lyric ecopoem(s) I write will be a performance of this score. Regarding these scores, Nathalie told me that they are a "way of editing things out and really kind of focusing on what I want to tell in a story"; in addition, one score potentially leads to multiple different sculptures, as well as a variety of musical performances.[18] Each one is an interpretation.

Miebach's work asks us to consider the relationship between science, data, and art or poetry. At the ASLE (Association for the Study of Literature and the Environment) 2023 seminar on ecopoetics led by Nicholas Bradley (University of Victoria) and Rina Garcia Chua (SFU), one of the questions raised was *How much science should the (eco)poet know?* Answers varied. There was an adamant *none at all* from a graduate student, who saw this resulting in a loss of any emotional tenor. From the two working poets who are also activists—me and a woman who works on water defence in Oregon—our response was *as much as necessary,* as long as the data does not overwhelm the art. This led to a more general discussion of the kinds of knowledge a poet brings into the back country and then into the poem—scientific knowledge

18 Private conversation with author, April 10, 2024.

drawn from the fields of biology, botany, ecology, geology; the social and cultural complications of concepts like “nature,” “the wild,” “wilderness,” “the back country”; knowledge of the ways in which the “back country” is itself curated and packaged to the hiker; our many languages that yield so many different words and worlds, with a particular concern for Indigenous languages rooted in place: yellow glacier lily, avalanche lily, dogtooth fawn lily, *Erythronium grandiflorum, Sk’émәth. Sxʷixʷ. Hʷikʷi. Máxa.*[19]

Nick condensed this question to *What does the poet carry in her backpack?* The answer might range from the material through the conceptual, from tools used to gather data (a compass, a loupe, recording technology, a map, a notebook) to knowledge of the anatomy of lichen, the Krebs cycle, symbiosis. The answer might determine how a poem like a Miebach sculpture might look and sound, which techniques and conceptualizations might yield an ecological witnessing or field notes.

Miebach insists on being true to the data so that it is still “legible” in her sculptures, where each element is a data point—bead, button, string, dowel, reed—and numbers control the form. The grid is also significant; different values—some meteorological, some human—are plotted along the X and Y axes in order to evoke an emotional tenor.

Miebach’s work also asks us to consider the role of the citizen scientist, as I described above in the case of iNaturalist. She is a

19 Turner, “Appendix 2B. Names of Native Plant Species in Indigenous Languages of Northwestern North America,” *Ancient Pathways, Ancestral Knowledge. Sk’émәth, Sxʷixʷ, Hʷikʷi, Máxa*: words for *Erythronium grandiflorum* in Upriver Halkomelem, Secwépemc, Sahaptin, and Ktunaxa.

citizen scientist herself in her collection of data, but she also draws on data supplied by a dispersed mass of observers to document, in the case of Hurricane Maria, a single, traumatic, impactful event.

Miebach's work is also inspiring in her use of the urgent cries for help made on Twitter during the worsening floods caused by Hurricane Harvey in Houston. Her incorporation of these distress tweets into *Harvey's Twitter SOS* profoundly maps minute human stories—little windows into the storm—onto the meteorological data and so interprets these numbers from a human perspective, telling stories from the data at hand.

I return again to my thinking on an oldgrowth specklebelly lichen poem. iNaturalist describes itself as an "online social network of people sharing biodiversity information to help each other learn about nature," a "crowdsourced species identification system," and an "organism occurrence recording tool."[20] In addition to basic data such as coordinates and clusters of communities, all verified at research grade, iNaturalist observations document in each instance the intersection of species—the human in the forest, the lichen thallus on a tree still standing or on a felled tree, each observation as if a periscope lowered into the old-growth rainforest, digitally sampling a moment as these species entwine. Each observation details coordinates, photographs, field notes by the observer, identification by the community; each observation offers a glimpse into the story of a lichen that has existed here since the last glaciation; the story of a complex ethical space in which loggers, RCMP, First Nations, activists, allies come together in urgent and profoundly contradictory ways.

---

20 "About," iNaturalist.

FIELD NOTES

Some ecological witnessing in poetry, especially in the twentieth century,[21] has taken a "field notes" style of observing contemporary ecological events, a style that I find appealing as a form of "documentary adequacy," to borrow a term from Seamus Heaney. I will consider here briefly just a few examples from the UK that I admire deeply. This discussion is not exhaustive, is not even an overview; it simply gestures towards this poetic technique or style, which is deeply observant, often draft-like, as if to present immediate impressions in the field, incrementally added to over time, as in a journal form.

By "documentary adequacy," Heaney describes poetry not as a game but as moral urgency, and poetry as trace:

> There is another kind of adequacy which is specific to lyric poetry. This has to do with the "temple inside our hearing"... it is an adequacy deriving from what Mandelstam called "the steadfastness of speech articulation," from the resolution and independence which the entirely realized poem sponsors. It has as much to do with the energy released by linguistic fission and fusion, with the buoyancy generated by cadence and tone and rhyme and stanza, as it has to do with the poem's concerns or the poet's truthfulness. In fact, in lyric poetry, truthfulness becomes recognizable as a ring of truth within the medium itself. And it is the unappeasable pursuit of this note, a note tuned to its most extreme in Emily Dickinson and Paul Celan

21 My Marxist cultural geographer friend N. scribbles in the margin: *Don't forget the 18th and 19th centuries. We have Jean-Jacques Rousseau, Humboldt, George Perkins Marsh, Charles Darwin, Henry Thoreau, Kropotkin, John Muir, and others doing ecological witnessing.*

> and orchestrated to its most opulent in John Keats—it is this which keeps the poet's ear straining to hear the totally persuasive voice behind all the other informing voices.[22]

Heaney first makes a connection between documentary adequacy and poetic form—an adequacy of form, the "rightness" of a poem in its sounding. The need for documentary adequacy—poetry's ability to document the savagery or myriad wonder of the world—is aligned with the form in which this is expressed. The right form must be found; that is where the authority of poetry is to be found. Other writers thinking about poetry have made similar observations. Terrence Des Pres writes that "the power base of poetry is poetry itself."[23] Helen Vendler notes, "Form is the necessary and skilled embodiment of the poet's moral urgency, the poet's method of self-revelation."[24] She also asserts a poem is not an essay, not a position paper, not an argument, not a speech, not a sermon. Mutlu Konuk Blasing in *Lyric Poetry: The Pain and the Pleasure of Words* (2007) also emphasizes, with Vendler, skilled embodiment in language as the basis of a poet's moral authority.

Regarding the adequacy of sound, Heaney gives the example of Yeats's refrain "Come build in the empty house of the stare," from his "Meditations in Time of Civil War" as well as the "sheer in-placeness of the whole poem as a given form within the language" in which the poem's form is necessary "to persuade that vulnerable part of our consciousness of its rightness in spite of the evidence of wrongness all around it."[25]

---

22 Heaney, *Crediting Poetry*, 48–51.

23 Des Pres, *Praises & Dispraises*, 230.

24 Vendler, *Our Secret Discipline*, xiv.

25 Heaney, *Crediting Poetry*, 52–53.

He uses form as synonym for sound, the poem's music—that when something sounds right, there is a greater inclination to believe it is true: Beauty is truth, truth beauty.[26]

While Heaney's emphasis is on music, I want to extend his concept of documentary adequacy to consider the idea of an ecological poem as trace or witness, carrying the same moral urgency through its emphasis on being "in the field," on recording the natural world, as if a series of footnotes or a tracing of a place, often returning to do so intermittently over many years or even decades. The tools of poetry assist in this documentation.

In Ted Hughes's *Moortown Diary* (1979),[27] which consists of a series of "notes"/poems that record his experiences working on his farm in Dartmoor in the early 1970s, he tells us in the preface that he used verse as a form because

> [i]n making a note about anything, if I wish to look closely I find I can move closer, and stay closer, if I phrase my observations about it in rough lines. So these improvised verses are nothing more than this: my own way of getting reasonably close to what is going on, and staying close, and of excluding everything else that might be pressing to interfere with the watching eye. In a sense, the method excludes the poetic process as well.[28]

---

26 I have discussed on my blog my concern with the expression of a direct link between moral rightness and a beautiful sounding: "documentary adequacy & poetic form."

27 An earlier version of this discussion of *Moortown Diary* and Sean Borodale's *Bee Journal* appeared on my blog, titled "poem as trace of an event 1."

28 Hughes, *Moortown Diary*, x.

Poem as loupe, to focus attention. He then describes being asked once to provide an editor of a magazine with one of these poems, or "notes," realizing that although it was raw, he couldn't rework it without having to "translate" it, thus destroying the original in the process. The original he now saw as "the video and surviving voice-track of one of my own days, a moment of my life that I did not want to lose... Altering any word felt like retouching an old home movie with new bits of fake-original voice and fake-original actions."[29] He describes the process of poetic revision as if the introduction of corruption—"fake-original voice"—a dubbing over of the raw event, or rather, the trace of this raw event. It's as if the original note were a snapshot or rubbing, still bearing molecular traces of the moment. In my experience, this is a true description of writing the first draft of a poem, when the words are still freshly inked. It might be employed for ecological witnessing in poetry, with a self-awareness of the process and "scientific" observation of the method built in, as well as Morton's discussion of an "ambient" poetics in ecological art, which, he argues,

> hardwires the environment into its *form*. Ecological art, and the ecologicalness of all art, are not just "about" something (trees, mountains, animals, pollution...). Ecological art *is* something, or maybe it *does* something. Art is ecological insofar as it is made from materials and exists in the world... But there is more to its ecological quality than that. The shape of the stanzas and the length of the lines determine the way you relate to the blank paper around them. Reading the poem aloud makes you aware of the shape and size of the room around you... The poem organizes space.[30]

---

29 Hughes, *Moortown Diary*, xi.

30 Morton, *The Ecological Thought*, 311–12.

Poems of the Romantic period, as with ecological poems, offer "metacritical commentaries on poetics itself"[31] where a poem functions like an aperture or opening, not a closing. The lyric poem offers a "contemplative materialism."[32]

Here is an excerpt from "Ravens," on a stillborn lamb. Hughes describes how the ravens are eating the lamb's corpse; this note is framed by the interest of a young child accompanying him in the field. We are asked to see through the child's eyes:

> Now over here, where the raven was,
> Is what interests you next. Born dead,
> Twisted like a scarf, a lamb of an hour or two,
> Its insides, the various jellies and crimsons and transparencies
> And threads and tissues pulled out
> In straight lines, like tent ropes
> From its upward belly opened like a lamb-wool slipper,
> The fine anatomy of silvery ribs on display and the cavity,
> The head also emptied through the eye-sockets.[33]

The note-like quality doesn't exclude technique: the use of simile ("like a scarf," "like a lamb-wool slipper"); the very fine use of

---

31 Morton, *The Ecological Thought*, 313. Andreas Weber observes, with reference to Gregory Bateson, that Romanticism was "first and foremost a scientific way of exploring the world as a subjective phenomenon. The first generation of Romantics in Germany and England (Coleridge, Hölderlin) were motivated by understanding how matter can be expressive of inwardness. They set out to build a first-person science, which remains incomplete" (Weber, *Enlivenment*, 150).

32 Morton, *The Ecological Thought*, 313.

33 Hughes, *Moortown Diary*, 27–28.

metaphor to describe the multiplicity of texture of the drawn-out lamb's "insides" (jellies, crimsons, transparencies, threads, tissues, tent ropes); the use of polysyndeton, that is, consecutive conjunctions ("jellies and crimsons and transparencies") so that the cumulative list sounds like a child's chanted enumeration.

I like his description of these "notes" as being about moving close and staying close: his insistence on paying attention. It suggests a moral dimension to the raw or transcript poem: An attempt at paying attention to the world as it is, and as it is perceived; to perceive and then document what is seen and heard, tasted, or touched, as closely as possible then becomes a way of sharing that knowledge with others through the lens of the poem.

And inevitably with each poet there is a different kind of seeing; each poem also carries a trace of the poet's mind with its idiosyncratic ways of viewing and interpreting the world. The worst of hypercapitalism's onslaught of ecological destruction occurs when we do not stay close, when we are disturbed and look away.

Another example of this approach is Sean Borodale's *Bee Journal* (2012), which similarly functions as a beekeeper's notebook, charting the progress of a hive. We are told on the volume's dust jacket that the "poems were written at the hive wearing a veil and gloves, and the journal is an intrinsic part of the kinetic activity of keeping bees." Each poem includes a date, and sometimes only a date, in the title, in keeping with the journal-like function of the poems. For example, this is from the opening poem, "24th May: Collecting the Bees":

> He just wears a veil, this farmer, no gloves
> and lifts open a dribbly wax-clogged
> blackwood box.
> We in our whites mute with held breath.

Hello bees.
Drops four frames into our silence.

The air is like mica
ancient with thin flecks;
distance viewed through a filter of thousands.
I am observed.

Each box has the pulsar of its source. Porous with eyes
we wait in the spinning sun. The light is Medusa,
sugar of frayed threads; a mesh, a warp-field, all
the skin of our heads.[34]

Here is a similar use, as in Hughes's *Moortown Diary*, of the lineation of verse to make notes, to slow down observation, and to frame the poet as observing "eye"/I; but also the poet as observed, indicating the subject-hood of the bees ("*I am* observed") And, as also with Hughes, close observation and careful description become paramount: bee-filled air "like mica / ancient with thin flecks" (what a beautiful image, to describe the frames of light-filled, bee-filled air as a slice of flecked stone); the boxes of bees like pulsars, an image which evokes light and sound as pattern, the thrum of energy emitted from each box; the layering of metaphor as if making attempt after attempt at a thick description of the bee-filled light: Medusa; mesh; warp-field.

POEMS LIKE MIEBACH SCULPTURES

More recently, in Canada, local, small-scale ecological witnessing is woven into a much larger political intervention in the face of the

---

34 Borodale, *Bee Journal*, 1.

sixth mass extinction, the incursion into planetary boundaries, and nearing tipping points. I think of Fred Wah and Rita Wong's *beholden* (2018), as well as Rita Wong's *forage* (2007); Adam Dickinson's *Anatomic* (2018); Stephen Collis's *Once in Blockadia* (2016); and Renée Sarojini Saklikar's epic SF three-volume poem, *The Heart of This Journey Bears All Patterns* (THOT J BAP) (2021–); anthologies such as the first three *Fire Season* anthologies (2020–2024), published by lecturers from Kwantlen Polytechnic University and Emily Carr University of Art + Design as limited series artist books that document art, poetry, and fire service ephemera each wildfire season in British Columbia; and *Worth More Standing: Poets and Activists Pay Homage to Trees* (2022), an anthology of tree poetry, edited by former Tofino poet laureate Christine Lowther.

Again, as with field notes or the concept of an ecological witness, I am not offering here a survey but simply three examples that I have found striking for going beyond a transcript-like approach, and which suggest the possibilities of an experimental poetics analogous to a Miebach sculpture that engages with the Anthropocene: Adam Dickinson's *Anatomic,* Fred Wah and Rita Wong's *beholden,* and Tiffany Morris's *Elegies of Rotting Stars* (2022).

While the International Commission on Stratigraphy has yet to formally acknowledge the Anthropocene as a geological era,[35]

35 Zhong, "Geologists Make It Official." On March 20, 2024, it was announced that this commission voted in February 2024 against adding the Anthropocene (the Human Age) to Earth's historical timeline, indicating the planet is still in the Holocene epoch, "which began 11,700 years ago with the most recent melting of the ice sheets." The vote was, however, contested. One of the dissenting scientists, vice-chair Martin J. Head, observed, "I feel this has been a missed opportunity to…

humans have already scored a legible signature in the geological record: plutonium from nuclear test sites; streaks of black carbon; technofossils—iPhones like twenty-first-century trilobites embedded in strata; chicken bones. And our carbon-fuelled military-industrial complex has similarly inscribed the human body. In his *Anatomic*, Dickinson takes the maligned lyric subject to a biological extreme, exploring the ways in which the poet's body is written by twenty-first-century technologies.[36] As prompts for this 2018 experimental collection, he sent off samples of blood, urine, feces (across the border, with some difficulty) to record and translate these signatures, which he then used as data for his poems. Biology as inscription is the dominant trope developed in this poetics. Dickinson observes:

> It seems to me that the effects of chemicals and microbes on the body constitute a form of writing. The human endocrine system, with its constant flow of hormonal messages, represents a kind of poetics—a poetics increasingly overwritten by the Anthropocene (our current historical moment in which humans have become biogeochemical forces on the planet). I have PCBs in my blood, which means I have the products of a multinational company inside me (Monsanto) [...] How can I use poetry to respond to this writing, make it legible and urgent, and rewrite it as a form of cultural critique?[37]

This trope is expressed in various guises throughout the book: "A hormone conjugates its subject"; "Real fruit smells

---

... recognize and endorse a simple reality, that our planet left its natural functioning state in the mid-20th century. A myriad of geological signals reflect this fact."

36 My discussion here of *Anatomic* is a revised version of a review I wrote of *Anatomic* for *Arc Poetry*, "An Anthropocene Poetics."

37 Dickinson, "'The Human Endocrine System.'"

are handwritten notes soaked with sweat and read by the light of a flesh wound."[38] The hormone, Dickinson notes, is a "compositional method, with its emphasis on concentration, cascade, and sequence."[39] In the long poem called "Hormone," which runs intermittently throughout the collection, we read:

> When I put food
> in my mouth,
> I am taking dictation.
> I am reading
> as I lick the glue
> on the envelope
> that holds the letter
> I have written
> about how you taste
> to me.[40]

In the concluding ten-page colour spread called "Metabolic Poetics," there are captions such as "Can writing function as a productive hormone disruptor within larger cultural narrative sequences? This is my urine. Its metabolites are messengers."[41] Such questions are not answered but act as theoretical prompts for the reader. The phrase "metabolic poetics" echoes Marx on the metabolic rift caused by the industrial revolution, in which the soil is depleted and contaminated, leading to an unsustainable circulation of materials and energy. Dickinson's poems transcribe this rift.

---

38 Dickinson, "Disruptors: *Mono-isononyl phthalate (urine): 1.0 ng/mL*," *Anatomic*, 77.

39 Dickinson, "'The Human Endocrine System.'"

40 Dickinson, "Hormone," *Anatomic*, 116.

41 Dickinson, *Anatomic*, 136.

Anatomic also expresses concern with the differential impact of this Anthropocene writing on bodies of various subject positions; there is acknowledgement of the poet's own white identity and privileged position in conversation with the impact of primary resource extraction on Indigenous bodies, bodies like litmus strips that register the ravages of hypercapitalism and are discarded as "externalities":

> In Aamjiwnaang First Nation, only a third of all babies are boys. The hockey team has been disbanded. Girls' softball was added. Refineries rim the community with pipes. Cholera, smallpox, the British, and the French split piles of young Anishinabek men. In unceded lipidscapes, offspring now flare with feedback.[42]

The poet points out in his notes that the community this poem describes "is surrounded by approximately 40 percent of Canada's chemical industry."[43] Anishinabek men are metaphorized as piles of split wood; bodies flare with chemicals. While the form of these poems is still relatively conventional—a mix of lineated and prose poems—the prompts are novel, as gestured to in the titles ("Lipids," "Disruptors," with sections of these poems given subtitles such as "*Polychlorinated Biphenyls, #156 (plasma): 1.56 ng/g lipid*") as is the conceptual notion of offering a transcription of the chemical analysis of one's own bodily fluids, which reveals the extent to which the chemical industry and its pollutants rewrite our bodies.

Dickinson's project offers an important conceptual contribution to the political ecology of bodies in the Anthropocene, lying within

42 Dickinson, "Lipids: *Polychlorinated Biphenyls, #156 (plasma): 1.56 ng/g lipid*," *Anatomic*, 39.

43 Dickinson, *Anatomic*, 145.

earshot of Bruno Latour's agent network theory; Jane Bennett's vibrant matter; and most closely resonates, perhaps, with Donna Haraway's cyborg ontology, where boundaries of organisms are breached and fluid and technology inscribes the body, while the act of choosing to interrogate and read this inscribed body within a collection of poetry offers us a microbial glimpse into the fissures where resistance begins.

Fred Wah and Rita Wong's *beholden: a poem as long as the river* shifts from the molecular to a riverine ecosystem, from the impacts of the Anthropocene within the human body to the impacts of the Anthropocene on the Columbia River. Part of a larger art installation on the Columbia, Wah and Wong collaborated to create a single scroll of paper, to be hung within a gallery space, charting the Columbia from its headwaters through its estuary as it opens onto the Pacific. A cut-out map of the river, with its printed cartographical notations positioned upside down, is inscribed on each bank with two poems, each one a single line that stretches the length of the river, sometimes crossing each other to reach the opposite shore. Wah's poem is in typeface while Wong's is handwritten.

In photographs of the installation, we see that it meanders through the gallery space, suspended from the ceiling at eye level so that you can meander with it, reading and dipping into it as you go; because this river project is recorded or transcribed on a single sheet of unfurling paper, there is a sense of movement and flow. For the book version of the poem, the effect of chopping this flow into discrete page frames necessarily dismembers both river and poems. On her decision to handwrite her poem, in a dialogue recorded in the book, Wong observes:

> I just had a feeling that I wanted to stay with the hand, with the flow, with the body. And the composition of writing

> something along the whole length of the map of the river, the representation of the river, not the river itself, I felt like I had to sit down and have long stretches of time just returning to where we were and trying to write through and around and over and under those moments.[44]

Handwriting slows the poet down and puts her in relation to the materiality of language and to the subject she addresses. Wah comments on the words they each chose to use, and how they came to select them, mentioning his sense of "difficulties" associated with the river, such as logging, trains, dams—difficulties mirrored in his sense of language. He gives the example of being on Lake Windermere, seeing a Canadian Pacific coal train rush past. He describes the word "diesel" as a gift, offering "the implications of power and oil"; that the materiality of the river requires "looking for the language" that might describe this."[45] He then links the poet's role to an "ethical responsibility" to look for "the right language" and to pay close attention, which returns me to Heaney's conception of documentary adequacy. Wong responds to Wah by noting that she saw not difficulties but the need for reciprocation, that when Wah heard the word "diesel," the words that came to her were "tule and bulrush, the little bits of life that have been here longer than the diesel train, and will be there much longer after."[46] This leads them into a discussion of "deep time." Wong observes that the tules exist within deep time, while the diesel is "a trickle in the context of that much larger river."[47] She also begins her discussion by considering what she does not know and identifies

44 Wah and Wong, *beholden*, 140.

45 Wah and Wong, *beholden*, 141.

46 Wah and Wong, *beholden*, 141.

47 Wah and Wong, *beholden*, 143.

the knowledges and languages of the "Salmon Peoples" who live along the Columbia. Later, she expresses caution regarding protocols and calls for relational, not extractive, processes:

> I worry that the structures that we're in, under capital, under colonization, tend to oversimplify and misrepresent things that are actually relational. They assume a mindset of access, entitlement, control, when the cultures we need in order to survive on this planet are ones that require we respect and learn from the earth's limits, working to foster the conditions for care, diversity and coexistence of life, rather than a capitalist race to exploit everything to the point of collapse.[48]

The First Nations who have existed for millennia along the river are signalled in her naming practice early on in her poem, in which she records "Pakisq'nuk (Columbia Lake First Nation), Kenpesq't (Shuswap Band) say the names: Ktunaya, Sinixt, Secwépemc, Okanagan, Syilx, neighbours in the basin before" while simultaneously, Wah's poem evokes the voice of the river, with inflections of Buddhist thought, "Columbia River starts humming its invisible Kootenay *qi* path breathing what exists through itself is called *as is* meaning. 'Going to the Water' hears the cadence as a wet prelude to Pacifica meanders slow and murmurs love this."[49]

Towards the middle of the river, and their poems, both swerve towards politics and Western boundaries. Wong addresses American imperialism, "through summer heat and choking dust storms through dolled up American imperialism that turns freedom into reservations imposes imaginary but political" while Wah turns towards "all

---

48 Wah and Wong, *beholden*, 146.

49 Wah and Wong, *beholden*, 2–3.

the forked tongues whispering Doctrine of Discovery."[50] Here, as with the previous pages I transcribed, there is an ironic disconnect, self-aware, of the printed map, a Western conceptualization of the river that necessarily crosses borders and boundaries, and ignores assertions of ownership, along the edges of which are inscribed lines of words not one's own (*Ktunaxa, Sinixt, Secwépemc, Okanagan, Syilx*), as well as critiques of political discourse (imperialism, Doctrine of Discovery). This speaks to the connection between language and place, and to the question of Indigeneity. What is the position of the non-Indigenous writer who writes of this land? How does such a writer become rooted in place? These poems in *beholden* lack roots, in that so much is unknown by the poets; the words have no rootedness in the river that they describe; they lack the fine granular texture of a knowledge of place that is gathered over many centuries and linked to a specific language. This the poets lament, while simultaneously acknowledging the "ethical responsibility to look for the right language"[51] and to consider their "debt," what they can reciprocate by means of poetry. As Rita Wong observes, "It's good for poetry to be humble about itself."[52]

Tiffany Morris, an L'nu'skw (Mi'kmaq) writer, as I noted earlier, describes the importance of the necropastoral for intervening in human exceptionalism. She also works within earshot of poetry and witness: "Poetry is one of our many processes of witness, and it happens regardless of style or iteration: in this case, both ecopoetry and speculative poetry have their modes

---

50 Wah and Wong, *beholden*, 53–54.

51 Wan and Wong, *beholden*, 141.

52 Wah and Wong, *beholden*, 143.

of witness."[53] And ecopoetry as witness to the climate crisis, she observes, is necessarily linked to a more hopeful speculation: "room to imagine a new world where an old one ends: one of healing, decolonization, and futurity." She brings the Mi'kmaq concept of *etuaptmumk*, "two-eyed seeing," to describe this duality:

> Etuaptmumk can be, in short, a method of decolonizing our thinking around the apocalypse. Holding these dualities in mind is important. We can also look to other modes of duality and interstices when we look to the future of poetry, ecopoetry, and speculative poetry: we can simultaneously see the hope in the shining green solarpunk future while holding sacred the fungal importance of decay in the necropastoral.[54]

In her poem "Re-wilding Under Those Conditions," Morris uses a mix of gothic language of decay, a technical vocabulary of climate change, and Mi'kmaq words and phrases to illustrate this two-eyed seeing, where the ravages of climate change are documented, yet not without hope for the "green solarpunk future":

> Stick this time—as in, half-formed century—with a pin
>   into the butterfly thorax, into embolism:
> there is not a word in every language for
>   extinction event
> but sometimes there are   a few words for burning
>   *neiamgla'tijig,*   they appear burning
> *nu'gwa'l'g,*   I set it
>   on fire

53 Morris, "Decolonizing the Apocalypse."

54 Morris, "Decolonizing the Apocalypse."

gaqoqtegl,   they are
                burned through
a cathedral into skeleton
    irritation into sensation
        ozone into nothing
    and it's not just forests —*nipugtl*—that burn, that fall.[55]

The phrase we have become so familiar with, "extinction event," is interrogated by placing it adjacent to a language which has no such phrase: "*neiamgla'tijig*" ("they appear burning"), "*nu'gwa'l'g*" ("I set it on fire"), "*gaqoqtegl*" ("they are burned through"). We phase shift through the poem from imagery of death: sticking of a butterfly thorax with a pin, symbol of a colonial method of collection and typology, through the forensic language of embolism. From this, to increasingly ominous, in context, words that lie adjacent to "extinction event," from an appearance of burning through setting on fire, to being burned through. (Extinction Rebellion Australia's animatronic kangaroo with its lower torso burned away to shear, smouldering bone.) The poet then observes, "There isn't much forest left   here in our territory / but there are   ashes, remnants, golf courses." She asks, What is more beautiful than these images of burning golf courses? The response: "things that grow / under these conditions (wildflowers probably? / mushrooms and moss / and all of it— / blooming   like seizing) / after the fire was gone."[56]

Throughout *Elegies of Rotting Stars*, a disturbingly grotesque imagery of decay documents the damage: "Downstream, a fish is bleeding / from the eye" while the sky is "the blue of a suicide / sluicing

---

55 Morris, "Re-wilding Under Those Conditions," *Elegies of Rotting Stars*, 17.
56 Morris, "Re-wilding Under Those Conditions," *Elegies of Rotting Stars*, 17.

through the budded / refuse of spring";[57] "the peeled / and raw bodies of trees" receive "metal stitches" in a "lesioned landscape."[58]

Yet beneath these explicit documentary images sounds the "mushroom hum"[59] of decay and reassembly, the necropastoral. This is foregrounded in the poem "In Strange Gardens" where a fig tree blooms from a stomach and there are "bones / wrapped in vines, growing an eye / or a mushroom":

> Listen:
> there are teeth that growl praise
> for rotting things and all the new
> that they might bring
> come spring, come hell
> come collapse, come dusk,
> stretching tubers, stretching petals
> that wrap us in their future
> regardless of whether or not
> we're breathing.[60]

WHAT WILL I CARRY IN MY BACKPACK?

What will I carry in my backpack, I ask myself, as I consider returning to Fairy Creek in the fall of 2023 to visit some of the sites documented in iNaturalist, to begin to gather, to muse, to listen for, maybe to write, my oldgrowth specklebelly lichen poem. All the

---

57 Morris, "Cigarette Reliquary," *Elegies of Rotting Stars*, 26.

58 Morris, "Flag Burning Against Storming Sky," *Elegies of Rotting Stars*, 19.

59 Morris, "There Are No Simple Hymns," *Elegies of Rotting Stars*, 13.

60 Morris, "In Strange Gardens," *Elegies of Rotting Stars*, 35.

necessary gear—my one-person tent and my sleeping bag, hatchet and multitool, hurricane matches, bear spray, notebooks and maps, headlamp, dried foods, pocket camp stove, first-aid kit, compass, whistle, flint, knife—all these small, crucial tools for basic survival.

I will carry the idea of a Miebach sculpture, its textural complexity, where each bead, dowel, ribbon is a datapoint, form determined by the tensions inherent in the data as her reeds respond to the numbers. She observes, in a keynote lecture in 2015, regarding those who work with craft, that you must "fail with [the material] a thousand times," "distort it and break it in a million ways in order to understand it."[61] In this way, you learn what the material can do, its strengths and breaking points, its flexibilities. And then she points out questions that she says she is always thinking about and working with in her studio, when using data:

1. How would our understanding of data change if we could touch it, hear it, taste it, feel it, and walk around it?

2. How do the mediums we use to translate data affect the way we understand it?

3. Do the digital and physical spaces through which we communicate data impose implied expectations on how the information will be consumed, accessed, and understood?

4. Are we being too polite with data?[62]

---

61 Miebach, "Keynote."
62 Miebach, "Keynote."

She cites Zadie Smith's observation in "Elegy for a Country's Seasons" (2014) that we lack "intimate words" for climate change; Miebach then calls for "a diversification of mediums, approaches, and spaces through which we speak about the weather or climate change in order to allow metaphors, analogy, and nuances to emerge within the science, and in my work that's very much what I'm trying to do."[63]

Poetry also looks for such intimate words. And I have similar questions: What might it mean to allow form to be determined by data, in a poem whose materials are words? What would it mean to be true to the data, where data is a portion of a poem's materials, data which I have been steadily assembling? Contoured maps with individual iNaturalist observations scattered along the coast, from Alaska to Oregon, including a small cluster at Fairy Creek: coordinates that record sites where oldgrowth specklebelly lichen has been found, recorded as little pink dots on the chiaroscuro of Upper Granite Creek.[64]

---

63 Miebach, "Keynote."

64 Neilson et al., "Without an Over-Arching Biodiversity Protection Act," 193, 194. Many of the sightings documented in TFL 46 may no longer exist. John Neilson, Loys Maingon, and Natasha Lavdovsky, in a 2022 article in the *Canadian Field-Naturalist*, describe their survey, using iNaturalist conventions, of 326 species in TFL 46, including "70 observations of 16 species that are considered vulnerable." Their survey was prompted following their realization that no comprehensive biological survey of at-risk species had been carried out by Teal-Jones or the BC government prior to the beginning of road-building and clear-cutting. Despite complaints these authors lodged in 2021 with the BC Forest Practices Board, the Minister of Forests Katrine Conroy, and Teal-Jones, logging continued: "Based on photographs of felled host trees in the Upper Granite Creek area [where many of the oldgrowth specklebelly lichen observations were made] obtained after the logging company was notified of the presence of the lichen, operations were unabated." Their article includes photographs of felled host trees carrying oldgrowth specklebelly lichen on its bark.

More recently, I have received coordinates of sightings at Bugaboo Creek from Joshua Wright, the young activist and filmmaker from Washington State who…

Photographs of lichen thalli grafted to bark or cupped in hands. A list of citizen observers and their observations. My notebooks from Fairy Creek, their pages warped from nights spent in the rainforest. My photographs. My hand-drawn maps of the camps: Roadside, which changed each time we visited; Granite Main; Landback Bridge. Instagram posts from @fairycreekblockade and @rainforestflyingsquad. Oldgrowth specklebelly lichen in and of itself, apart from these digital, numerical, textual, symbolic representations, if only to hint at its being or to sense it as a retreating negative presence. Do I even want to be true to the data? Yet as Miebach says, the data are materials and need to be tested, just like reeds or clay, to see what they can yield.

I will carry Heaney's idea of documentary adequacy, Wah's search for the "right words" so that he can speak to the river, an observation within earshot of Zadie Smith's "intimate words," Wong's reminder of reciprocity and humility, a reminder to ask, What can my poem give back? This speaks also to Robin Wall Kimmerer's discussion of reciprocity in *Gathering Moss* and to her interest in the voices of the mosses themselves:

> The names we use for rocks and other beings depends on our perspective, whether we are speaking from the inside or the outside of the circle. The name on our lips reveals the knowledge we have of each other, hence the sweet secret names we have for the ones we love. The names we give ourselves are a powerful form of self-determination, of declaring ourselves sovereign territory.

... first detected from his survey of satellite images that logging was gearing up in the Fairy Creek watershed and initiated the protests; and near Truck Road 11, shared by Rutabaga, who is a Fairy Creek long-timer I know from both forays to camp and Freeskool organizing in Vancouver.

> Outside the circle, scientific names for mosses may suffice, but within the circle, what do they call themselves?[65]

We have Linnaeus classification (*Pseudocyphellaria rainierensis*);[66] its common name, "oldgrowth specklebelly lichen"; a technical description:

> Thallus foliose, large, loosely appressed to pendulous, 1–2 cm across, brittle when dry; lobes 0.5–3 cm broad; upper surface gray or pale bluish-gray, smooth or irregularly wrinkled; lower surface whitish to light brown, tomentose, with scattered conspicuous *pseudocyphellaria*, 0.2–0.6 mm in size; primary photobiont a green alga, with internal cephalodia containing the cyanobacterium photobiont; lobules and coralloid isidia present; apothecia rare, reddish-brown, with thalline margin; medulla white to gray; cortex K+ yellow; medulla K- or brownish, all other spot tests negative.[67]

Tomentose. Pseudocyphellaria. Internal cephalodia. Coralloid isidia!

We have words for its endangered status (COSEWIC status—Special Concern; SARA designation—"Special Concern"; Conservation Status on the BC List—"Blue," Rank S2S3, N2N3, G3G4).[68]

---

65 Kimmerer, *Gathering Moss*.

66 Bureau of Land Management, "Management Recommendations," 2. "*Pseudocyphellaria rainierensis* Imshaug was first found in Mount Rainier National Park in 1948 and was described by Henry Imshaug in 1950 (Imshaug 1950). It is in the order *Lecanorales*, suborder *Peltigerineae*, family *Lobariaceae* (Tehler 1996)."

67 Bureau of Land Management, "Management Recommendations," 2.

68 The website Biodiversity of the Central Coast (https://www.centralcoastbiodiversity.org) defines some of these terms. Blue List species "are of special concern because they have biological or life-history characteristics that make them particularly vulnerable to natural or human-caused disturbance." COSEWIC stands for…

We have chemical signatures, data which Natasha Lavdovsky has used to generate a soundscape—"Each lichen... will have a particular tonal sound or chord."[69]

But what do they call themselves?

SYMPOIESIS (MAKING-WITH)

In *Staying with the Trouble: Making Kin in the Chthulucene* (2016), Donna Haraway points out a brief two-page article that appeared in *Natural History* in 2001, written by Dorion Sagan and Lynn Margulis—famous for her theory of symbiogenesis, the theory that accounts for how chloroplasts and mitochondria contain genomes separate from their host organisms. She proposed that these organelles were once independent organisms who merged with larger cells. In their article, Margulis and Sagan describe a "compound beauty found in a termite's gut."[70] The "compound beauty," *Mixotrichia paradoxa*, although it appears at low magnification as a "single-celled swimming ciliate," has five genomes:

> [I]nside each nucleated cell, where one would expect to find mitochondria, are many spherical bacteria. On the surface,

...Committee on the Status of Endangered Wildlife in Canada, and SARA for Species at Risk Act (a federal list). Species "listed as endangered, threatened, or of concern by COSEWIC" are recommended to be protected under SARA. As of March 2024, BC has no SARA of its own, despite many promises to enact one by the NDP government. S2S3: Subnational 2 (imperiled) 3 (special concern, vulnerable to extirpation or extinction). N refers to "National"; G refers to Global. G4: Global rank, 4, "apparently secure."

69 Lavdovsky quoted in Acker, "Artist Finds New Population."

70 Margulis and Sagan, "The Beast with Five Genomes."

> where cilia should be, are some 250,000 hairlike *Treponema spirochetes* (resembling the type that causes syphilis), as well as a contingent of large rod bacteria that is also 250,000 strong. In addition, we have redescribed 200 spirochetes of a larger type and named them *Canaleparolina darwiniensis*.[71]

They describe this complex—paradoxical—creature as the "poster animal" of symbiogenesis. Haraway suggests a different term as a lens for thinking about our entangled relations with, and dependencies upon, all species on Earth: *sympoiesis*, or "making-with." She traces the term to a Canadian environmental studies graduate student, M. Beth Dempster, who suggested "sympoiesis" in 1998 as a term for

> collectively-producing systems that do not have self defined spatial or temporal boundaries. Information and control are distributed among components. The systems are evolutionary and have the potential for surprising change.[72]

As Haraway observes, sympoiesis is "a word proper to complex, dynamic, responsive, situated, historical systems. It is a word for worlding-with, in company."[73] As in all her work, Haraway seeks out unusual kin, making the strange familiar, encouraging us to consider lively entanglements and the myriad ways in which all organisms are in the process of co-making the world. *M. paradoxa* is added to her expansive list of "companion species," as yet another tactic to undermine the boundedness of human exceptionalism.

---

71 Margulis and Sagan, "The Beast with Five Genomes."

72 Dempsey quoted in Haraway, *Staying with the Trouble*, 62.

73 Haraway, *Staying with the Trouble*, 58.

OLDGROWTH SPECKLEBELLY LICHEN—LICHENOUS FORM

I am just beginning to learn about the morphology, anatomy, physiology, phylogeny of lichens, about their symbiotic, sympoietic, and communal ways of being in the world. What might be a lichenous form in poetry? And what will this poem on oldgrowth specklebelly lichen look like, within the larger ecosystem of a book that is rooted in Ada'itsx? How might the microecosystem of the poem feel and sound? What will be its acoustic niche? What rhythm? What form?

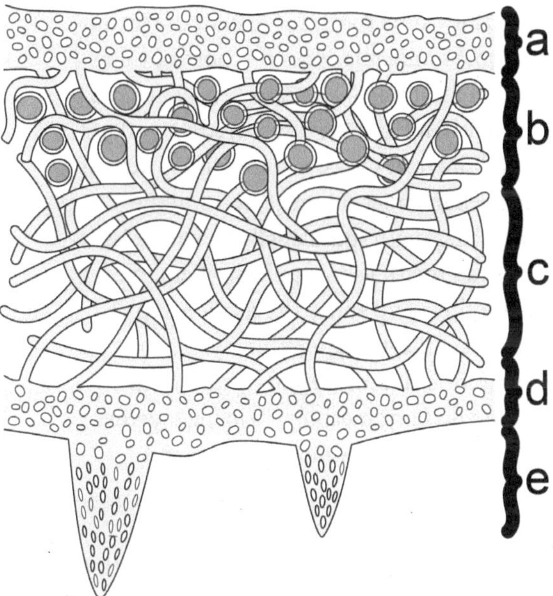

Schematic cross-section of foliose lichen: (a) the cortex is the outer layer of tightly woven fungus filaments (hyphae); (b) this photobiont layer has photosynthesizing green algae; (c) loosely packed hyphae in the medulla; (d) a tightly woven lower cortex; (e) anchoring hyphae called rhizines where the fungus attaches to the substrate. *Credit: Nefronus, Wikimedia, CC-4.0.*

Lichens are commonly thought of as symbiotic communities; the fungus provides structure, while the photobiont—either green algae or cyanobacteria, or both—uses the sun's energy to transform carbon dioxide into organic carbon sugars. The thallus, or body, of a foliose (leaf-like)[74] lichen typically has four layers: an uppermost protective cortex formed of thickened fungal hyphae; an algal layer, in which the algae are embraced by fungal filaments, like a green marble clasped in macramé; another layer of loosely woven fungal hyphae, called the medulla; and a lower cortex. The cyanobacteria can be held on the upper or lower surface of the thallus, in "small pustules called cephalodia."[75] The lower cortex often has rhizines, little roots that anchor the thallus to its host. The thallus absorbs minerals and water borne by rain and dust; the cyanobacteria fix atmospheric nitrogen, which can benefit the tree. More recently, it has been discovered that other kinds of bacteria and basidiomycetes yeast—found in the lichen's cortex—form part of the lichen's microbiome.[76] Some of the rich nutrients required by oldgrowth specklebelly lichen for its survival are provided by old-growth yellow cedars, where trees such as amabilis fir grow at their drip zone. The relationship of fungus, green algae, cyanobacteria, basidiomycetes yeast, host tree, nurturing tree is symbiotic, a term created by the German mycologist Heinrich Anton de Bary, meaning, "a living together of dissimilar organisms."[77] Lichens are complex beings, and

---

74 Oldgrowth specklebelly lichen is foliose; other lichens can be crustose (crust-like) or fruticose (shrub-like), amongst other forms.

75 Wikipedia, "Lichen Morphology," accessed August 3, 2023, https://en.wikipedia.org/wiki/Lichen_morphology.

76 Aschenbrenner et al., "Understanding Microbial Multi-Species Symbioses"; Spribille et al., "Basidiomycete Yeasts."

77 Wikipedia, "Symbiosis," accessed April 23, 2025, https://en.wikipedia.org/wiki/Symbiosis.

the "first ancestors of lichens with characteristic morphology can be traced back to the Devonian 400 million years ago."[78]

I turn to the renowned lichenologist Trevor Goward's beautiful sequence "Twelve Readings of the Lichen Thallus."[79] He suggests that form—in particular, form as species—is "more in the nature of a verb":[80]

> Effectively living form is the species perceived at two time scales: first in organismic time—the individual at home in its own life history... and second in evolutionary time—the individual as participant in the billion-year stage play of life.[81]

Form, on this view, is a process—a "verb"—not static. This works beautifully for thinking of a poem: the poetic form as process, unfolding through time, across the length of a book, as it is written, and as it is read through time, by one reader, by many, now and by later generations, at each reading layered with new meanings, linked to earlier—and later—readings and literary traditions. The poem evolves.

I spoke recently with Trevor, who was in the midst of writing a scientific paper on lichen as dual ontology, as emergent. He said to me, "In society we tend to go one way or the other, science or the arts. And there are very few people who struggle to meet somewhere, to quite meet in the middle, but we try. Some of us try." I mentioned to him that everything he says about lichen, I could say about a lyric

---

78 Aschenbrenner et al., "Understanding Microbial Multi-Species Symbioses."

79 Trevor Goward has been the co-curator of the lichen collection at the UBC Herbarium for over thirty years.

80 Goward, Essay XII, "Twelve Readings," 29.

81 Goward, Essay XII, "Twelve Readings," 29.

poem. He observed that if he weren't writing for peer review, he'd be using poetry and music. And later, while discussing his newest project, Edgewood Wild,[82] he noted that it was intended above all for "people who feel like the time we've entered really should be talked about and probed from all manner of perspectives, certainly I would say not including but above all poetic perspectives."[83]

In his twelve lichen essays, every time he writes "lichen thallus," I read "poem"; the parallels are striking.

For example, he describes the lichen thallus[84] as a "portal" (in Essay IV, "Re-emergence") or "conceptual doorway":

> Lichens, but especially macrolichens, exist at a kind of conceptual doorway, a portal. When we look out this portal in one direction, through the microscope, what we see is multiplicity: the lichen as its parts, as fungus, as alga, as symbiosis, as ecosystem. But when we peer through the same portal in the other direction, at macroscale, what comes into focus now is unity: the lichen as emergent property, as physiologic entity, as organism.[85]

Here he speaks to scale (spores, algae; macrolichen clinging to a tree bole), to part versus whole (algae and fungal hyphae versus lichen thallus), and to the flickering of our own perception and

---

82 Edgewood Wild is a website (https://edgewoodwild.org) "dedicated to brainstorming one of the most pressing issues of our age: societal reconciliation with the Living World that sustains us." Accessed November 6, 2024.

83 Private communication with author, June 20, 2024.

84 A lichen thallus is the structural body of a lichen that is not involved in reproduction.

85 Goward, Essay IV, "Twelve Readings," 1.

conceptual apparatuses through which we think about the thallus, as in Wittgenstein's duck-bunny, now one, now the other perspective coming into clear focus. I am also reminded of Timothy Morton's reference to Coleridge's "Effusion 35," as a good poem for thinking with. Goward's essays show us how complex a "technology" the lichen thallus is for thinking with: about scale, networks/systems, parts and whole, species within the process of evolution, ecosystem, built community, transcription, archive. He refers to this morphing feature as "its unsettling capacity for transmutation even at the slightest shift in perspective," a shift requiring that the thinker hold several perspectives simultaneously in mind.[86]

A former UBC student of mine, Derek Woods, now a professor in environmental media at McMaster University, is a long-time friend of Trevor Goward.[87] Derek offers an intriguing reading of lichen as technology or "prosthesis"; he builds on ideas presented in Merlin Sheldrake's *Entangled Life*, where Sheldrake speculates on the ant as prosthesis when a fungus takes over its body in order to propagate, or when termites cultivate fungi for the digestion of cellulose, a "prosthetic metabolism." In order to address his concerns about the scaling up of the concept of symbiosis from macroscopic lichen through ecosystem/Gaia, and to resolve the inherent contradictions in the concepts of autopoiesis and symbiogenesis (the boundary between organism and symbiotic ecosystem), he argues that we might consider

---

86 Goward, Essay 1, "Twelve Readings," 3.

87 Derek worked as a field assistant searching out oldgrowth specklebelly lichen in northern Vancouver Island during a survey conducted by forest ecologist W.J. Beese for Western Forest Products Inc.; the subsequent report was published in 2008–09. The survey attempted to determine the presence of OGS lichen in TFL 6 and TFL 19. He also describes, in the essay "Prosthetic Symbiosis," driving up to Goward's home, in the Clearwater Valley, which was under an evacuation alert during the fire season of 2017, to rescue Goward's large collection of lichen.

symbiosis as "a kind of prosthesis or technological process" and lichens as "nonhuman technologies":[88] "Symbiogenesis is not a matter of organisms using one another like nonliving tools or machines, but a fundamental technical process in which one autopoietic life form externalizes functions into another."[89] Derek develops the concept of prosthesis as a "kind of minimal ecological relation: a threshold between ecological and biological registers and a technical process that mediates between ecological relation and biological self-relation."[90]

Derek's concept of lichen as prosthetic technology works intriguingly with the idea of a poem; the poem as prosthesis is worn or inhabited by the reader's body/consciousness. The poem is already well along this path of the lichen thallus as technology for thinking with. Keats described the poem's ability in terms of negative capability ("no irritable reaching after fact"). Poetic language is steeped in ambiguity, figurative language as a turning away from the literal, while simultaneously embracing it, as it embraces multiple meanings. The poem pries us out of our left hemispheric mindset, as documented by Iain McGilchrist: the whole, the gestalt, the musical, complex rhythm, wordplay, emotion are all embedded in right hemispheric styles of perceiving the world, in a refusal of what Goward calls "our largely unconscious tendency to emphasize the single perspective over the multiple."[91]

Goward also speaks to the lichen thallus[92] as a microcommunity:

---

88 Woods, "Prosthetic Symbiosis," 159.

89 Woods, "Prosthetic Symbiosis," 160.

90 Woods, "Prosthetic Symbiosis," 160.

91 Goward, Essay 1, "Twelve Readings," 3.

92 I am using "lichen thallus" here as Goward uses it, to denote what in common language we call "lichen." Goward's point is that fundamentally there is no lichen, no name for lichen, if we take seriously his argument of the lichen thallus as portal, community, built system, ecosystem. Yet at times he also reverts to the common…

> what, I ask, is a lichen if not a kind of community writ small: an imponderably complex, internally consistent, self-sustaining ecosystem composed of who-knows-anymore-how-many lichen forming fungi, algae and bacteria?[93]

Within the context of Fairy Creek, this works loosely by way of analogy (I am not suggesting any strict 1:1 correlation between lichen thallus and Fairy Creek community[94] or between lichen thallus and poem). Although I only made seven or eight visits through the fall of 2021, for a few days each time, I witnessed a constant questioning and negotiating of the nature of the community, which was itself in constant flux of folks who came and went; of our ways of interacting with one another, and with the matriarchs and Elder Bill Jones; of relations between Indigenous and non-Indigenous allies (sometimes fraught); of our encounters with the RCMP, C-IRG, and Teal-Jones; of our decision-making processes; of our housekeeping (Who will wash the dishes? Who will take on the hard labour of collecting water from Renfrew Creek?); of our ethical engagements with the

---

... term, "lichen." And at times, I do also. This gestures towards lichen as word, concept, organism, technology, ecosystem, as it flickers in and out of conceptual categories. Yet there is lichen: as emergent organism, more than the sum of its algae, fungi, cyanobacteria, and so on.

93 Goward, Essay 11, "Twelve Readings," 1.

94 Derek points out important concerns regarding the loose application of symbiotism to larger scales such as ecosystems and Gaia, particularly as this concept is ubiquitous among many contemporary social theorists and utopian visionaries (lichen as utopian symbiotic community). At the same time, he attempts to theorize a non-utilitarian form of symbiosis as prosthetic technology, not algae as standing reserve used by fungus. My experience of the many difficulties and quarrels in establishing an equitable and just community at Fairy Creek speaks to his concerns. A. Laurie Palmer's *The Lichen Museum* (2023) offers a thoughtful example of the interest in lichen as model for queer communities and as challenge to the inhabiting of time and public spaces within a capitalist system.

Indigenous history of so-called Canada, with the Pacheedaht,[95] on whose traditional territory we stood, and with our more-than-human kin, with Grandmother and Grandfather Trees.

In the vein of a community, Goward asserts the *built* quality of a lichen thallus: "Lichens are built, not grown; and in this they have more in common with ecosystems, say, and enduring human relationships."[96] Poems are also built, out of breath, vocalizations, graphemes, inked letters, words; I think of Wah's "right words," Miebach's "intimate words." Goward is kin to poet in this sense, lichenologist seeking out patterns and right words: throughout his twelve essays he offers a rich description of the lichen thallus. For example, with reference to the cortex, he notes that it

> varies across a wide range of attributes: thickness, compaction, permeability, opacity, pigmentation, crystalline chemistry, hyphal alignment, surface texture. Sometimes it bears tiny hairs (tomentum, dew hairs), while other times it wears a coat of calcium oxalate crystals (pruina), dead cortical cells (epinecral layer) or, indeed, a see-through polysaccharide negligee (epicortex). No classification system will ever do justice to the synergistic complexity of the lichen cortex, which even across the length and breadth of a single thallus can vary in bewildering degree.[97]

---

95 As I have already noted, Fairy Creek was, and continues to be, a complex ethical space. There were also internal disagreements among the Pacheedaht, divided as so often by hereditary leadership in opposition to a colonial band council, an artefact of the Indian Act, which continues to divide and conquer. See Morin, "'We're Not Going Anywhere.'"

96 Goward, Essay IX, "Twelve Readings," 2.

97 Goward, Essay X, "Twelve Readings," 3.

Opacity, hyphal alignment, tiny hairs, *a see-through polysaccharide negligee!!!*

Another example appears in his offering of neologisms for the "undesignated macrolichen structures seemingly integral to macrolichen carbon economy": arterials, cortical vents, dew hairs, isidalia, micropores, rain cups, scleridia, sorsidia, tartaria, undulidia.[98] *Rain cups! Isidalia! Undulidia!!*

A poem might also be thought of as a community, in that poems and poets are always in conversation with other poems, other poets, contemporary and historical, with conventions and genres. A community is a conversation. A poem is dialogic. A poem is also an ecosystem, as is a lichen.

In Goward's third essay, "Credo," he speaks of the lichen thallus as oscillating between organism and ecosystem; that it is in fact both, simultaneously, which forces us, if we wish to "think seriously about lichens . . . fundamentally to move outside the comfort zone of 'common sense.'"[99] As ecosystem, the lichen embodies "the requisite level of biotic diversity" as well as a "definite trophic structure in the form of producers (algae), consumers (fungi) and decomposers (presumably fungi and bacteria) . . . living lichens are much more helpfully conceived of as compact, interactive, fully-functioning ecosystems complete, more or less, unto themselves."[100]

From a structural perspective, the words of a poem are the result of synchronic choices (syntactic; words placed side by side generating

98 Goward, Essay X, "Twelve Readings," 8.
99 Goward, Essay III, "Twelve Readings," 1.
100 Goward, Essay IV, "Twelve Readings," 4.

meaning) and diachronic evolutions: this word, as it has developed through time; this is Emily Dickinson's flickering of one choice over another embodied in her fascicles. Julia Kristeva's juxtaposition of the tensions between the semiotic (rhythms, patterns, emotional resonances that begin in the womb, in a wash of maternal language) and symbolic (words as symbols that generate meaning, convey concepts)[101] also suggests the ongoing exchange of materials and energies within an ecosystem. At one point, Goward cites Bateson's beautiful and startling observation: "We commonly think of animals and plants as matter, but they are really systems through which matter is continually passing."[102]

A poem (and again, this is a loose analogy) also organizes sounds, letters, phonemes, syllables, words; it composes, consumes, decomposes, causes to interact, and become more than the whole of its parts; it redistributes musical vibrations and emotional energies, from language to poem, from poem to reader. The poem also exists within not simply a conceptual but a material ecosystem, from plant fibres used to make the paper it is handwritten or typed upon, to the chemical elements of the ink, the food ingested to power the writer, sunlight and carbon now redistributed as hieroglyphs on a page, now bound into pages, and circulating within a human-based system of exchange, however tenuously, at the margins of the capitalist-cultural economy. The poem—as with the poet—is a system through which language and materials are continually passing.

The lichen thallus is described by Goward as emergent:

> Emergence, says the physicist, is what happens when a system exceeds some critical threshold of internal

101 Kristeva, *Desire in Language*.

102 Bateson quoted in Goward, Essay v, "Twelve Readings," 1.

> complexity, and suddenly reconfigures to a wholly new level of organization. To qualify as emergent in biology, this new level of organization should at once be radically novel, fully integrated, self-sustaining, and capable of evolving. Its functionality, moreover, should be based less on any specific attributes of the component parts and more on the particular nature of their relationship. That the lichen thallus meets all of these criteria seems to me self-evident.[103]

He could be describing a lyric poem: ink splotches, vowels and consonants, phonemes, words, phrases, sentences and fragments, lines, line breaks, stanzas, metaphors, metonyms, similes, images, anaphoric and other rhetorical patternings, assonances, alliterations, rhythms, slant and half rhymes, tropes, ideas—at some point reach a "critical threshold of internal complexity" and become "radically novel, fully integrated, self-sustaining," and "evolving" in the sense of generating new meanings, new poems, by those who are reading, and interacting with not-yet-written poems in the distant future:

> Westron wynde when wyll thow blow
> the smalle rayne downe can Rayne
> Cryst yf my love were in my Armys
> And I yn my bed Agayne.[104]

This brief sixteenth-century song, probably a remnant of a poem in Middle English composed hundreds of years earlier, has seen many adaptations, allusions, and modifications over the centuries. An incomplete list of subsequent reworkings and popular references

---

103 Goward, Essay III, "Twelve Readings," 2.

104 Wikipedia, "Westron Wynde," accessed April 23, 2025, https://en.wikipedia.org/wiki/Westron_Wynde.

include musical versions by Igor Stravinsky, The Limeliters, Current 93, and literary allusions such as those found in Virginia Woolf's *The Waves* and in the title of Thomas Pynchon's first story, "The Small Rain."[105]

The many allusions to and reworkings of this tiny lyric might also be characterized as a conversation; Goward theorizes the lichen thallus as both "conversation" and as "place" in Essay V:

> [Lichen] by their very ability to establish and grow have more to tell us about a particular habitat, its changing moods, than we're likely any time soon to fully absorb. Learning to "read" the environment through the lens of macrolichens requires, of course, that we first learn to "read" macrolichens themselves.[106]

How might a poem be a place? I have addressed this briefly with reference to *beholden*, rootedness, and Indigenous language that is grounded in specific land. I'm thinking also of song rooting community in place in the Kaluli's singing of *tok* in the 1970s, in the Saami *joik*, and in the songspirals of the Aboriginal Peoples in Australia.[107]

---

105 Wikipedia, "Westron Wynde."

106 Goward, Essay V, "Twelve Readings," 2.

107 Steven Feld, in his 1972 book *Sound and Sentiment*, studied the rich poetic vocabulary arising from the aural environment of the Kaluli of Papua New Guinea, describing it as a form of knowing (acoustemology). Feld noted the Kaluli would compose a *tok* or "poetic map," which drew singer and listeners together in community, a song that was also a journey unfolding through time, stitching the emotional lives and memories of individuals together and their identity as community to the land as places were named and sadness evoked.

The Saami *joik* is perhaps similar, "like a holographic, multi-dimensional living image" of place, establishing community through song (Länsman quoted in Burke, "The Sami Yoik.")

Bawaka Country et al. have written of songspirals: "Songspirals, commonly known as songlines, are rich and multilayered articulations, passed down through…

How might a poem attempt to embody the complexities of Fairy Creek, where the neoliberal exigencies of the social contract to log are challenged on the ground, at the blockade; where different conceptions of the law struggle with their own interpretations and rejections, and, in the case of Indigenous protestors and their allies, a completely different conception of law, including Indigenous law, the "laws" of Pachamama, of nature, of more-than-human kin, of bees and oldgrowth specklebelly lichens, who are themselves engaged in their own murmurous conversations?

Goward writes of the lichen's ongoing conversation in relation to complex (cybernetic, that is, positive feedback) systems:

> [T]he inner workings of the lichen have the form of a conversation between the constituent parts. Now we're getting somewhere. In effect cybernetics invites us to visualize the lichen as an infinitely detailed transcription of a very long "meeting" for which the thallus has not only acted as stenographer but also now provides the filing cabinet. On the agenda, and hence duly recorded in the thallus, are certain actions taken in response to an ongoing, but ever varied, interplay of environmental variables—rain, dry, damp, warmth, chill, chemistry, and so on. Hence we have the lichen thallus seen as document: the ways and moods of the weather through the seasons and, indeed, across the years.[108]

I love this description of a lichen as a conversation and a transcription—"infinitely detailed"—where the lichen thallus becomes the archive of an

---

...the generations and sung by Aboriginal people to wake Country, to make and remake the life-giving connections between people and place—people co-becoming as place" (Bawaka Country et al., "Gathering of the Clouds," 296).

108 Goward, Essay v, "Twelve Readings," 2.

ongoing process that has taken place over years, possibly over millennia; in the case of the Fairy Creek oldgrowth specklebelly lichens, Goward suggests they are descendants of communities stretching back to the last ice age. A poem can also function as document/transcription/archive, where the form itself bears traces of its own history and evolution in form; capable of "thick description"; poem as archive, poem as *fonds*.

Goward is thinking towards a complex reading of the lichen thallus[109] that embodies these and other concepts—community, conversation, scale-free network, transcription, microecosystem, portal, technology for thinking. As well, he is seeking terms to describe this, aware of our conceptual limitations and our "overwhelming allegiance to words" while also asserting the reality of the oldgrowth specklebelly lichen, the thing in itself, outside of the conceptual, verbal, narrative mapping of the human:

> The words by which we describe existence to ourselves can never actually contain it. Words are synaptic, catalytic, metaphoric: they signify, but they never convey. The map is not the territory, and neither is the word the thing. This is the first thing to understand about species.[110]

---

109 For a beautiful reading of lichen as a "mad surface" and trope for the entwining of nature-culture, see Orchid Tierney's *looking at the Tiny: Mad lichen on the surfaces of reading* (2023), a fittingly tiny volume that has accompanied me twice in my visits to Fairy Creek: "lichens are embedded with signs and interpretation. semiotics entrap me too: lichens are open culture chambers, biosocial destroyers of rocks and stained glass windows. wow. forget it. we're not living in the anthropocene. it's the lichencene. and lichens' power lies in their surface spreading of small catastrophes" (Tierney, *looking at the Tiny*, 3).

110 Goward, Essay VII, "Twelve Readings," 2.

Lyric poetry approaches this gap between map and territory, if obliquely, as it often incorporates narrative, while embodying tension between lyric present and narrative impulse, between now and time unfolding, organism and ecosystem, part and whole, single and multiple meaning(s), tiniest and most infinite of scales. Goward observes that we have great difficulty with very large and very small scales, although we have abstraction, equations, and tools, such as a microscope or a telescope, to describe this range; "organismic life," however,

> occupies roughly 11 orders of magnitude, ranging from a fraction of a micron (bacteria; viruses aren't usually thought of as alive) to tens of hectares, as in the rooting systems of clonal trees like Trembling Aspen (*Populus tremuloides*) or the (no doubt discontinuous) mycelial mats of the Honey Mushroom (*Armillaria ostoyae*). Measured along the time axis, life is bookended at the small end by biochemical time (measured in milliseconds or less) and at the large by geologic time (measured roughly in millions of years).[111]

Within this range, we are further bounded by our senses, such as sight; we can only perceive the "visible" (to us) portion of the light spectrum, oblivious without our human-made tools to that which lies beyond, to the ultraviolet and the infrared. In this eleventh of the twelve essays, Goward presents a charming diagram of scale, most of which we can barely conceive of, where he marks out various points, its descriptive key in itself a prose poem:

> A through J, the approximate spatial scales at which a person, if expanded or shrunk, would (A) collapse into a black hole, (B) create her own gravity, (C) lose the ability to dissipate heat

111 Goward, Essay XI, "Twelve Readings," 6.

> quickly enough to prevent lethal overheating, (D) survive a long fall, (E) walk on water, (F) stick to a wall, (G) float in air, (H) behave like a gas, (I) occupy multiple locations simultaneously, and (J) feel the strong force on her face.[112]

To identify each of these spatial scales provokes thought. And each of these examples might be incorporated into a poem, using poetic tools to attempt a "translation" of such an experience that organisms that exist at other scales might know—what it feels like to stick to a wall (a gecko), to float in air (a dandelion seed), to occupy multiple locations simultaneously (mycelia).

These are some ideas on lichenous form that I carry in my backpack.

112 Goward, Essay XI, "Twelve Readings," 6.

*The chickadee's alarm call can signal nuanced variations of danger and urgency. Humpback whale song can travel for thousands of miles through the dark oceans. Ravens and crows grieve—*kiaaw kiaaawwwww. *Humans are not the only species that create poetry and song, nor the only species that mourn their dead. The* Umwelten *of other kin. Acoustic niches and acoustemology. Humans are governed overwhelmingly by sight; our metaphors confirm this. Yet sound contours the* Umwelten *of so many of our more-than-human kin and lies at the heart of lyric poetry.*

UMWELT

The chickadee's alarm call, after which it is onomatopoeically named, has been described as incredibly complex, capable of signalling nuanced variations of danger and urgency. Humpback whale song can carry for up to 16,000 kilometres (10,000 miles) through the dark oceans, their songs often continuing for twenty-four hours or more. Scientists have documented the grieving practices of ravens and crows—*kiaaw kiaaawwwww*. Humans are not the only species that creates poetry and song; there are many forms of culturally transmitted song, linked to each species' way of being in the world. As Ed Yong has observed, "Earth teems with sights and textures, sounds and vibrations, smells and tastes, electric and magnetic fields. But every animal can only tap into a small fraction of reality's fullness. Each is enclosed within its own unique sensory bubble, perceiving but a tiny sliver of an immense world."[1] That "sensory bubble," resultant sensory data that a given organism's sense organs yield, is its Umwelt, "specifically the part of those surroundings that an animal can sense and experience—its *perceptual* world."[2] Coined by Jakob von Uexküll

1 Yong, *An Immense World*, 5.

2 Yong, *An Immense World*, 5.

in 1909, German for "environment," *Umwelt* refers to the sensory world that is accessible to an animal—everything that it can sense and experience. Yong points out that Uexküll perceived animals "not as mere machines but as sentient entities, whose inner worlds not only existed but were worth contemplating. Uexküll didn't exalt the inner worlds of humans over those of other species."[3] The human species is governed overwhelmingly by sight; our metaphors confirm this. Yet sound contours the *Umwelt* of so many of our more-than-human kin, just as it lies at the heart of lyric poetry. Yong has pointed out that many sensory biologists have roots in the arts, "which may enable them to see past the perceptual worlds that our brains automatically create," that to approach the *Umwelten* of other organisms requires "what psychologist Alexandra Horowitz calls 'an imaginative leap.'"[4]

SONGS OF THE HUMPBACK WHALE

Their songs thrummed through the wooden hulls of ships in the nineteenth century; their voices were recorded as "singers" in the whaling logbooks.[5] Sailors imagined them as sirens, as mermaids, as sea canaries.[6] First Nations and Inuit have "been hearing them through the hulls of their boats for millennia."[7] The earliest recordings of humpback whale songs were made in the 1960s by the US Navy, inadvertently, as they deployed hydrophones to listen for the movement of Soviet submarines. My sister has heard them singing while she swam underwater off the coast of Maui. As for myself, I

3 Yong, *An Immense World*, 6.

4 Yong, *An Immense World*, 13.

5 Janik, "Whale Song," R109.

6 Payne, "A Change of Tune," 44.

7 Gray et al., "The Music of Nature," 1.

have only ever heard recordings: *Songs of the Humpback Whale*, the 1970 five-track LP, which was later excerpted and sent into space on *Voyager* in 1977. In 1979 an imprint of the LP was made by *National Geographic*[8] and sent out to all its subscribers. I have a faint memory of discovering as a child this flimsy disk, stamped into a square of black plastic and interleaved among glossy photographs and densely printed columns of text. I placed the square of black plastic onto my parents' turntable and out swam *Megaptera novaeangliae*.

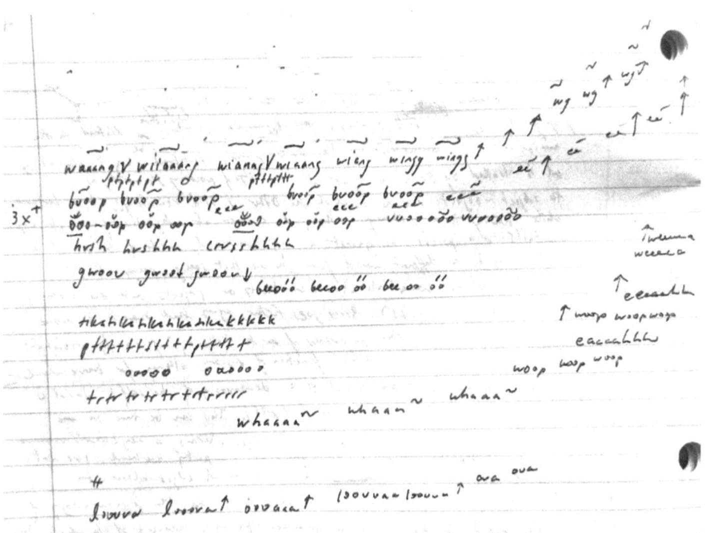

Transcription of *Songs of the Humpback Whales. Credit: Kim Trainor.*

How to transcribe these slow, languorous songs? I tried recently, using only ink, letters, and other random symbols, scored across a page of my

8 Strongman, "Forgotten Audio Formats." This was a flexible Eva-tone recording known as a "soundsheet" or "flexi disc"; you could detach the perforated sheet from the magazine and play it on a turntable.

notebook. I found I didn't want to use words with semantic content, although I was not entirely successful; I wanted to carry more a sense of the sounds' texture, their spareness conveyed by scoring on paper.

Unlike my rough transcription, spectrograms provide a less impressionistic, more quantitative, graphic representation of frequencies—a sound print. Payne and McVay describe the process of documenting the songs of humpback whales: "Once the spectrograms were made, the hundreds required for each song were carefully matched, glued to large sheets of paper, and photographically reproduced."[9]

I like how these spectrograms are shorn of any human semantic content, unlike the use of the alphabet in my own sketch, while the relative black thickness and width of the lower frequencies, contrasted with the delicate scratches and plumes of the higher ones, hint at something of the original song. Roger Payne interprets them using the vocabulary of human song—subunits or pulses combine into units, then units into phrases. A series of similar phrases, unbroken, can be called a theme; "several distinct themes combine to form a song."[10] A song session, with no more than a minute's pause between songs, can last for hours. In short, "subunit < unit < phrase < theme < song < song session."[11]

Katy Payne has identified refrains that form "rhymes," and she speculates that, in longer songs, these rhymes may serve a mnemonic purpose, helping the whales to remember long complex songs:

> One possibility is that whales, like human bards, sometimes use rhymes to help recall their lines in a long

---

9 Payne and McVay, "Songs of Humpback Whales," 592.
10 Payne and McVay, "Songs of Humpback Whales," 591.
11 Payne and McVay, "Songs of Humpback Whales," 591.

> oral performance . . . What do the song changes, and the preference for novelty that they seem to reflect, mean in the life of humpback whales? What drives tomorrow's song to be just a little different from yesterday's, and all singers to keep up with the latest version? Can we speculate about this, and about whales' use of rhymes, without thinking of human beings and wondering about the ancient roots in nature of even our aesthetic behavior?[12]

Payne considers whales as kin, with both human and whale song rooted in a distant past. This invites us to conceive of whales as sentient, capable of intent, communication, and creation for its own sake. Gray notes that humpback whales have a range of seven octaves but that they tend to use musical intervals similar to human scales; similarly, they balance percussive or more noise-like elements with pure tones as in Western symphonic music, while the "tone and timbre of many whale notes are similar to human musical sounds," even though they are capable of a vast repertoire of sounds that are less pleasant to human ears.[13]

I've noted Jane Bennett's observation in *Vibrant Matter* that the human impulse to anthropomorphize is not necessarily an unethical move; it can offer a more empathetic attempt at understanding the lives of more-than-human kin, as well as the material objects of this world, the apparently inanimate matter to which we might not attribute any form of agency or sentience we would recognize. While anthropomorphization might imply an inability to see these beings outside of a human frame, the frame might also function as a window into another world. That is, to hear and interpret a humpback whale's vocalizations as song may widen our conception

12 Payne, "A Change of Tune," 46.

13 Gray et al., "The Music of Nature," 53.

of whales as possessing a form of consciousness, capable of intent, communication, and creation for its own sake. Much recent research into whale songs and calls has documented that cultural knowledge can be passed down through generations in other species. Whales perceived as sentient singing beings should not be treated as resource, as in the past: "In the 1960s, tens of thousands of whales were slaughtered every year, mainly for soap, oil and pet food. Humpback whales, which numbered around 100,000 in 1900, had been hunted mercilessly and fewer than 7,000 remained."[14]

The scientists still don't know why humpback whales sing. They think it is only the males who sing, but even that is not certain; there has been speculation that their songs are a form of lekking—the males displaying rituals of courtship. Humans may also have learned to sing in order to court, to convey coded data in mnemonic form, to formalize ritual and heighten emotional tenor, all these; yet also simply to sing—for the physical pleasure of resonance, vibration, beauty, intimacy, as voice enters landscape and other beings, in a profoundly intimate way that sight cannot.

BIOSONIFICATION

I'm listening to track 1, "*Picea* (Spruce)" by German artist Bartholomäus Traubeck. A bass piano chord opens the track, followed by a trickling of individual soprano keys. Another single deep note is played several times while the highest soprano notes are sounded, one or two at a time, slightly off-kilter. It continues in this vein, notes spilling, slipping across one another, high and low, dissonant, not following any recognizable pattern of key or technique. For his album *Years*, Traubeck

---

14 Lewis, "'It Always Hits Me Hard.'"

took slices of trees and rigged a contraption that could "play" the tree rings of different species on a vinyl turntable. Initially a piece of performance art, he then created an album of seven tracks, featuring seven different trees—*Picea* (Spruce), *Fraxinus* (Ash), *Quercus* (Oak), *Acer* (Maple), *Alnus* (Alder), *Juglans* (Walnut), and *Fagus* (Beech). The album's Bandcamp page describes the technique Traubeck used:

> A tree's year rings are analysed for their strength, thickness and rate of growth. This data serves as basis for a generative process that outputs piano music. It is mapped to a scale which is again defined by the overall appearance of the wood (ranging from dark to light and from strong texture to light texture). The foundation for the music is certainly found in the defined ruleset of programming and hardware setup, but the data acquired from every tree interprets this ruleset very differently.[15]

The data provided by the tree rings is translated into piano notes. As a technique it troubles the "binary" of nature and culture, and the extent to which the tracks are the tree rings' soundings. Consider that each tree ring is an archive of years of plenty or of drought, of infestation or of health. Traubeck, in an interview with Data Garden, has observed of his process,

> I set a rule-set for the compositions by programming and building this machine which has some kind of internal rules of how it works so it can't just produce any sound but then again the composition is actually then being made by the tree's data, which is not really random. Some people would say it is random but I think it's not because it has a very special structure and follows certain

15 Traubeck, *Years.*

> rules that derive from other systems, like ecological systems. But there is always a rule-set to find in there.[16]

The music we hear is a co-making; the tree has provided the data in its rings which function as an archive of its growth over time while Bartholomäus has contributed an algorithm and a machine to read and translate this data into sound, including the choice of a piano to be the tree's "voice." He observes, "the sound is coming from the wood but it's also coming from me somehow."[17] The Data Garden interviewer makes an interesting observation that the music also is a representation of time, a "reverse timelapse" as the scan of the tree rings moves from its outer rings inward, towards the oldest (youngest) tree rings at its centre. Traubeck describes his desire to challenge the nature-culture binary, in that all technology is ultimately an extreme version or "result" of nature, and he sees his research as the merging of biological and digital in the area of bioelectronics: "I went further and tried to see plants or trees as part of manifested algorithms. DNA is like a program that's run and depending on which environment it's running it will develop differently."[18]

My former student Derek Woods, who introduced me to Traubeck's work, told me that when he plays Traubeck's music to his own students, they begin with a discussion of indexicality—what exactly is the relationship between tree rings and the sound we are hearing? To speak to the title of one of the articles I rely on below in my discussion of PlantWave, is Traubeck "forcing" these tree rings to produce music or is it a gentler kind of sounding, a facilitating or co-making of music? To what extent might it be

16 Traubeck, "Interview."
17 Traubeck, "Interview."
18 Traubeck, "Interview."

thought of as a violent act, to wrench sound from a tree that has already experienced violence in its logging. Derek told me his students are often wildly polarized in their stance on this question.[19]

Towards the end of "*Picea* (Spruce)" comes a more intricate plucking of notes in the upper register while the bass resounds more insistently, the lowest keys resonant; the piece ends on an upward ring of high-pitched notes. This track is guided by the data of the tree rings of a slice of spruce tree, but the music sounds familiar; it could be the composition of an avant-garde musician. The effect of the piano is to distance the original source of data, even though a piano is typically made of the very wood—spruce—that here is being made to sound.[20]

Working around the same time as Traubeck, in 2011, the sonic artist Mileece was placing electrodes on plants to detect changes in their bioelectric variations, running them through an amplifier that translated the impulses into binary code where software animated them, producing sound. Asked about the paradox of taking biofeedback, which is "natural," and then translating it into "artificial" sound, Mileece makes an argument similar to Traubeck's:

> In terms of the plant music with the organic versus the electronic stuff, I don't find it paradoxical as much as I find it symbiotic because the sonification of those signals in that context creates such crazy music. And I could never have made it nor could anybody else... I do think plants are sentient. I know they're sentient. No one in science can answer to you what consciousness is. No one. But what we... like to say is consciousness is derived from having a central processing unit

19 Private conversation with the author, June 20, 2024.

20 "Wood Types on Pianos." A quality piano's sounding board is usually made of spruce.

> as in the brain, which plants do not have. But they do have conglomerations of tiny cells that function like brains because they can take information, they can assess information, and they can make decisions about that information. And they can update it in real time. The intention is just to relay whatever they're feeling. And do it in a way that people can understand.[21]

As noted here by Mileece, little progress has been made on the hard problem of consciousness, despite ever finely tuned technologies that can scan the activities of the human brain. At most, as philosopher Philip Goff discusses in his work on panpsychism, we must reply upon on our own intuition of what it feels like to *be* this singular thinking sentient person. And we must think beyond the human-centric model of consciousness aligned with a central nervous system, as pointed out by Adamatzky in his work on the speculative language of fungi.[22] Artists such as Traubeck and Mileece generously

---

21 "Meet the Sonic Artist Making Music with Plants," 4:40.

22 Adamatzky, "Language of Fungi." Adamatzky observes that we associate neuronal activity (spike potential) in terms of a nervous system, but that other organisms also exhibit such potential: hydrozoa, slime moulds, protozoa, and fungi. He outlines contemporary research into the language of "creatures without a nervous system and invertebrates" (2), who use communicative techniques such as intracellular signalling, chemotaxis, and pheromones, observing that "[p]lant communication processes are seen as primarily sign-mediated interactions and not simply an exchange of information" (2). For example, he addresses chemicals as "words." This is reminiscent of Adam Dickinson's treatment of hormones and pheromones, as well as other chemical compounds, in *Anatomic*.

Adamatzky points out that the importance of this research lies in that "a modified conception of language of plants is considered to be a pathway towards 'the deobjectification of plants and the recognition of their subjectivity and inherent worth and dignity'" (Gagliano cited in Adamatzky, 2). Adamatzky asks of electrical spiking in fungi, "Are the elaborate patterns of electrical activity used by fungi to communicate states of the mycelium and its environment and to transmit and…

extend their intuition of sentience to more-than-human kin and seek to engage in a co-making of the world through their sonic art.

The intersection of digital and organic data to produce sound was also being pursued by Joe Patitucci and Alex Tyson of PlantWave in 2011. PlantWave developed out of a zero-waste record label called Data Garden, which "released digital albums via download codes on handmade printed artwork embedded with seeds that could be planted and grown into flowers."[23] This led to an installation at the Philadelphia Museum, "Data Garden Quartet," which consisted of four harmonizing plants. Patitucci and Tyson noted their goal was "to foster an awareness of plants as living organisms."[24] Jon Shapiro, Data Garden's produce development manager, observes, "it has allowed me to look at other life forms and appreciate their aliveness in a different way."[25] He stresses that the aliveness of plants "isn't necessarily human," and that the sounds we hear are mediated: These artists measure fluctuations in electrical resistance between two points within a plant, fluctuations influenced by water movement or photosynthesis, data which is then converted into pitch that in turn is fed through a choice of instrument via software:

...process information in the mycelium networks? Is there a language of fungi?" (4). In order to answer these questions, he applies techniques similar to those used to decode Pictish: "(i) type of characters used to code, (ii) size of the character lexicon, (iii) grammar, (iv) syntax (word order), and (v) standardized spelling," with a focus on i, ii, and iv (4).

He studied four different kinds of fungi: ghost fungi (*Omphalotus nidiformis*), Enoki fungi (*Flammulina velutipes*), split gill fungi (*Schizophyllum commune*), and caterpillar fungi (*Cordyceps militaris*). His conclusions are that the electrical activity suggests a fungal lexicon of up to fifty words (with a core vocabulary of fifteen to twenty words), and that word lengths are roughly equivalent to those of some human languages such as English or Russian.

23 "Who We Are: History."

24 Haigney, "The Lessons to Be Learned."

25 Haigney, "The Lessons to Be Learned."

The variation in the connection is largely related to how much water is between those two points, which changes a lot as the plant is moving water around while it's photosynthesizing," Shapiro said. "Then we graphed that change as a wave, and then we translate that wave into pitch, so then essentially we're getting a stream of all these pitch messages coming from the plant." The pitches then enter the device's software, which features different electronic instruments—the flute, harp, piano, guitar, bass and some synthesizers among them—that you can elect for the plants to "play," then scaling them to be harmonious. A symphony (of sorts), generated by algorithms and leaves.[26]

Their choice of electronic instruments is traditional here, and the results tend to sound synthy; they have commercialized their software and hardware so that folks can experiment with the music of plants on their own, but there's a limited number of sounds that can be produced with the commercial equipment. In theory, a more sophisticated software program and MIDI board can translate given pitches into a wide range of sonic materials, including into other natural sounds, such as samplings of the *quork* of a raven, *hoo-hoots* of an owl, the *feeee-beee* of a chickadee, the scratching of a dark-eyed junco in the undergrowth, rainfall tapping on leaves, river run, rustling leaves, thunder, in addition to human-generated sounds such as the percussive sounds generated from tapping spoons on a tin pot, sticks on metal cans, blowing across the rim of half-filled mason jars, and so on.

In my work on *walk quietly / ts'ekw'unshun kws qututhun*,[27] an Indigenous, artist, and scientist guided walk, my collaborator, the musician and

26 Haigney, "The Lessons to Be Learned."

27 Williams, "Hul'q'umi'num—ts'ekw'unshun qututhun." *ts'ekw'unshun kws qututhun*, "walking with respect and honour along the shore," is a term that was provided to…

composer Hazel Fairbairn, took field recordings of Hwlhits'um (Canoe Pass), as well as data from the bioelectric activity of flora at this site in Ladner, BC, at the mouth of the Fraser River estuary:

> Working from the line *Mukw'stem 'l' utunu tumuhw 'o' slhiilhukw'tul*—"Everything is interconnected," the soundscape for "Hwlhits'um | signs" weaves together filter-swept field recordings made at Brunswick Point, MIDI data captured from the bioelectric activity of plants—used to trigger samples of birds and voices—with melodic fragments and electronica generated from spectrographs of maps and images from the film.[28]

Hazel ran the bioelectric data through a MIDI board programmed with a variety of recorded samples of birds and human voices at the site; she also used images from my poetry film and generated electronica from their spectrographs. It was important for us to incorporate the voices of these plants, however mediated, transformed, or conceptual, as part of the textural weave of Canoe Pass.[29]

... Amy-Claire Huestis by Cowichan Elder Dr. Luschiim Arvid Charlie for our project. It was relayed to us by Hul'q'umi'num language teacher and knowledge holder Jared Qwustenuxun Williams, who explained that Arvid Charlie "broke it down further talking about how *ts'ekw'un* is the root word meaning to treat something with love, care, and respect. He used the word in reference to family, friends, and the earth. So I think it fits perfectly, as the suffix shun refers to the foot or walking."

28 Fairbairn, "Everything is Interconnected," 22. *Mukw'stem 'l' utunu tumuhw 'o' slhiilhukw'tul*, "Everything is interconnected," is a Hul'q'umi'num phrase taught to us by knowledge holder Jared Qwustenuxun Williams, and which he gave us permission to use in the subsequent poem and film I created for *walk quietly*.

29 The film can be found on the Walk Quietly website (www.walkquietly.ca) and on the ASLE website, as part of the ASLE virtual showcase, "Watery Ecologies": https://www.asle.org/stay-informed/asle-spotlight/watery-ecologies.

More recently, there has been an interest in biosonification on the West Coast of Canada. I first heard Ruby Singh's work at Lobe 4DSOUND Studio in East Vancouver, at a performance of his Polyphonic Garden for the spring equinox in 2023. The website describes the studio as

> [a]n array of speakers across the ceiling and under the floor, in conjunction with custom-designed vibroacoustic floor panels, [which] entirely surround the listener in an immersive and haptic listening experience. Using 4DSOUND technology, sound ebbs and flows, forming sonic environments holographically and without perceivable sources.[30]

Hazel and I entered the darkened studio in stocking feet, after removing our shoes in the lobby and placing them in low cubicles ranged under a long bench. Many audience members had already arrived—at most the studio has a capacity for perhaps forty people—and were seated on the wooden floor that had been scattered with soft cushion-backed chairs; around the edges of the room, some folks had stretched out supine on matts. Thin banners of cloth hung from the ceiling, spot lit in different colours; this gave the impression of entering a subterranean realm, as if lying beneath the tentacles of a sea jelly.

The room becomes a choreographing tool in itself, as the composer must consider the 4D effect of experiencing immersive sound, sound moving all around, coming from above, and vibrating through the speakers embedded in the floor. Because these performances are so complex, they are pre-recorded, but the immersive experience is such that you feel as if the speaker—in this case, Ruby Singh—is speaking to you live.

---

30 "About," Lobe Studio.

As with Mileece and PlantWave, Singh uses biosonification to "raise" songs from Indigenous flora and fungi, "transforming bioelectricity into midi data to inform pitch and rhythm."[31] The performance we heard that night was later released as an album, *Polyphonic Garden Suite II*,[32] which engages with West Coast ecology, old-growth logging, and Fairy Creek:

> The emerging melodies are then mixed with field recordings and unique instrumentation (tambura, mohan veena and fujara). Singh tempers keyboards with the songs of coastal wolves, orca, and birds (western screech owl, thrush, robin, song sparrow). To further deepen these sonic landscapes, the midi data of plants and fungi trigger the songs of their animal cohabitants: a Cottonwood tree triggers the call of the Song Sparrow that lives within its branches; bull kelp triggers the song of orcas.[33]

Whether we use the word "forcing" or "raising," both point to the agentic intent of the musician in contrast with the apparent passivity of the organism itself from which a sounding is "extracted." This is iterative, in the most negative interpretation, of the ongoing extraction of old-growth trees from the forests adjacent to the Fairy Creek watershed where ancient yellow cedar and Douglas fir were seen by the logging industry and the BC government as standing reserve. Yet this music is, on the most positive interpretation, and in the spirit in which it is intended, hypnotic and mysterious and speaks to spirit as much as to the blurring of nature and culture and to the idea of co-making.

---

31 "Interactive Polyphonic Garden."

32 Singh, *Polyphonic Garden Suite II*.

33 Singh, *Polyphonic Garden Suite II*.

There are seven tracks: "Amrit Vela," "A Wolf in Cedars Clothing," "Fairy Creek Lament," "After the Fires," "Lost in the Grasslands," "Cotton Song of the Sparrow," and "Shorelines." Regarding "Fairy Creek Lament," Singh writes:

> In BC less than 1% of Old Growth Forests are left standing and even with so few intact ecologies surviving, they are still being logged and destroyed for short term gain. The second single from *Polyphonic Garden Suite II* was created from field recordings from Fairy Creek, on the lands of the Pacheedaht First Nations, site of one of the largest cases of civil disobedience in canada's shortsited [*sic*] history...May we begin to choose new paths that understand our interdependence with this world and show care for all that surround us.[34]

This track begins briefly with the sound of birdsong, over which an ethereal flute and wavering synthetic notes thread songlines. After about two minutes, a deeper throbbing bass note is introduced. It continues in this vein, ending as it begins with birdsong and wind. At the Lobe performance, within the dimly lit studio, Singh's voice would introduce a piece, guiding us from one ecological zone to the next and then yield to the sounds of each zone, biodata of field recordings tempered by human agency as they triggered pitch and rhythm. Colours from spotlights shifted, dimmed, re-emerged, and video images were projected onto the cloth banners. The effect was mesmeric.

The track "After the Fires" speaks to our current moment as wildfires sweep through British Columbia each summer and persist into the fall:

---

34 Singh, "Fairy Creek Lament." Description for Singh's YouTube video.

> Amidst the hottest months and largest fires in documented history, the recordings and biosonifications for After the Fire were collected from the smoldering earth in Nłeʔkepmxcín lands in the summer of 2021. The first growth after fires in these territories trigger synth pads, including sage, alfalfa flower, and the tender shoots of fireweed. Field recordings of "dune boom," a phenomenon wherein wind over sand dunes plays the landscape like a flute, create the low humming sound throughout the track. Fire is a dangerous element that brings grave destruction but it also provides the right alchemy for change, transmutation and nourishment for forests.[35]

This piece includes field recordings, as he notes, of "dune boom," where the landscape is "played like a flute." The low humming or quavering tone that is heard throughout the piece is haunting, more so knowing its origin. Again, as with "Fairy Creek Lament," I find many points of convergence with my own work, as my sequence "Seeds" works with the concept of serotiny—the need for heat or fire that some organisms require in order to transform and thrive.[36]

Joe Patitucci of Data Garden notes that Data Garden tries to avoid anthropomorphization of plants.[37] As I observed earlier, the use of the term "forcing" of plants in the article's title is revealing and suggests some discomfort with the idea that human interaction in

---

35 Singh, "After the Fires." Description for Singh's YouTube video.

36 My collaborator Hazel, after our attendance at Singh's Polyphonic Garden performance, applied for a residency at Lobe Studio so that we could adapt and perform a sequence of films from my "Seeds" sequence in November 2024.

37 Haigney, "The Lessons to Be Learned."

the "translation" of plant sounds is somehow a contamination of the plants' own sounds and agentic volition. As my former student Derek observed to me, some of his students perceive the "forcing" of music from tree rings as a form of violence, doubly so in the context of the tree having been first cut down in order to "play" it. The more positive, hopeful reading of these experiments is that such experiments allow for a deeper connection with our more-than-human kin. Mileece observes this, as does Data Garden's Jon Shapiro, who notes the appreciation of the aliveness of plants that is engendered by their work. And as Stuart Derdeyn notes in his *Vancouver Sun* review of Singh's work, "Connecting to the root structure of a cedar tree and then plucking and tapping it to produce beats or defining the sonics of a lobster mushroom not only provides a treasure trove of useable data. Singh also feels that it yields up a means to hear the natural world calling out to us. Depending on the degree to which the 'composers' communicate, the results can be surprising."[38]

Singh indicates that Polyphonic Garden and a twin album *kraKIN* were seeded in residencies in Desolation Sound and the Octopus Islands, but also notes,

> You don't need to go far, because the natural world is everywhere, even in us... We made synth patches from everything from the howls of coastal wolves and orca songs to turning local woodpeckers into hi-hats or raven songs into something you could play on a keyboard. All told, the creations came from two years of field recordings and bio-sonifications done in six specific biomes around BC.[39]

---

38 Derdeyn, "From Mushroom Jazz to Bark-Rocking Beats."

39 Singh quoted in Derdeyn, "From Mushroom Jazz to Bark-Rocking Beats."

Singh speaks to "After the Fires" or "Fairy Creek Lament" as songs of "post-calamity regeneration" and argues for the "need to exercise our imaginations to achieve a sustainable future."[40]

Natasha Lavdovsky's art converges along lines similar to those of Ruby Singh, as to Nathalie Miebach's: similar to Ruby Singh, in that her work uses field recordings of organisms at Fairy Creek; similar to Nathalie Miebach's in that she generates a "score" that is used to create the soundscape. I've described how Natasha presents on her website an image of thin layer chromatography, a method for chemically analyzing the chemical markers found in lichen. This produces an image that looks like test tubes seen through a violet aquarium. She describes her technique for generating her "Music for Lichens (In Progress)" in this way:

> This image shows a "Thin Layer Chromatography" (TLC) plate, which was the starting point of the *Music for Lichens* soundscape series. Illuminated with UV light, this TLC plate—which is a thin ceramic plate used to chemically analyze biological material—shows the chemical markers of 18 different lichens. To make this plate, I processed tiny samples of lichen species from a seaside tree through a chemical analysis called thin layer chromatography. Each column (rising from the circles at the bottom) shows the particular acids present in that lichen. I translated this visual data into a musical composition, with the pitch determined by the height of the spot, and the tone generated from lichen micro-sounds or field recordings from the lichens'

40 Singh quoted in Derdeyn, "From Mushroom Jazz to Bark-Rocking Beats."

> habitat. Combining this tonal composition with layers of audio collected from the local ecosystem, the result is a music soundscape made for lichens and inspired by their chemistry and using the sounds they make when they move.[41]

Pitch is "the auditory attribute of a sound" while tone (or timbre) is "more about a sound's quality."[42] A classical guitar and a clarinet play a middle C: This is their pitch, the frequency at which the sound vibrates and enters your ear. The tone is the quality of the sound—its thickness or reediness, something of its texture and emotional resonance.[43] Based on this description, Lavdovsky's technique seems to involve generating a series of pitches based on the height of each column in the TLC, where the tone is generated by the ambient sounds she recorded in the forest, whether background audio or what she calls "lichen micro-sounds." There is no strict indexical aspect to her compositions, as there is with Traubeck's. I love how she describes these pieces as music *for* the lichen—a reciprocity, as of giving back to the lichen what she has received from them.

On Bandcamp, Lavdovsky has released several of her compositions, such as "The Sound of Lichen Chemistry: An Old-Growth Cedar Branch."[44] It is accompanied by the following TLC plate, which diagrams the chemical markers and identifies the different lichen being sampled, such as *Hypogymnia duplicata, Alectoria sarmentosa, Pseudocyphellaria rainierensis.*

---

41 Lavdovsky, "Music for Lichens (In Progress)."

42 Sloan School of Music, "The Fundamentals of Pitch Versus Tone."

43 Sloan School of Music, "The Fundamentals of Pitch Versus Tone."

44 Lavdovsky, "The Sound of Lichen Chemistry." Other compositions include "Music for Lichens on a Salish Sea Beachside Fir Tree" and "Music for Lichens on a Pacific Oceanside Fir Tree."

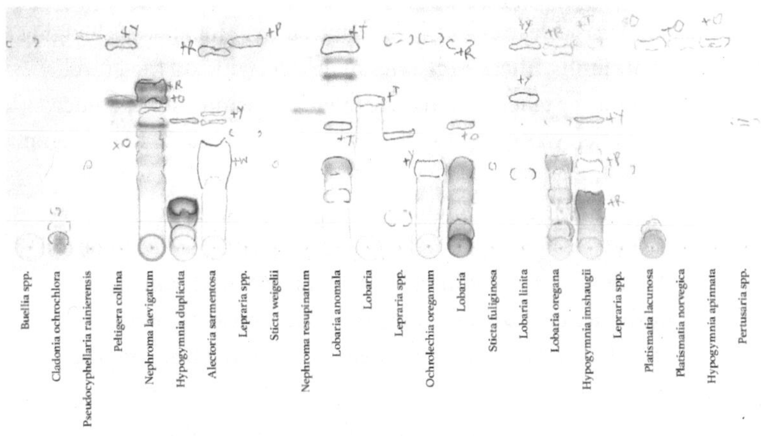

"The Sound of Lichen Chemistry: An Old-Growth Cedar Branch." *Credit: Natasha Lavdovsky.*

The 3-minute-and-19-second-long track is free to download. I recommend listening to it on headphones for the full effect. It begins with a thin crackling ribbon of sound, which could be mistaken for creek water or the snapping of a fire. Beneath this a deep ethereal hum emerges, as if the thrum of a blue whale like a deep-sea accordion bellows. Then synthetic bursts, at intervals, as if sound filtered through a distortion in space, like a Doppler effect. As the piece progresses, the deep ethereal hum slowly increases in volume, filling both ears as it deepens while the intermittent jangling synthetic bursts like static discharge continue.

I wasn't sure at first if Tasha was using a technology such as PlantWave to capture electric signals emitted by the lichen. She clarified this for me when I asked, sharing that this initial sound was generated by (re)hydrating *Alectoria sarmentosa*:

> When I found this blown-over old-growth cedar tree laying across the logging road at the edge of a freshly logged clear

> cut, I was awestruck by how much lichen biomass was hanging off its limbs. There were piles of lichen laying on the gravel around the fallen tree, having fallen in a winter storm. Since the lichen was going to decay into the road/ditch, I took some of the most plentiful lichen, *Alectoria sarmentosa* (witch's hair lichen), and brought it home to experiment with. In the past when I had hydrated piles of salvaged lichen... I noticed that the lichens would move and create sound from their movements while absorbing the water/mist. The micro-sounds that you hear at the beginning of that track are the barely audible crackling movements that a pile of dry *Alectoria sarmentosa* makes after I spray it with water. The droning sound in the background was created with the help of sound designer Joe McMurray, from field recordings that I made in the forest area around that fallen cedar near Fairy Creek. There are field recordings of flies, songbirds, marbled murrelets, ravens and water, all digitally manipulated and layered to create a deep hum, representing the life-forms that share the ecosystem with these lichens on this cedar tree branch.[45]

While I learned how these tiny lichen sounds were created by Tasha for her piece, by hydrating *Alectoria sarmentosa,* I think, I will have to ask Trevor Goward about lichen micro-sounds. Robin Wall Kimmerer has described the tiny popping sound as sphagnum moss releases its spores. When I do a quick Google search, I find an online community already engaged in the question of what lichen might sound like. From "Sound Material, Sound Art," I find: "the sound of blowing over the top of a glass bottle," "bell-esque." From a Reddit post titled "what sound would lichen make if it would have a voice?": "A soft whispering. Feathery giggling when you touch it," "meep,"

45 Email from Natasha Lavdovsky to author, November 1, 2024.

"Teeny tiny grumpy muttering." My collaborator Hazel tells me of an instrument called a geofon, which detects tiny vibrations, and wonders if it might be possible to use this to record micro lichen sounds.

ACOUSTEME

Sound is a kind of knowing and a becoming part of place. Steven Feld, the ethnomusicologist who documented the songs of the Kaluli in Papua New Guinea in the 1970s, coined the term "acoustemology,"

> to join acoustics and epistemology, to argue for sound as a capacity to know and as a habit of knowing ... a new all-species way to talk about the emplaced copresence and correlations of multiple sounds and sources.[46]

Sight, by contrast, assumes necessarily a distance between self as observer and that which is observed; vision offers gestalt, a rich source of spontaneous information. Gerard Bruns has argued that the gap or distance, the sense of apartness generated by sight, also creates a lack of empathy—one is separate from the observed other. And you have control; you can shut your eyes. By contrast, sound enters you. Bruns argues that this entry can be violent and overpowering; one cannot so easily close one's ears.

Yet sound is also intimate. The Other calls to you and the sound of their voice is tactile, a vibration and resonance in your bones. Sound waves, as ephemeral as light, made by one body, are received by another. The sound of the Other enters you. This is not metaphor. A call, a cry, emitted by one body is carried through the medium

46 Feld, *Sound and Sentiment*, xxvii.

of air in the form of waves. Acoustic waves perceived by humans range from 20 hertz (with a wavelength in air at atmospheric pressure of 17 metres) to 20 kilohertz (1.7 centimetres).[47] Beyond this range lies, to us, the imperceptible—ultrasound, infrasound.

The sound of your voice, standing next to me, ranges from approximately 100 to 400 hertz, with a wavelength that ranges from roughly 1 to 3 metres.[48] You call me by my name and the acoustic waves you have created enter and cause to vibrate the small bones inside my ear—malleus, incus, stapes. Here is the intimacy of lyric poetry.

While the Gay'wu Group of Women, speaking of the radical alterity of more-than-human kin, "incomprehensible to humans," indicate that we can at least be aware that they have knowledges and experiences beyond us; listening can offer an intimate connection, an opening of awareness and a kind of knowing.[49] Kimmerer recalls the tiny *pop pop pop* of sphagnum moss sporophytes releasing their seed into the bog, which leads her to observe that listening is a form of intimacy. As Steven Feld observes, sound is an intimate form of knowledge: "Sound both emanates from and penetrates bodies; this reciprocity of reflection and absorption is a creative means of orientation, one that tunes bodies to places and times through their sounding potential."[50] This is knowing as an opening of self to other, allowing sound of another's alterity to enter, or tune you.

---

47 Wikipedia, "Sound," accessed August 20, 2023, https://en.wikipedia.org/wiki/Sound.

48 Wolfe et al., "Voice Acoustics."

49 Gay'wu Group of Women, *Songspirals*, 298.

50 Feld, "Sound Worlds," 184.

WHAT DO THEY CALL THEMSELVES?

Robin Wall Kimmerer offers a version of *etuaptmumk* in her book *Gathering Moss,* and in her practice, drawing on both her scientific training as a biologist with a specialization in mosses and forest ecology and in her embrace of Indigenous knowledges, drawn from her reconnection with her heritage as an enrolled member of the Citizen Potawatomi Nation. She describes her relationship with the quiet voices of mosses as an integration or braiding of intimacy, relationship, subjectivity, objectivity, scientific knowledge, and Indigenous knowledges—although note that Kimmerer argues that Indigenous knowledge *is* scientific knowledge, so she rejects in fact the distinction, insisting rather on Indigenous knowledge as a form of scientific knowledge not yet wholly recognized by the established Western scientific community.[51]

In her essay "Learning to See," science is symbolized by her hand loupe, which magnifies the tiny moss anatomies. Sight is foregrounded, both in this hand lens and in the use of other tools for quantitative measurement: "We record light and pH, collect data on all the moss species, calling out their names."[52] The taxonomy of Linnaeus offers another layer of our approach to mosses; the formality of this taxonomy sorts them into families, as does the precise, scientific descriptors of the moss anatomy and life cycle: sporophyte, gametophyte, acrocarp, pleurocarp, dentate, serrate, serrulate, ciliate, plicate, complanate. "With words at your disposal, you can see more clearly. Finding the words is another step in learning to see."[53]

---

51 Kimmerer, "P-Values and Cultural Values."

52 Kimmerer, *Gathering Moss.*

53 Kimmerer, *Gathering Moss.*

Kimmerer indicates that as humans we know the limits of our vision, of our *Umwelt*, and have developed ways to extend our sight such as satellite imagery or electron microscopes, yet "at the middle scale, that of the unaided eye, our senses seem to be strangely dulled."[54]

Elaine Scarry discusses this at length in her discussion of tools as extensions of the human body, and thus the extension and redistribution of human sentience.

Poetry, as possibly with *etuaptmumk*, seeks to counter habituation—both the reliance on and the distractions of—certain kinds of habituated technology that diminish sight and hearing, through a practice of attention: "Attentiveness alone can rival the most powerful magnifying lens."[55] Kimmerer offers an example that many have experienced, of having to learn to see that which is right before you. She recounts searching for sea stars on the Pacific coast, but her narrowly focused, pinpoint attention worked against her; then she notes, "A Cheyenne elder of my acquaintance once told me that the best way to find something is not to go looking for it."[56] When she adopted a more receptive form of attention, she began to notice the sea stars everywhere. This is vigilance, a broadband receptiveness, an opening. I cannot think now of this story without being reminded of the heat dome in the summer of 2021, the die-off of sea stars and mussels along the tide line, all along the west coast of southern British Columbia, and of the wasting disease that has afflicted sea stars

54 Kimmerer, *Gathering Moss.*
55 Kimmerer, *Gathering Moss.*
56 Kimmerer, *Gathering Moss.*

since the 1970s on the Pacific coast of North America. Such wideband attention and receptiveness are needed more than ever.

Kimmerer tells us, take time, attend, listen at the edges of our perception and at the extremities of our scale; this is intimacy: "Mosses and other small beings issue an invitation to dwell for a time right at the limits of ordinary perception."[57]

EYE YIELDS AT A DISTANCE, SOUND GATHERS WITHIN

I return to Seamus Heaney, describing his first home as analogous to a bucket of water that shivered with every tremor and vibration, attuned to the world's signals, to resonance and sound. Kimmerer describes hearing the faint *pop, pop* of sporophytes bursting in sunlight and releasing their seed. She observes, "Learning to see mosses is more like listening than looking."[58] Lying in my tent each time we visit Fairy Creek, the darkness makes me intensely aware of the sounds of the rainforest—a shiver of water droplets when wind gusts through salal branches; sharp retort of hail, softened to a hush on the nylon fly; the dim constant rushing of Renfrew Creek. An owl's soft hoots. Ravens, either their *quork quooork* as they call to one another, or that ethereal plucking sound, like water drops distorted as they plonk into a well, *toookkk, tokk.* Rustling movements at the edges of my zippered tent. Towards dawn, the songbirds begin their chorus—but spare, and then Foxtrot begins to snore. I can zip the tent closed and the trees—yielded to me by my eye at a distance, establishing a subject-object relation—are removed from sight. But sound easily slips through—the raven's sudden, startling *quork, quoorrrk* soaks in as waves, vibrations

57 Kimmerer, *Gathering Moss.*

58 Kimmerer, *Gathering Moss.*

that have travelled through the mist-laden air, make resonate the small ossicles in my ear, make the forest thrum within the cavity of my chest.

In *The Material of Poetry*, Gerard Bruns notes, "the poet's relation to language is one of listening or hearing and not just speaking or writing."[59] Drawing on Emmanual Levinas, Bruns argues that poetry prioritizes listening as a "mode of responsibility."[60] He summarizes Stanley Cavell's argument that

> our relation to the world, and to others in it, is not one of knowing—knowing as objectification or conceptual determination—but one of acknowledgement and acceptance, being open and responsive to people and to things rather than trying to get a grip on them. Responsiveness to others and to things *in their irreducible singularity* calls for an intimacy that cognition rules out.[61]

Levinas, according to Bruns, reads this intimacy as "proximity," "where we exist in the mode of being touched rather than in the cognitive mode of grasping or opposition."[62] Cognitive grip or grasp can be linked to the manipulation or handedness of the left hemispheric style of processing the world, as identified by McGilchrist, and is linked by Bruns to sight and the subject-object divide in which the Other is held remotely, at a distance, while hearing is a gathering within, and a form of subjectivity:

> [hearing] implies or entails a porous, as against a self-contained, mode of being, and it also implies a different world from the

---

59 Bruns, *The Material of Poetry*, 42.
60 Bruns, *The Material of Poetry*, 43.
61 Bruns, *The Material of Poetry*, 43.
62 Bruns, *The Material of Poetry*, 43.

> one that seeing, perception, observation, or conceptualization constructs or projects onto the screen of consciousness.[63]

Bruns goes further, arguing that there is a more disturbing quality of this porousness, which he characterizes as a decomposing of the self: "Sound is invasive... Sound bleeds the self."[64] This can be true in a human-made environment—car alarms, a neighbour's lawn mower, the deep thumping bass of a party overhead. But I've not found this in the forest—sound edges closer to intimacy and touch—I will come back to the phenomenology of the forest in my discussion of Merleau-Ponty's concept of *la chair*—"the flesh"—of the world. The intimacy of sound can be an offering, "a different way of seeing, when visual acuity is not enough."[65] The "alterity" of sound, vibrations that bypass the objectifying function of vision, allows for the intimacy of touch, even transcendence.

WHAT WE DO NOT PERCEIVE, WE DO NOT KNOW

Just as Umeek speaks of *isaak* and respect for beings, Kimmerer also observes that "all beings are recognised as non-human persons, and all have their own names"; it is a form of respect to call a being by its name.[66] As noted earlier, she asks, "[O]utside the circle, scientific names for mosses may suffice, but within the circle, what do they call themselves?" Here she begins, obliquely, to consider the address to the "thing in itself." We don't have internal access to what the moss "calls itself": what it is like to be a moss,

---

63 Bruns, *The Material of Poetry*, 23.

64 Bruns, *The Material of Poetry*, 45.

65 Kimmerer, *Gathering Moss*.

66 Kimmerer, *Gathering Moss*.

to truly know moss? We only have our perceptions of moss and the names we give moss (as can be said of oldgrowth specklebelly lichen): "but what do they call themselves?" We are aware of our perceptual limitations, even more so as we become aware that more-than-human kin have different perceptual apparatuses that yield a distinct, sometimes utterly different, *Umwelt* from our own.

Consider sight, for example, which has evolved in myriad complex and beautiful ways: from patches of photo-receptor proteins ("eyespots") that can detect light, or "ambient brightness," which allows them to regulate circadian rhythms—to the most complex image-processing eye, where the eyespot has deepened and invaginated as a cup to catch the spill of light, a seal of transparent cells forming a cornea to focus light on the back of the retina. Our own narrow human range of wavelengths runs from red through violet. But what of the infrared, the ultraviolet? Night vision, depth perception, eyes placed at the side, not the front, of the head: All of these will yield different qualia and therefore different perceptions of the world.[67]

How and what does a chickadee see? A peregrine falcon? A raven? The Pacific treefrog tadpole has eye lenses that change shape to accommodate its metamorphosis from water to land, its eyes moving to the front of the head as the lenses compress. What of the sight of a dragonfly, a Chinook salmon, a blue whale? It has been reasoned that eyes tend to develop with the ability to detect a narrow range of wavelengths in the visible spectrum due to the fact that

> the earliest species to develop photosensitivity were aquatic, and water filters out electromagnetic radiation

67 Wikipedia, "Evolution of the Eye," accessed August 20, 2023, https://en.wikipedia.org/wiki/Evolution_of_the_eye.

> except for a range of wavelengths, the shorter of which we refer to as blue, through to longer wavelengths we identify as red. This same light-filtering property of water also influenced the photosensitivity of plants.[68]

Each eye is startling, beautiful, fearsome, some with more or less acuity, more or less access to the range of sensory data beyond our own.

Ed Yong points out that many animals in fact have much poorer vision than humans; the visual field, in particular its acute zones, "determine where it sees *well*."[69] He provides the example of cows, who don't move their heads to look at you because their visual fields wrap around their heads and "their acute zones are horizontal stripes, giving them a view of the entire horizon at once." He observes this is also true of animals in flat habitats: rabbits, water striders, fiddler crabs.[70] Touch, he argues, might be a way for humans to imagine how other creatures see—just as we can feel a breeze simultaneously on lips, collar bone, knees, we can imagine "what it might be like to fuse the omnidirectional nature of that sensation with the long range of sight. Vision can extend in any direction and every direction, can envelop and surround."[71]

Another example Yong offers of different *Umwelten* is that many species are able to perceive ultraviolet wavelengths, which range from 10 to 400 nanometres, including many birds, fish, reptiles, rats, gerbils, insects; similarly, "reindeer, dogs, cats, pigs, cows, ferrets, and many other mammals can detect UV with their short blue cones. They

---

68 Wikipedia, "Evolution of the Eye."

69 Yong, *An Immense World*, 72.

70 Yong, *An Immense World*, 72.

71 Yong, *An Immense World*, 73–74.

probably perceive UV as a deep shade of blue rather than separate colour, but they can sense it nonetheless."[72] In the example of reindeer, he points out that they can "quickly make out mosses and lichens, which reflect little UV, on a hillside blanketed by UV-reflective snow."[73] Flowers also make use of "dramatic UV patterns" to attract bees.[74]

Each sensory organ and its cells offer varied access to a spectrum of sensory data. Consider hearing: The human range runs from 20 Hz to 20 kHz. Blue whales have a far greater range, from 7 Hz through 35 kHz. Pigeons can hear "infrasound" that falls as low as 0.5 Hz; as a result, "they can detect distinct storms, earthquakes, and even volcanoes."[75] Bats use echolocation by which they navigate. Shore birds like western sandpipers and dunlin use the magnetic field to navigate, possibly relying on

> subtle, fundamentally quantum effects in short-lived molecular fragments, known as radical pairs, formed photochemically in its eyes. That is, the creatures appear to be able to "see" Earth's magnetic field lines and use that information to chart a course between their breeding and wintering grounds.[76]

In his discussion of the ability of some species to detect surface vibration, Yong describes the research of the biologist Rex Cocroft, who guesses perhaps 200,000 insect species use surface vibrations for communication, and who has made recordings of treehoppers:

---

72 Yong, *An Immense World*, 93.

73 Yong, *An Immense World*, 94.

74 Yong, *An Immense World*, 94.

75 Wikipedia, "Hearing Range," accessed May 7, 2024, https://en.wikipedia.org/wiki/Hearing_range.

76 Hore and Mouritsen, "How Migrating Birds Use Quantum Effects to Navigate."

> The song of *Stictocephala lutea* resembles a scratchy didgeridoo. *Cyrtolobus grammatanus* melds a hooting monkey with mechanical clicks... *Potnia* lures me into a false sense of security with a mundane *brum-brum-brum* train, which then ends with a shocking half moo half scream.[77]

To return to sight, tetrachromats have an extra cone to detect colour. Yong notes, "Tetrachromacy doesn't just widen the visible spectrum at its margins. It unlocks an entirely new *dimension* of colours."[78] This ability is common in most birds[79] but in humans only present in some rare women who possess four cones to perceive colour, as opposed to the usual three. These women have the ability to see 100 million colours—that is, 100 times the spectrum most humans see. Concetta Antico, a trained artist who has this fourth receptor, observes:

> I see colors in other colors. For example, I'm looking at some light right now that's peeking through the door in my house. Other people might just see white light, but I see orange and yellow and pink and green and some magenta and a little bit of blue. So white is not white; white is all varieties of white. You know when you look at a pantone and you see all the whites separated out? It's like that for me, but they are more intense.[80]

Sound, compressed underwater, offers three-dimensional information to whales, as soundwaves rebound and locate objects in the dark ocean. In

77 Yong, *An Immense World*, 194.

78 Yong, *An Immense World*, 97.

79 Yong, *An Immense World*, 115. Yong points out that flowers evolved their colours to attract insects, based on the design of the insects' eyes, calling eyes "living paint brushes" that have been shaped by evolution.

80 Concetta Antico quoted in Tsoulis-Reay, "What It's Like to See 100 Million Colors."

Listening to Whales: What the Orcas Have Taught Us, Alexandra Morton imagines what the experience of orca echolocation might be like:

> Echolocation is like running your hands over your lover's face in the dark. Although you can't see the details, your sense of touch fills in the gaps. But with its remarkable echolocation, a whale can not only "see" in the dark ocean; she can actually see inside a number of objects, including other whales [...] Floating in a boat off the coast of Vancouver Island, you'd never know any of this was going on. Whale sounds usually don't make the transition from water to air. When the wind wasn't blowing, Johnstone Strait could be so quiet that I could hear raven calls miles away. Yet without my hydrophone, I would have been deaf to the symphony of oceanic sound beneath my feet. Water itself began to sound different to me. In full flood Blackney Passage roared like an avalanche. Pebble beaches chattered; shrimp feeding in kelp beds crackled like frying bacon. Rock cod issued adorable low, serious grunts. Rain hissed. Herring burbled. Streams gurgled. I soon realized the vast amount of information a whale could pick up just by listening.[81]

This intense desire to imagine what it might be like to echolocate informs her methodology and shares the ethical imperative of *etuaptmumk*. Morton describes needing to adapt her own life to the rhythms of the wild animal she studies: "it's the only way you'll begin to understand how your subject encounters the world. We land-locked humans experience our surroundings primarily through our eyes: land and vision. A killer whale's aquatic world comes to it almost

81 Morton, *Listening to Whales*, 90.

exclusively through its sense of hearing: water and sound."[82] And as Bruns observes, sight sets up a particular manipulative subject-other relationship that sound eludes; with sound, the orca is attuned to multi-dimensional space. Of the distinctions between humans and orcas, Morton notes, "Our cultures are so far apart that only the most open mind will be able to cross the interspecies void."[83]

QUALIA

From the Latin adjective *qualis*, "of a sort, of what kind," something it is like to experience a colour, a taste, a sensation, an emotion. The quale of blue: I lie beneath the cobalt-blue tarp drawn taut over my one-person tent at the base of Stawamus Chief and light pools blue under cedar and fir. Cool of the forest. Cedar's dry sweetness as it warms in the sun. I sip Laphroiag and taste woodsmoke and liquid peat. Qualia offer us access to the world beyond, each quale a portal: the needling sting of a tattooist's pen that pierces my skin and injects black ink to form the tip of a crow's wing; burn of scotch on my tongue. As I write this, I'm listening to the original 1979 analogue recording of *Songs of the Humpback Whale*, translated into a digital format, posted to YouTube, now played on my laptop—miraculously, the haunting calls and groans travel from the ocean depths of the 1970s, penetrate the static of the recording, reconstitute waves, and resonate in the small bones of my ear to create my experience of this song, in the year 2022. What is it like for me to hear this song?

As a human, I see within the frequencies of red to violet, not infrared, not ultraviolet. I am not one of the tetrachromats, capable of perceiving possibly a hundred times more subtle variations of colour than other

82 Morton, *Listening to Whales*, 2.

83 Morton, *Listening to Whales*, 1.

humans. I hear within the range of 20 Hz to 20 kHz, and less of the higher range, as I grow older. What other sensations and information might be floating in the air, in the medium I breathe and look through and taste, that I have no organs to perceive? And how does my brain, with its complex gyri, interpret the data that my senses collect and reframe as qualia, as pattern, as narrative, as song? How does the brain of a chickadee or a blue whale interpret the same data? Or the brain of *Orcinus orca*, with its "exquisite level of cortical folding"?[84] An orca, a humpback whale, a black-capped chickadee might process qualia in somewhat different ways, or be capable of experiencing qualia I cannot, yielding a somewhat or very different world.

I have begun to try in my own practice to use the tools of poetry to explore—to model—my own experience of consciousness, of these qualia, this pooling of blue in the shadow of cedars, this pure sweet two-toned call of the chickadee. I have also used these poetic tools to attempt to model, in a sympathetic understanding, the experience of what it might be like to be a raven or of the order Hymenoptera, to be a photosynthesizing sea slug, *Elysia chlorotica*, or a paper birch tree, *Betula papyrifera*. It will always be a failure at a fundamental level, but the attempt is key.

Consciousness is most simply defined by Nagel,[85] as having the experience of *being like*—for example, does the honeybee or the paper birch sapling or the blue whale experience what it is like to be itself? To exude the sweet liqueur in a Nootka rose, to receive at the edge of ultrasound a

84 Crawford, "Killer Whales Are Non-Human Persons."

85 See Thomas Nagel's "What Is It Like to Be a Bat?" (1974) for his influential definition of consciousness, which places emphasis on qualia; he argues that there is consciousness in an organism where the organism has a feeling of what it is like to be that organism.

call that has travelled a thousand kilometres through the dark Pacific, to feel the papery chalk-white skin stretch and peel in sunlight?

A flight of winged seeds. Here, on this scorched ground.
Embryonic roots split the seed coat. Take hold in thin
mineral soil.
Micro-organisms enter the wounds. *Inonotus obliqua.*
Phellinus igniarius. Nectria galligena.
A shoot, through mineral waste. A clearing. Blue.
Sunlight. A leaf and a leaf. Stitch carbon to water. Leaves.
Leaves greening. Carbon to carbon. Lignin. The heartwood.
The sapwood runs.
Roots in darkness. Plaits mycelium. Sends signals, sugars.
Links to kind.
Carbon to carbon.
Crackling of root tips in underground channels.
Root tips reaching out to fungal threads, through dark soil.[86]

What is it like to feel a Pacific windstorm rush through your limbs on the Juan de Fuca Trail?

blue   blued   bluuuue   resonant resin   res
tympan tam   tam   tam tamp   tamp
suck   whoosh hushhh   husshhhhhhh

salt   *siit*   *siit siiiiiit*   *tuuxupt* pitch tok tok
o o   o tam tam tamp tamp tamp
suck whooosh   husssssshhhhh   hussshhhhhh
siit siiiiiit siit sit ka   ka   ka.[87]

86 Trainor, "Seed 20: T, *k'i*, betula," *A blueprint for survival.*

87 Trainor, "Seed 10: Siit, Tuuxupt, Sitka Spruce," *A blueprint for survival.*

There are many theories of consciousness: as illusion, epiphenomenon, software running on a parallel processor; as generative of the universe; as adaptive trait that allows one to distinguish self from not-self, to navigate safely through a dangerous environment; as a communal adaptive trait to allow for the sharing of ideas and collaborative work; as integrated information network that, at a certain point, achieves lift off, emergence; as a "hard problem" that neuroscientists will eventually explain away; as the elemental constituent of all matter. Some of these are compatible, or at least, kin: Variants of panpsychism resonate with integrated information theory and theories of adaptation and collaboration. Calvo et al., in their work on plant sentience, argue that a frame shift is necessary:

> The reason that any element of consciousness or awareness is commonly discounted in plants is that virtually all responses in plants are very much slower than our perceptual time frame which operates on an image length of about a tenth of a second.[88]

As such, a human researcher may be looking for reactions or movements indicative of animal sentience. But trees don't need to move to gather or catch their food, so they move—grow—much more slowly and graze on sunlight. Similarly, the absence of a typical animal nervous system—centralized brain, spinal cord, nerves, synapses—does not mean necessarily the absence of consciousness. Panpsychism posits more of a continuum—it is not all or nothing.

The jellyfish *Clytia hemisphaerica,* with a gene called GCaMP spliced into it, capable of producing a green fluorescent protein, becomes a tiny illuminated bell-shaped flower, its neurons glowing as it feeds,

---

88 Calvo et al., "Integrated Information."

contracts, floats. We split off from its branch of the evolutionary tree over 600 million years ago. Instead of a concentrated cluster of nerve cells or brain, *Clytia* has a nerve net, distributed across the inside of its gauzy bell. Here is a different kind of circuitry:

> It's hard to put yourself into the mind of a jellyfish—their life cycle of polyps and spores is utterly alien, their weird array of sensory organs have no analogues to our own. *Clytia* have specialized balance organs called statocysts; other species of jellyfish have sensors called rhopalia that detect light or chemical changes in the surrounding water. Researchers have observed some things that could be thought of as akin to our emotional states; for example, *Clytia* display a unique set of behaviors when spawning, and they perform their feeding action more quickly when they're hungry.[89]

What might it be like to be *Clytia hemisphaerica*? What might it be like to be a plant, asks Paco Calvo. He compares our human situation, attempting to imagine what it is to be a plant—or, let's say, a tree, *Betula papyrifera,* to that of Jackson's Mary—the neuroscientist of Frank Jackson's 1982/1986 thought experiment in which he posits a neuroscientist called Mary who studies to the smallest detail the human processing of colour but exists in a world of black and white. The experiment asks, With this vast body of knowledge, what *doesn't* Mary know about the experience of colour—can she truly know what it feels like to see the colour of tangerine, mustard, dusky rose? Calvo asks,

> Once having mastered all of plant neurobiology, would we still be missing some information that proves crucial to our capacity to put ourselves in the shoes of a plant? Well, this

89 Katwala, "A Gene-Tweaked Jellyfish."

> depends on what we mean by "all of plant neurobiology." It can be a lot! As with Mary's potential of imagination (Churchland, 1985), we may be surprised by how radically our plant neurobiology conceptual framework could change, and how deep our capacity to introspect could go.[90]

An ecological poetry might try to embody this capacity for imagining, and for presenting a potentially alien inner life in a distinct form that cannot be paraphrased or translated without loss, as meaning is carried in the very form (a lichenous form?). It might allow us to crack open hardened human paradigms: a nervous system and brain; a range of frequencies and light waves we are able to perceive; what music is, what language; our speed and agency and subjectivity entwined; our sense of time; our experience of what it is like to be human. As Nassar and Barbour argue, we need a more generous consideration, a more free-ranging imagining, of a tree's "rootedness"[91] and experience of time, from the fleeting 150 years' lifetime of *Betula papyrifera,* which, for a tree, burns through life, to thousand-year-old Grandfather Tree in Fairy Creek.

I return to the image of the ancient Sitka spruce cut down and strapped to a flatbed truck—its cross-section of light and dark rings, each marking a season, a year, years of drought or abundance, what Nassar and Barbour call an "embodied history."[92] Agency, they caution, does not necessarily require mobility. Trees, they argue, ask us to consider multispecies justice:

> In the era of the Anthropocene, new ontologies of nature are needed: ones that are able to accommodate and take

---

90 Calvo, "What Is It Like to Be a Plant?," 220.

91 Nassar and Barbour, "Rooted."

92 Nassar and Barbour, "Rooted."

> account not only of individual species and their competing interests, but also of environments, and relations that undergird and enable the emergence of species.

Ecuador's constitution (2008) recognizes the rights of Pachamama, Mother Earth, "to exist and to maintain and regenerate its cycles, structure, functions, and evolutionary process."[93] We are entangled, as are the mother trees Suzanne Simard describes with their intermingling mycorrhizal networks. Consider a poem as an artifact that can extend the human body, redistribute the benefits—imagine the myriad forms—of consciousness in our more-than-human kin, as in our own.

Which qualia elude us utterly because we cannot perceive them, because we have no sense organ or made tool to perceive? We can at least know that we have a distinctively shuttered, human vision of the world. Vigilance, however, asks us to imagine our way towards more-than-human kin. What are the senses of a Sitka spruce that has grown in place at the edge of the Pacific for hundreds of years, making infinitesimal mycelial links to the plants and other trees around it? As Kimmerer asks, What does the tardigrade perceive, in the forest of mosses? What worlds do the tardigrade and the Sitka spruce inhabit, with their abilities to endure at different and alien scales to our own, to flourish in austere environments, to sip nutrients from soil and air, sodium from the salt breeze, to endure the pressurized environment of the depths of the sea and the vacuum of space, to enter a dormant tun state, to wake again, to live in a forest of mosses, to live and grow 270 feet tall for 1,000 years at the edge of the Pacific?

---

93 Surma, "Ecuador's High Court."

7. BLUE THINKS ITSELF WITHIN ME

Consideration of the phantom hemlock looper, minute green inch worm, this little worm, this "thing in itself." Philosophical accounts of human perception of the world and the "gap" between thing and language or representation. Merleau-Ponty's conception of la chair, *"the flesh," and* le chiasme, *"the chiasm"; Graham Harman's theory of the role of metaphor (via Ortega y Gasset) in object-oriented ontology (OOO); Philip Goff's theory of panpsychism—consciousness as the constituent element of matter. Rainforest teems with consciousness.*

> My body is a sort of open circuit that completes itself only in things, in others, in the encompassing earth.
> —DAVID ABRAM, *The Spell of the Sensuous: Perception and Language in a More-Than-Human World* (1997)

> As I contemplate the blue of the sky... I abandon myself to it and plunge into this mystery, it "thinks itself within me," I am the sky itself as it is drawn together and unified, and as it begins to exist for itself; my consciousness is saturated with this limitless blue. —MAURICE MERLEAU-PONTY, *Phenomenology of Perception* (1962)

> Strange as it might sound at first hearing, there doesn't seem to be a candidate for being the intrinsic nature of matter other than consciousness. —PHILIP GOFF, *Galileo's Error: Foundations for a New Science of Consciousness* (2019)

INCHWORM

Here is (not) the thing in itself.

I am lying on my stomach on the warm cedar planks of the deck that surrounds the yurt on Cortes. I rest on my forearms, notebook open, sketching the outlines of this book that has not yet been written. Call of a raven, far distant, *quorrrk..... quorrrk.* The air is still and hot. At some point I become aware of a speck or twist of green, inching, spindling its way down an invisible thread, a tiny patch of brilliant emerald in my field of vision when I look up from the page. I focus. It reaches the deck—grey planks of weathered cedar; it lies there, motionless. Emerald resolves to segmented body, shot through with lighter horizontal stripes of cream and yellow. At one end, it appears to have two fleshy disks that could be eyes, punctuated by black dots like pupils in the centre of each. Suddenly it raises itself, its middle portion lifted up as if by a tiny hook and propels itself forward on invisible sticky feet. Elongates. Raises itself up, slowly inching its way across the plank.

I return to my notebook. Slashes of black ink accumulate—dots, loops, line by line. Some words are scratched out. Others added, above or below a line. Hand-drawn arrows. Numbers. I have forgotten about the tiny inchworm.

I look up. It has moved about two feet and reached one of the posts that secure the awning above the yurt's front door. It prods and moves side to side with its head, then rears itself onto its hind legs, attaches itself to the post, and begins to inch its way up. I go back to my writing.

All day, all week, as we encounter them, we gently ease them onto a fingertip and place them on leaves, on trunks, on a shady patch of earth surrounding the yurt. They come in and out of focus.

One day, I take photographs of the inchworm as it moves, stretches, inches its way up onto one end. I'd never before looked so closely at these little inchworms. They were so small it was difficult to focus on them as they moved. The photographs allowed for stillness and detail of observation through enlargement: horizontal bands of emerald green and cream rimmed in a slightly darker green; the surface of the worm's body gleaming in sunlight. A torso divided into slightly rounded segments, most noticeably striated when viewed from above. Looking closer at what I think is the head, I see it has not two but four black dots, set within a darker moss green. No, not four dots—eight? The tail end has a row of similar black dots. Little protuberances—stubby legs, two at the tail end, two more just a little farther along where it lifts itself up into a loop; another four towards the front, but more delicate looking—the back four legs seem to do the heavy lifting. They stick firmly onto the cedar plank and the whole front of the body lifts and quivers, levitating, moving this way and that, sensing which way to move, until it decides on a direction, and then the back end heaves itself forward. It can also lift itself up entirely on its hind legs, so that it can pull itself up onto a leaf or a branch.

I took several videos, which remind me now of its sensing, curious, exploratory movement—its ability to stretch itself straight as a stick, levitating above the cedar planks while its back sticky feet remained attached to the wood; to raise itself up, vertically, into a question mark; to swivel around, from one side to the other, sensing which direction to take.

While it was automatic for me to take photographs and videos with my iPhone, I didn't try to draw the inchworm—why didn't I? It is not usually part of my toolbox, but I have come to learn, when observing tiny, delicate morphology, simply a sharp pencil and the human eye can record a clarity of structure that even the miraculous iPhone camera cannot.

Curious to discover what it is, I google "little green inchworm BC" and find hundreds of possibilities, quickly narrowing it down to a few: Hemlock looper (*Lambdina fiscellaria*)? Western hemlock looper (*Lambdina fiscellaria lugubrosa*)? Western oak looper or Garry oak looper (*Lambdina fiscellaria somniaria*)? I post a series of photographs to iNaturalist, which suggests this little green inchworm might be the larva of the phantom hemlock looper moth, *Nepytia phantasmaria*. Later, my ID receives a "research grade" confirmation, as others with more experience in the system verify my guess. It is a larva of the class of geometer moths, family Geometridae, order Lepidoptera, its name derived from "the Ancient Greek *geo* (*γεω*, derivative form of *γῆ* or *γαῖα*, 'the earth'), and *metron—μέτρον*, 'measure' in reference to the way their larvae, or 'inchworms,' appear to 'measure the earth' as they move along in a looping fashion,"[1] which is why they are also called loopers or spanworms. This

1 Wikipedia, "Geometer Moth," accessed March 20, 2022, https://en.wikipedia.org/wiki/Geometer_moth.

family contains approximately 23,000 species of moths; 1,400 species from six subfamilies are indigenous to North America.[2]

There are other ways to approach this little inchworm. Its full Linnaeus classification is Animalia, Arthropoda, Insecta, Lepidoptera, Geometridae, *Nepytia, N. phantasmaria*. Its binomial name is *Nepytia phantasmaria*; its MONA (Moths of North America) number, 6907.[3] In French, it is called *arpenteuse verte de la pruche*.

I find a generalized diagram of the family Geometridae, side view, and a technical description of its body. I learn to say longitudinal markings, not horizontal. Crochets at the ends of prolegs to "cling to foliage, bark, silk," the tip of my finger. Spiracles for respiration. Prothoracic shield, thorax, abdomen, legs, prolegs. The head with its own precise clutch of terms: *lobe, frons, labrum, mandibles, stomata*—"six simple light-sensitive eyes arranged in a curved row"—on each side of the head, *clypeus, antenna*. Salivary glands within the head, I read, produce silk, "a proteinaceous substance used for aerial dispersal, construction of shelters (tents, feeding webs, and cocoons), escape from predators, and other things."[4]

2 Wikipedia, "Geometer Moth."

3 Wikipedia, "*Nepytia phantasmaria*," accessed April 24, 2025, https://en.wikipedia.org/wiki/Nepytia_phantasmaria.

4 Bugwood Wiki, "Caterpillar Morphology," accessed March 31, 2022, https://wiki.bugwood.org/Archive:Caterpillars/Morphology.

I could search for it in prehistory: The oldest looper found was preserved in amber, dating to approximately 44 million years ago, in the Eocene:

> In 2019, the first geometrid caterpillar in Baltic amber was discovered by German scientists... it measured about 5 mm (0.20 in), and was estimated to be 44 million years old, dating back to the Eocene epoch. It was described as the earliest evidence for the subfamily of *Ennominae*, particularly the tribe of *Boarmiini*.[5]

Here is perhaps a descendant of the tribe of Boarmiini that now works its way towards me across the cedar planks of the yurt.

I find a technical description of the phantom hemlock looper on a Canadian government website, where it is described as a "common and occasionally destructive solitary defoliator":

> Head, green with ten prominent black spots. Dorsum yellowish green with a faint green middorsal stripe; subdorsal stripes white edged on either side with a fine dark green line; supraspiracular area green with a pair of wavy, broken dark lines; yellow spiracular area green with a pair of wavy broken dark lines; yellow spiracular stripe.[6]

It is found throughout British Columbia; spends winter in the egg stage; larvae emerge in late May. They pupate in August, the moths emerging in September and October, when the cycle begins again,

5 Fischer et al., "Geometrid Caterpillar."

6 Natural Resources Canada, "Phantom Hemlock Looper."

a single moth laying "up to 115 eggs singly or in small groups on undersides of needles."[7] Their main hosts are amabilis fir, grand fir, Rocky Mountain Douglas fir, Sitka spruce, western hemlock, and western red cedar. In photos on the government site, the looper spreads out in a stiff line along a twig, disappearing into green foliage, its cream-coloured longitudinal stripes imitating the colour of the wood.

I have found only a few photographs of the eggs and pupa of the Hemlock looper, which shares its common name. The US Forest Service writes that all western hemlock eggs begin green; the viable eggs turn bronze as they mature while parasitized eggs turn black. Previous year's shells are clear.[8]

Years ago, when I lived in Montreal and my daughter was very little, her father brought home from his classroom a monarch butterfly chrysalis in a slim glass container. The caterpillar had attached itself to a branch inside the case, uppermost. I missed seeing it emerge, but at some point, when I thought to look, the monarch had hatched, its wings slowly opening and closing like a heartbeat. The chrysalis was still attached to the branch overhead, torn, transparent, and beneath it lay a small drop of blood. No, not blood—a dark red liquid, meconium—leftover pigments and metabolic wastes expelled by the monarch. I imagine there is a similar process for a phantom hemlock moth.

---

7 Natural Resources Canada, "Phantom Hemlock Looper."

8 Dickinson and Kohler, "Western Hemlock Looper," 4.

Apparently, they come in waves, intermittently, every few years. There have been outbreaks documented in BC: 1956–57, 1982, 1994, 2001, 2020. I find a news report from 2020: Provincial forest entomologist Babita Bains observes, "Both species of moths are native to the area, and outbreaks happen periodically... This is just a natural part of succession. It's important for recycling of nutrients and trees, so a lot of the tree mortality we will see—there are benefits to it."[9]

I remember my music collaborator Hazel mentioning this, as she lives past Deep Cove, farther along Indian Arm. She said when the moths emerged and began to fly that year, it resembled a snowstorm.

My notes become cryptic:

> *predictive egg sampling*
> *sex pheromones?*
> *wing patterns of adult moth*

I find images of its soot-coloured patterns on papery, chalky wings. How strange—to think that the little green looper I saw on Cortes, tiny green worm, with its sensing of the air, its purposeful movements, its clearly intentional decisions—to move forward, to lie still, to reject a bamboo leaf, to spin down on a thread of silk from overhead—metamorphosed into this moth with its feathered antennae and delicate chalk-coloured wings marked as if by soot.

9 Bains quoted in Fatur, "Looper Moth Outbreak."

I have found the source of my cryptic note on pheromones, with reference to the phantom's cousin, the western hemlock looper.

> After dusk, females release pheromones to attract males... During an outbreak, bodies of adults that die shortly after mating can accumulate in massive numbers on the ground, in streams, and on the leeward shore of ponds and lakes. A report of the northern Idaho outbreak in fall 1937 observes, "in some areas the ground was actually white with their dead bodies, and small streams were even clogged and dammed."[10]

White with their dead bodies. Like snowfall. White as snow.
White petal, white blossom, bloomed from green inchworm.
Twig. Needle. Earth measurer. A loop. A question mark.

This is (not) the thing in itself.

ÉCART | *MIND THE GAP*

There is a gap, between the observing subject, and that which is observed.

There is me, lying on the deck of the yurt, ribs pressed into weathered cedar planks, making small black abstract marks of ink in a notebook, when I suddenly become aware of this tiny green inchworm. How long has it been in my peripheral field of vision, sharing this small space of

10 Dickinson and Kohler, "Western Hemlock Looper," 6.

earth and time, before I see it—so that it clicks into focus? And then I give it my attention, or it holds my attention. Its paler, cream-coloured longitudinal stripes, its stubby prolegs, its looping movements. I hear a raven call; I return to my notebook. The inchworm comes in and out of my awareness. I can refocus my attention, the way an iPhone uses square targets to lock onto a face or an object in the foreground of an image, sharpening, blurring, sharpening. Zoom in: I can research this inchworm—google "small green inchworm," do an image search, post a photograph of it to iNaturalist for suggestion of species based on its geotag, and later receive confirmation of my guess. I can describe its colours and markings, its ways of moving, its life cycle. I learn the etymology of its family name, Geometridae—"earth measurer."

I lose focus. I scribble diagrams in my notebook. I check to see if I have a cell signal. I lose myself for a time as I sift miscellany, look for patterns in my research. The sun slips forward onto the backs of my knees, my thighs. Then I think of the inchworm again and look for it: It has worked its way down one of the posts that holds up the awning over the front door. It has its own material, sensual, purposeful life. It carries on.

I am not a pure idealist; I do not think there is only the human correlator who brings the world into focus, into existence even. But in some ways I am, in practice, to the extent that my own experience of the world exists for me through my perceptions. Here I am, writing this book, trying to think through this gap between observer and observed, with a focus on how this plays out in poetry with an ecological slant.

On Cortes, as I sat on the rocks by Hague Lake, I drew a diagram, which I'm using to navigate this chapter.

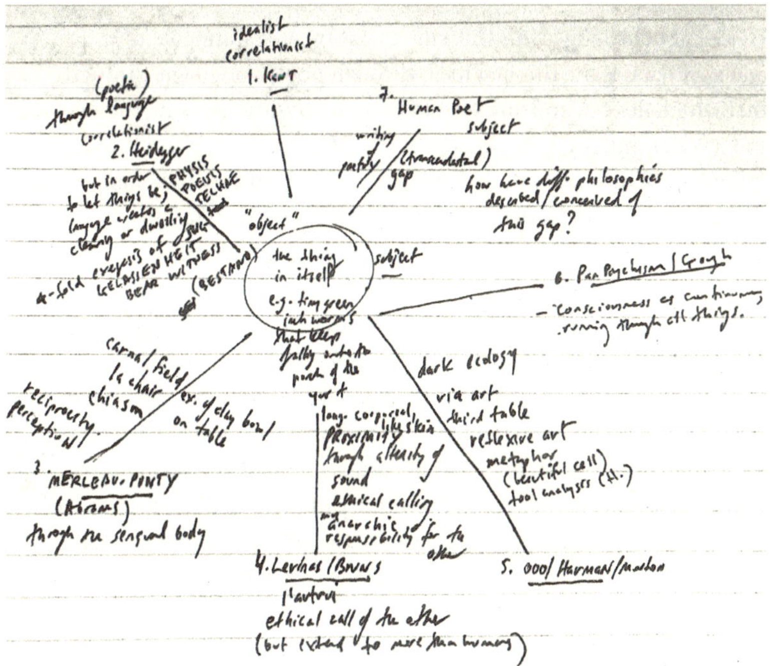

The thing in itself. *Credit: Kim Trainor.*

I am not a philosopher nor a historian. I offer only the briefest of sketches of each of these schools of thought, particularly for those who are unfamiliar with them, sifting their words for ideas that may be of relevance for thinking about the lyric ecopoem.

For Kant, we cannot cross over or bridge this gap; the thing in itself is always dark; only the correlator, or individual human consciousness, can bring it into human focus, within a human framework. Descartes's perception of animals as mechanical and lacking a soul leads us towards an instrumental vision of the natural world, which constructs a barrier to everything beyond the knower.

Heidegger challenges this thinking of nature as standing reserve, and approaches the thing in itself through poetic language, through that which lies beyond any system of metaphysical thought, in order to let things be, to blossom forth. Merleau-Ponty, and the extension of his ideas in the ecological writings of David Abram, suggests we approach the thing in itself through the sensual, perceiving body; that there is a reciprocity of perception.

Levinas writes of the ethical call of the other across this gap, to which one must respond; this relationship is governed by the visual, by the presence of another's face, and situated firmly within the human realm. But might it be extended to our more-than-human kin? As a challenge to this visual bias, Gerald Bruns, in *The Material of Poetry*, explores the alterity of sound, the alterity of the other as experienced through sound that collapses the gap between knower and known, seeing and seen, enters one's own body; we are permeable beings.

Graham Harman through his object-oriented ontology (OOO) extends Heidegger's work; of especial use to ecopoetry is Harman's discussion of the role of metaphor in approaching the thing in itself, as described by Ortega y Gasset in an early essay on aesthetics in 1914. Timothy Morton, an adherent of OOO, considers the role of art and this gap between observer and observed, with reference to the first iteration of Romantic poets and in his discussion of reflexive art and dark ecology.

I conclude with Philip Goff's work on panpsychism, on consciousness as the intrinsic nature of all matter, an appealing idea that ties into Merleau-Ponty's thinking on *la chair*, or the "carnal field," as described by Abram. Throughout, I consider how they are implicated and entangled in my own practice as a poet.

DESCARTES | GHOST IN THE MACHINE

For Descartes, there is both the gap that lies in his distinction between humans and all other animals and the gap created by placing so much emphasis on the human knower. Regarding the gap between humans and all other animals: Descartes believed that only humans are ensouled; non-human animals are then perceived as "machines, devoid of mind and consciousness, and hence lacking in sentience," a "mechanical philosophy" that came to replace Aristotelian physics in the eighteenth century.[11]

As such, the inchworm's ability to reject the offer of a leaf, to stretch up on its prolegs to scout the terrain, to stiffen upon my touch—that is, "to respond via their sense organs in a situationally appropriate manner"—must be explained as purely mechanical function.[12]

In his *Discourse on Method,* Descartes sketched out a theory of animal as complex machine, using mechanical analogies to describe animal behaviours: Swallows that arrive in the spring operate like a clock that tells time; similarly, the "actions of honeybees are of the same nature, and the discipline of cranes in flight, and of apes in fighting, if it is true that they keep discipline."[13] He also rejects the possibility of a continuum of emergent consciousness on the part of animals. It must be all or nothing:

---

11 Hatfield, "René Descartes."

12 Hatfield, "René Descartes," The New Science, para. 7.

13 Descartes, "Animals Are Machines," 17.

> The most that one can say is that though the animals do not perform any action which shows us that they think, still, since the organs of their body are not very different from ours, it may be conjectured that there is attached to those organs some thoughts such as we experience in ourselves, but of a very much less perfect kind. To which I have nothing to reply except that if they thought as we do, they would have an immortal soul like us. This is unlikely, because there is no reason to believe it of some animals without believing it of all, and many of them such as oysters and sponges are too imperfect for this to be credible.[14]

As a machine fashioned by God, he argues, the relative sophistication and complexity of an animal is not surprising. He suggests that we might even think humans are such machines—and in fact, many of our functions, such as a heartbeat and so on, are essentially no different than those of animal automata and require no deliberate thought. Descartes writes, "I suppose the body to be nothing but a statue or machine made of earth, which God forms with the explicit intention of making it as much as possible like us."[15] This mechanical theory of the body accounts for all animal functions, from digestion and circulation of the blood through the reception of information through senses (sounds, tastes, heat, and so on), through cycles of waking and sleep.[16]

The difference between this human machine and all other animals, however, can be determined by two tests, according to Descartes: First, the test of speech, that is, the ability to use symbolic language to share our thoughts with others, and second, the ability to

14 Descartes, "Animals Are Machines," 17.

15 Descartes quoted in Lokhorst, "Descartes and the Pineal Gland."

16 Descartes quoted in Lokhorst, "Descartes and the Pineal Gland."

act upon knowledge, to use reason to determine certain actions. Using these two methods, we can "recognise the difference that exists between men and brutes."[17] And the ability to use reason and symbolic language is contingent on having an immortal soul, which according to Descartes, was lodged in the pineal gland.

What does this all mean for the looper inching its way across the deck of the yurt on Cortes in the summer of 2021? Do loopers have a pineal gland? For Descartes, it would be inconceivable that a looper has a soul because his only measure for this is human anatomy and physiology, human language and reason. Therefore, the looper is a purely mechanical creature, an automaton, complex by virtue of its creation by God, but without sentience or capacity of perception or volition. Descartes is unable to consider that consciousness might arrive by multiple evolutionary paths or exist upon a continuum.

The second gap opened by Descartes's methodology is the emphasis placed on the human knower, "as a means to determine the scope and possibilities of human knowledge."[18] This influential method—the interrogation and introspection of the knower—comes to be adopted by philosophers such as Berkeley, Hume, and Kant,[19] yet

---

17 Descartes, "Animals Are Machines," 14–15.

18 Hatfield, "René Descartes," Legacy, para. 3.

19 And challenged by later writers. Andreas Weber, pitching his concept of an "enlivenment" to mend the neoliberal wreckage caused by a Cartesian enlightenment that divides the world between *res cogitans* and a dead *res extensa*, observes, "Enlightenment-style thinking can be defined by its omission of what marks life at its very core: the intertwining of matter and desire. For…

> [t]hese authors came to different conclusions than had Descartes concerning the ability of the human mind to know things as they are in themselves. Hume and Kant especially—and each in his own way—rejected the very notion of a metaphysics that reveals reality as it is in itself.[20]

KANT | DAS DING AN SICH (THE THING IN ITSELF)

Kant makes a distinction between the "representation of appearance" and the thing in itself:

> the things that we intuit are not in themselves as they appear to us . . . if we remove our own subject or even only the subjective constitution of the senses in general, then all the constitution, all relations of objects in space and time, indeed space and time themselves would disappear, and as appearances they cannot exist in themselves, but only in us. We are acquainted with nothing except our way of perceiving them.[21]

That is not to say that the things cease to exist entirely if we do not perceive them, but that our perception of them in space and time ceases to exist. A priori constructs of space and time act as a matrix within

. . . Enlightenment thinking, there is either matter—accounted for in terms of science and technology—or desire—reserved for humans and their endeavors, language, and culture" (Weber, *Enlivenment*, 16). Tim Lilburn, in his 1999 essay collection, *Living in the World as If It Were Home* similarly cautions, "The point is not to counter one ontology with another, materialism, for instance, for idealism: each grasps in a way that skews the object. The point is to not allow ontological loyalties to shape seeing" (43).

20 Hatfield, "René Descartes," Legacy, para. 3.

21 Kant, *Critique of Pure Reason*, 168, section A42/B60/A43.

which the human mind slots all things and it cannot perceive things without such a matrix; a posteriori sensations, or "empirical intuition," generate a variety of perceptions that may differ from person to person. This perception or empirical intuition adheres to the subjective perceiver under local conditions, within the matrix of space and time. But the thing in itself "would still never be known through the most enlightened cognition of [its] appearance, which is alone given to us."[22]

This distinction between the appearance of a thing as filtered through a priori categories and a posteriori sensations, and the thing in itself, has come to be called "transcendental idealism," transcendental in that these a priori categories or "tools of understanding" are said to transcend any individual human perceptions and are shared by all human subjects.[23] Blumenau cites Bertrand Russell's analogy of blue-tinted spectacles: If all humans were born with blue-tinted spectacles, the things in the world would all have a bluish tinge, but

> philosophers, once they have realized that these tinted spectacles (since we *all* wear them, we might call them "transcendental spectacles") are an irremovable part of our visual equipment, will come to understand that we cannot know what the colours of the world are *really* like because they can only reach us as mediated by our "transcendental spectacles." The philosopher will know that he is receiving signals from outside; he will be aware that there is something "out there" which is sending the signals; but he will also know that the signals he is capable of receiving depend on the nature of our receiving apparatus.[24]

---

22 Kant, *Critique of Pure Reason*, 168, section A42/B60/A43.

23 Blumenau, "Kant and the Thing in Itself."

24 Blumenau, "Kant and the Thing in Itself," para. 8.

Which then leads to this crux: If *das Ding an sich* ("the thing in itself") is unknowable, how can we know it exists at all? We are then inching towards the realm of a pure idealism. Perhaps we have no choice but must rely on intuition or risk pure solipsism—a leap of faith that some *thing* is providing us with the appearance of this thing in the world, the thing in itself. Nonetheless, it is the human perceiver, the human subject, who sits firmly in the centre of Kant's philosophy; object-oriented ontology will come to challenge this central position of a correlationist subject.

But for now, what does Kant's theory of thing in itself mean for my tiny looper? A priori, I can only intuit it as an object in space and time: I imagine it as if plotted within the three-dimensional matrix of a *Neuromancer*-ish virtual web, the transcendental matrix of human intuition. Further Kantian categories could be applied: of quantity (unity, plurality, totality), of quality (reality, negation, limitation), of relation (substance and accident, cause and effect, activity and passivity), of modality (possibility and impossibility, existence and non-existence, necessity and contingency).[25] The looper is one thing: It is "real," it *is* (as opposed to *is not*). This is a category of looper (substance) but shows patterns distinct from other loopers and caterpillars (accidents?) There seems to be cause and effect: I touch it gently with a fingertip and it stiffens.

A posteriori, the perceptions I recorded earlier still apply: its stubby prolegs; the various colours—apple green, emerald, lime; the fine gossamer of its thread as it spun down from the awning; its straight measuring-tape body sensing the air, then looping into a question mark as it moved along the weathered cedar planks of the yurt's deck.

---

25 Blumenau, "Kant and the Thing in Itself."

Maybe my friend Foxtrot perceives it differently. I am using my phone to take a short video of it as it loops its way forward along the planks. She says, "Whatcha doin', Kim?" I say, "I'm taking a video." She says, "Whatcha takin' a video of Kim?" I say, irritated, "Of this looper." She says, "Why are you taking a video of it, Kim?" I say, "Because." She keeps asking and I keep answering, until we dissolve in laughter. What is the looper to Foxtrot? What has she perceived of it? What is it to either of us? What are we to the looper? There is, in this theory of Kant's, a fundamental darkness that privileges the human subject and orients all things to the human mind's a priori concepts and categories, a matrix of human perception. I'm not sure Kant would particularly care what the looper is, in and of itself.

HEIDEGGER | DAS DING AN SICH (THE THING IN ITSELF)

In his later writings, Martin Heidegger edged closer towards an interest in the other in its own being, as a way of knowing that rejected what he saw as twentieth-century technological framing of "nature" as *Bestand*, or "standing reserve," that is, something objectified, to be managed, in order to secure its presence and make it available to humans: A forest is timber, a river is hydroelectricity, salmon are tins on a grocery shelf.[26]

In "The Question Concerning Technology," Heidegger defines technology as a means to an end and as a human activity; it is instrumental: "The manufacture and utilization of equipment, tools, and machines, the manufactured and used things themselves, and the needs and ends that they serve, all belong to what technology is. The whole complex of these contrivances is technology."[27] In

---

26 Foltz, *Inhabiting the Earth.*

27 Heidegger, *The Question Concerning Technology,* 1.

his discussion of small-scale, handcrafted technology—"handcraft manufacture"—he describes how the material, the form, the purpose, and the maker are all responsible for "starting something on its way into arrival" where technology is a form of revealing.[28] There is some exploration of etymologies—briefly, technology is in "the realm of revealing, i.e., of truth"; the word "technology" comes from the Greek *technikon*, from *techne*, "the name not only for the activities and skills of the craftsman, but also for the arts of the mind and the fine arts. *Techne* belongs to bringing-forth, to *episteme* and to *poiesis*; it is something poietic"[29] and a form of knowing. Poet, and poetry, derive their names from *poiesis*, or "making," as in an opening up or revealing of truth, *aletheuein*: "[*Techne*] reveals whatever does not bring itself forth and does not yet lie here before us, whatever can look and turn out now one way and now another." Technology is also a form of making and revealing; however, he argues this conception of technology "might apply to the techniques of the handcraftsman, but that it simply does not fit modern machine-powered technology."[30]

What is it that is different about modern technology? Heidegger names the coal mine, the industrial forest, industrial agriculture, the power plant, the hydroelectric dam. This kind of modern technology, he argues, is not a revealing but a commanding forth:

> This setting-upon that challenges forth the energies of nature is an expediting [*Fördern*], and in two ways. . . . It expedites in that it unlocks and exposes. Yet that expediting is always itself directed from the beginning toward furthering

28 Heidegger, *The Question Concerning Technology*, 4.

29 Heidegger, *The Question Concerning Technology*, 6.

30 Heidegger, *The Question Concerning Technology*, 6.

> something else, i.e., toward driving on to the maximum yield at the minimum expense. The coal that has been hauled out in some mining district has not been supplied in order that it may simply be present somewhere or other. It is stockpiled; that is, it is on call, ready to deliver the sun's warmth that is stored in it. The sun's warmth is challenged forth for heat, which in turn is ordered to deliver steam whose pressure turns the wheels that keep a factory running.[31]

He presents a similar argument regarding a hydroelectric plant placed in the Rhine, in which the river is no longer a river but a "water power supplier."[32] Humans become caught up to an extent in the standing reserve also:

> The forester, who, in the wood, measures the felled timber and to all appearances walks the same forest path in the same way as did his grandfather is today commanded by profit-making in the lumber industry, whether he knows it or not. He is made subordinate to the orderability of cellulose, which for its part is challenged forth by the need for paper, which is then delivered to newspapers and illustrated magazines. The latter, in their turn, set public opinion to swallowing what is printed, so that set configuration of opinion becomes available on demand.[33]

Humans "ensnare" nature, where nature becomes an "object of research, until even the object disappears into the objectlessness of standing-reserve."[34] This calling forth into standing reserve is an

31 Heidegger, *The Question Concerning Technology*, 7.
32 Heidegger, *The Question Concerning Technology*, 8.
33 Heidegger, *The Question Concerning Technology*, 9.
34 Heidegger, *The Question Concerning Technology*, 9.

enframing, or *Ge-stell*, a rigorous ordering that is also a concealing, that "blocks the shining-forth and holding-sway of truth."[35]

The night we left Landback Bridge, we walked down the mountain through clear cuts and slash piles: old-growth forests, biodiverse, ancient trees that have grown in place for centuries—and, in some cases, generation after generation, back to the last glacial age without interruption—wiped out in a summer.

And with the loss of the trees comes the loss of so many other species, like oldgrowth specklebelly lichen (*Pseudocyphellaria rainierensis*), which in itself is evidence of the age of this forest. Oldgrowth specklebelly lichen, as I've already noted, requires environments of rich nutrients to thrive, near ancient yellow cedars, near oceans. It spreads incrementally, slowly. It draws crucial nutrients from the cedars, nutrients taken in from the sea air and which younger cedars cannot provide. I repeat again Trevor Goward's observation on the documentation by artist Natasha Lavdovsky of a widespread presence of oldgrowth specklebelly at Fairy Creek:

> When you find a population as large as [this one], it means that the forest has been there for thousands of years. I'd be astonished if anyone is able to find evidence of charcoal. [Those trees] have been standing in place since glaciation.[36]

35 Heidegger, *The Question Concerning Technology*, 15. Andreas Weber offers a variation on Heidegger's thinking here when he writes that we must "supplant the concept of *techné*, which deeply marks the Anthropocene with its optimism towards human stewardship of the Earth, with the concept of *poiesis*. This poiesis is not about a language game. It is rather the element that brings forth reality" (Weber, *Enlivenment*, 11).

36 Goward quoted in Acker, "Artist Finds New Population."

Slash pile near Landback Bridge, TFL 46, Ada'itsx / Fairy Creek. *Credit: Kim Trainor.*

Clear cut near Landback Bridge, TFL 46, Ada'itsx / Fairy Creek. *Credit: Kim Trainor.*

What has taken 10,000 years to nurture has taken twenty-five years to destroy, or a single summer. On northern Vancouver Island,

> nearly half of the original oldgrowth forest land base within the horizontal and elevational range of Oldgrowth Specklebelly has been harvested, most of it within the last 25 years. In a rainforest region where wildfire is rare, industrial-scale forestry thus stands as by far the most important cause of decline in Oldgrowth Specklebelly—both as a result of habitat loss per se, and, in the long term, of on-going fragmentation of the remaining oldgrowth islands.[37]

---

37 "Species Profile: Oldgrowth Specklebelly Lichen."

The BC government continues to allow Teal-Jones to log old-growth trees and employs the RCMP to support the financial interests of a private company, weaponizing injunctions against Indigenous people and complex entangled ecosystems.

I've described seeing this on my second visit to Fairy Creek, as we participated in a convoy to bring Elder Bill Jones to a ceremonial site at the recently fallen Waterfall camp. We made it only halfway there, stopped several times by metal barriers on two different FSRs as we drove past clear cuts and slash piles on precipitate slopes, until at last we arrived at a manned access point, guarded by white pickup trucks, engines idling, headlights on. The ruins of a land defender camp torn apart in a raid lay strewn to one side, and we salvaged what materials we could find—water jugs, tarps, some camping equipment. The company's guards sat inside their pickups and denied the Elder access to his own hereditary land, telling him that any access to this land would be "at the pleasure of Teal-Jones."

I've described Red Dress camp, along Granite Main, the forest service road that leads up to Landback Bridge and the former River camp, where defenders placed red dresses on the slash piles and stumps of one of the clear cuts, each red dress a symbol of a missing or murdered Indigenous woman or girl; memorial and accusation, the dresses extend far up the mountain, as far as the eye can see. As we descended the night we left, they bruised the blue, ashen dusk.

The Heideggerian commentator Bruce Foltz observes,

> Technology, however, is not only a way of revealing. In disclosing entities, it also involves an establishment and determination of their being. Challenging and provoking

> entities into disclosure, it delimits the manner in which they can be present. As revealed by technology, entities are [forced to] manifest by what Heidegger calls "stock" or "standing reserve" (*das Bestand*). In a technological age, the very being of an entity is to be on call as a resource or standing reserve, to be "in stock" for further disposal: the being of entities thereby consists in their constant availability to ordering and delivery.[38]

Kant, and Descartes before him, posit "nature" as something brought into being through, and made accessible to, human subjectivity, "constantly present to subjectivity in its measurability and calculability."[39] Heidegger: "human willing too can be in the mode of self-assertion only by forcing everything under its dominion from the start, even before it can survey it... The earth and its atmosphere become raw material."[40] This is the dominant neoliberal hypercapitalist mode of approaching the natural world and more-than-human kin. This approach is described by Heidegger as assuming the natural world is "present at hand."

Foltz notes how the natural world "has been measured and weighed; photographs have been taken from outer space; and the Earth itself has even been calculated to be a kind of spaceship. In addition, it can be forced to manifest as a stockpile of energies and resources."[41] The iconic photographs of Earth taken from Apollo 8—*Earthrise* on December 24, 1968, or the *Blue Marble* image taken on December 7, 1972, by the Apollo 17 crew, 29,000 kilometres from the Earth's surface—render the Earth present to the human subject: It is grasped by instantaneous visual gestalt. While these photographs have played

---

38 Foltz, *Inhabiting the Earth*, 8.

39 Foltz, *Inhabiting the Earth*, 12.

40 Heidegger, "What Are Poets For?," *Poetry, Language, Thought*, 111.

41 Foltz, *Inhabiting the Earth*, 14.

a role in suggesting the fragile vulnerability of life on Earth, they also present Earth as object and resource: Spaceship Earth.[42]

Tree farm licence 46 (Ada'itsx / Fairy Creek)—three distinct yet overlapping conceptual and physical spaces[43]—provides a stark example of this vision of nature as standing reserve: As TFL 46, the forest is chattel and denied agency; the courts and the police reinforce this subject/object distinction, unable to see and respect the forest's agency. As TFL 46, the trees are reduced to a stumpage fee—a percentage of any revenue generated by cutting down the forest; the stumpage fees go to the government, in exchange for the logging company's right to clear-cut the land and make short-term profit from it; the courts weaponize injunctions—the protection of "private" property—to support private for-profit interests over the rights of Indigenous Peoples as caretakers of this land, and the inherent worth of the trees and the diversity of species as subjects that are both self-presenting and withholding.

On southern Vancouver Island, the stumpage fee for cedar was $22.14 per cubic metre as of March 1, 2021, and $80.87 per cubic metre as of November 1, 2022, as specified in the BC government's *Coast Appraisal Manual*.[44] Typical coastal old-growth yellow cedar (*Chamaecyparis*

42 Garrard, *Ecocriticism*, 182. "The concept of 'Spaceship Earth' was in fact proposed by architect, inventor and cosmologist R. Buckminster Fuller... who took the Earth image as a figure for the possibility of the total, cornucopian management of the planet in human interests."

43 As TFL 46, it is a parcel of Crown land; as Fairy Creek, it is a watershed named under colonial naming practices; as Ada'itsx, it is a place where the Pacheedaht have deep, enduring roots.

44 The BC Government Timber Pricing Branch's *Coast Appraisal Manual* for 2021 (amended on November 1, 2022) lists the stumpage rate for south island cedar as...

nootkatensis) grow into true giants in the wet, moderate coastal valleys; some are over 2,000 years old. One of the largest, named St. RandAlly, that fell in 2004, was measured at 61 metres (200 feet) in height, with a circumference of 13.08 metres (almost 43 feet) and a diameter of 4.16 metres (13.7 feet). Its crown spread was 16 metres (52.5 feet) and its stem volume estimated to be 175 cubic metres.[45] At the stumpage rate of $22.14 per cubic metre, the government would have received something in the vicinity of $3,874.50 for such a cut tree prior to November 1, 2021, and roughly $14,152.25 after.[46] Old-growth coastal "logs" can "fetch around $350 per cubic metre for lumber-quality logs and $700 per cubic metre for high-end grades."[47] At the higher end of this range, 175 cubic metres would yield $122,500.[48]

...$80.87 per cubic metre; see the Ministry of Forests, Lands, and Natural Resource Operations (FLNRO)'s Memorandum of February 24, 2021, "Average Sawlog Stumpage Rates by District and Species ($/m3) Effective March 1, 2021" for the previous rate of $22.14 per cubic metre. Rates for cedar harvest on the north island are even lower.

45 Koep and Hughes, "World's Largest Yellow Cedars."

46 Nicholson, "British Columbia Tree Costs Surge." BC has seen a huge increase in stumpage rates as a result of competition from the US market.

47 Pawson, "Money Trees." As of 2018. As of May 2023, the BC Government documents the average price per cubic metre of a D-grade old-growth cedar, for the one-month period ending May 2023, at $826.29; an old-growth D-grade cedar with 175 cubic metres would sell for $144,550. In the month ending May 2023, the province records selling a total volume of 33,206.24 cubic metres, at an average of $301.34/m³, grades D through Y. That's just over $10 million for one month for roughly 190 trees (assuming 175 m³ per old-growth tree). Timber Pricing Branch, "Coast Log Market Reports."

48 Bourgon, "How Thousand-Year-Old Trees." Prices vary according to the species and the quality of the wood. Bourgon writes of a growing problem of old-growth tree poaching, in which "forest investigators have found themselves fielding cases in which more than 100 trees were stolen at once." Such thefts (no different, I would argue, than those sanctioned by the BC government and our social contract to log), Bourgon notes, are "greased by the ease of globalized trade... [Chen Hin] Keong...

A 2,000-year-old yellow cedar, named after two forestry engineers; a volume of 175 cubic metres; a monetary value of perhaps $122,500; a stumpage fee ranging from $3,874.50 to $14,152.25.

A tree with rings of lightwood and darkwood and lightwood, ring after ring, heartwood and sapwood and cambium, through centuries of being. Mycelia entwined, feathered mosses, fairy parachutes, oldgrowth specklebelly lichen at the drip zone, clinging to the trunks and branches of companion trees.

Heidegger suggested that the earth is self-emergent, source of *physis*, that which blooms or blossoms forth, yet also simultaneously withdraws:

> In Heidegger's thinking proper, the earth is not only that in which plants take root and upon which houses are built but also the human body, the sound of a word or the script of a text, the bronze or clay that upholds a sculpted surface.

... [head of the Global Forest Trade Program at TRAFFIC International] likens a piece of furniture to a cell phone—minerals are extracted from one place, everything cobbled together piecemeal in another. Often, when an inspecting officer opens a container of cargo, he or she is sorting through legally sourced items to find the illegal material buried in the middle or hidden underneath."

This is analogous to the "artisanal" cobalt found in your iPhone, which has inevitably been touched by human rights abuses, child labour, and possibly the slave trade, somewhere along the supply chain.

> In each case, the earth is what bears and gives rise to what comes to light only by remaining intrinsically dark itself. The earth is the sound that carries the words of a poem and secretly permeate its meaning, but they withdraw into mere phonemes—incapable of bearing a poem or any meaning whatsoever—when explicitly examined and investigated.[49]

For humans, language can articulate openness and the correspondent obligation for humans to bear witness. I like the idea that there is an ethical imperative to witness and create a space for other beings so as to leave them be, beyond human interest and interaction. Heidegger observes,

> It is language that tells us about the nature of a thing, provided that we respect language's own nature. In the meantime, to be sure, there rages round the earth an unbridled yet clever talking, writing, and broadcasting of spoken words. Man acts as though *he* were the shaper and master of language, while in fact *language* remains the master of man. Perhaps it is before all else man's subversion of *this* relation of dominance that drives his nature into alienation.[50]

The caveat here is "provided that we respect language's own nature," which provides some insight into the emphasis, in his later writings, on the important role of poetry, which, of all forms of language use, allows for language to be itself, and to point towards its polysemous, subversive, polyvocal nature. An opening might be possible within such language, for considering, however

49 Foltz, *Inhabiting the Earth*, 14–15.

50 Heidegger, "What Are Poets For?," *Poetry, Language, Thought*, 146.

mediated, the blossoming of other beings, while at the same time, respecting their withdrawnness, their fundamental darkness.

Related to the concept of openness, and letting things be, is the idea of "attunement." Greg Garrard writes, "We learn resistance to the instrumentalism or en-framing (*Ge-stell*) that discloses being always in its narrow and reductive terms. We seek *attunement* to the demand beings put on us to disclose them without constraint. We learn, that is, to let beings be."[51]

The phantom looper moth, *Nepytia phantasmaria, arpenteuse verte de la pruche,* apple green, splashes of ink, slips down on gossamer thread, slips into my field of vision, comes into focus—a fine dark green line, supraspiracular, faint green middorsal—blurs into needle, a flower, a twig, a flurry of snow.

MERLEAU-PONTY | *LE CHIASME, LA CHAIR (CHIASM, FLESH)*

> As I contemplate the blue of the sky I am not *set over against* it as an acosmic subject; I do not possess it in thought, or spread out towards it some idea of blue such as might reveal the secret of it, I abandon myself to it and plunge into this mystery, it "thinks itself within me," I am the sky itself as it is drawn together and unified, and as it begins to exist for itself; my consciousness is saturated with this limitless blue. —MAURCIE MERLEAU-PONTY, *Phenomenology of Perception* (1962)

---

51 Garrard, *Ecocriticism*, 35.

Qualia, Merleau-Ponty argues in his last, incomplete manuscript, *The Visible and the Invisible,* are not distinct or atomistic but integrated, woven within the fabric of the world. Of the quale red, he observes,

> this red is what it is only by connecting up from its place with other reds about it, with which it forms a constellation, or with other colors it dominates or that dominate it, that it attracts or that attract it, that it repels or that repel it... The red dress *a fortiori* holds with all its fibers onto the fabric of the visible, and thereby onto a fabric of invisible being. A punctuation in the field of red things, which includes the tiles of roof tops, the flags of gatekeepers and of the Revolution, certain terrains near Aix or in Madagascar, it is also a punctuation in the field of red garments, which includes... the dresses of women.[52]

Not only is this quale a shifting quality of red in relation to many other reds, it is also dependent upon context, and within each context, "a momentary crystallization of colored being or of visibility."[53] The red dresses snagged on the slash piles in a clear cut at Ada'itsx / Fairy Creek flicker between the red of spilled blood, the red of #landback, the red of an open wound, the red of the medicine wheel, the red of salmon flesh become tiny rents in the world, portals from visible to invisible, part of "a *flesh* of things."[54] In a comment inserted within brackets in his last, fragmented manuscript, Merleau-Ponty writes, "One can say that we perceive the things themselves, that we are the world that thinks itself—or that the world is at the heart of our flesh. In any case, once a body-world relationship is recognized, there is a ramification of my body

---

52 Merleau-Ponty, *The Visible and the Invisible,* 132.

53 Merleau-Ponty, *The Visible and the Invisible,* 132.

54 Merleau-Ponty, *The Visible and the Invisible,* 133.

and a ramification of the world and a correspondence between its inside and my outside, between my inside and its outside."[55] We can extend this to our more-than-human kin, each in its own *Umwelt*, with its own body and sensory perceptions, a part of this thinking, pulsing fabric. Words that Merleau-Ponty uses at times for this correspondence are *synthesis*, *symbiosis*, and *simultaneity*.

In his phenomenology, Merleau-Ponty works towards resolving both the opening that the individual can make to receive the other, while acknowledging at the same time the other's withdrawnness, their inaccessibility or mystery, and the ethical call this entails. The Pacific northwest ecophilosopher Ted Toadvine argues that we might consider our "immanence to nature" as not simply a limitation or "ineliminable blind spot" but rather the very condition required for us to have any access or approach to nature.[56] We inherit the "sedimentation of a perceptual tradition," and this tradition or "screen" is not so much a screen as constitutive of our ability to perceive anything at all: "Nature, therefore, is precisely what discloses itself *through* our expressive acts, and as requiring such expression for its disclosure."[57] Toadvine also cautions us to consider whether placing the body at the centre of our relationship with the world is simply another anthropomorphic move that displaces Descartes's *cogito* with human body. Yet he praises Merleau-Ponty's phenomenological perspective, which "means describing our access to nature in a fashion that respects both its autochthonous meaning and its transcendence."[58]

---

55 Merleau-Ponty, *The Visible and the Invisible*, 133.

56 Toadvine, *Merleau-Ponty's Philosophy of Nature*, 11.

57 Toadvine, *Merleau-Ponty's Philosophy of Nature*, 15.

58 Toadvine, *Merleau-Ponty's Philosophy of Nature*, 16.

There is a constant entanglement or dialogue between body and sensible world. Merleau-Ponty:

> The question is always how can I be open to phenomena which transcend me and which nevertheless exist only to the extent that I take them up [*reprends*] and live them?[59]

While Heidegger takes as fiat the ability of human language to create such an opening, Merleau-Ponty still asks, *How*? If we are silted up with this tradition's residual sediment, if it is nevertheless a very condition of our ability to take up this world, how can I remain open to the world's self-expression, and from the perspective of a poet, how can I write a poem that offers acknowledgement of its more-than-human being that always transcends me?

Toadvine argues, "Merleau-Ponty is explicit... that defining the thing as a correlate of the body and our life does not exhaust its meaning, since it does not disclose the 'non-human element' that it harbours."[60] There is the someone who perceives the thing, but there remains still "a genuine *in-itself-for-us*."[61] Merleau-Ponty describes this "non-human element" as aloof, self-sufficient, and disinterested in the sensor; it is "hostile and alien, no longer an interlocutor, but a resolutely silent Other, a Self which evades us no less than does intimacy with any outside consciousness."[62] I would resist this need to characterize the "non-human element" (more-than-human kin) as hostile or alien—this is part of the sludge of Western and colonizing traditions that has consistently perceived the natural

---

59 Merleau-Ponty quoted in Toadvine, *Merleau-Ponty's Philosophy of Nature*, 52.
60 Toadvine, *Merleau-Ponty's Philosophy of Nature*, 58.
61 Merleau-Ponty, *Phenomenology of Perception*, 322.
62 Merleau-Ponty, *Phenomenology of Perception*, 322.

world as hostile and dangerous force. Elsewhere Merleau-Ponty characterizes perception as communication or communion, which is a more helpful description.[63] I think back to a conversation I had over Signal this week[64] with a settler-ally at the Unist'ot'en Healing Camp, who said, when I asked her whether there were bears in the camp, and if volunteers bring anything to scare them away,

> Oh, this is black bear and grizzly bear country, but we don't scare them away. Black bear is little brother, and grizzly bear is big brother, and we welcome them. But we say very loudly when we walk into the woods to our tents, *hello little brother, hello big brother, I'm coming, wooo-hooooo, I'm on my way.*

This made me recall the first time I encountered little brother—no, little sister—on the Juan de Fuca Trail, with her two young cubs swinging on a log as she turned over clumps of seaweed at the high-tide line, searching for food. She turned and looked directly my way—she was sensing, aware, focused, as much a consciousness perceiving me as I was one perceiving her. Toadvine interprets Merleau-Ponty in such an instance as suggesting that this "resistance and aloof aspect of the thing is precisely what gives it the status of an in-itself in our experience, what rejects the body's advances even while remaining, in some sense, correlated with it."[65]

While Toadvine cautions against a simple substitution of the body for *cogito*, David Abram is less cautious, embracing Merleau-Ponty's concepts of attunement, and his later development of *le chiasme* and *la chair* in his last, unfinished manuscript, *The*

63 Merleau-Ponty, *Phenomenology of Perception*, 320.

64 Perhaps this was in 2021 or 2022. I did not record the date.

65 Toadvine, *Merleau-Ponty's Philosophy of Nature*, 58.

Visible and the Invisible, as foundational for an ecological phenomenology, in which the body is permeated and diffuse:

> the boundaries of a living body are open and indeterminate; more like membranes than barriers, they define a surface of metamorphoses and exchange. The breathing, sensing body draws its sustenance and its very substance from the soils, plants, and elements that surround it; it continually contributes itself, in turn, to the air, to the composting earth, to the nourishment of insects and oak trees and squirrels, ceaselessly spreading out of itself as well as breathing the world into itself, so that it is very difficult to discern, at any moment, precisely where this living body begins and where it ends... the body is my very means of entering into relation with all things.[66]

The trees sip oxygen, carbon; absorb sunlight and minerals drawn from the sea; breathe out oxygen en masse; I breathe in oxygen, exhale carbon dioxide; the thread-like hyphae of mycorrhizal networks take up potassium, calcium, zinc, magnesium, water; the tree makes carbohydrates stitched from carbon and sunlight, produces leaves. I eat the fruits and nuts of plants, the huckleberries, the thimbleberries, the hazelnuts, the chokecherries; I scatter seeds as I walk through the forest. The Sitka spruce senses my steps, drips sap, tastes salt in the air; a dark-eyed junco darts through the undergrowth of salal. Little sister turns to look at me, pauses, then resumes her task at hand. Sunlight scatters through atmosphere, burns blue, is absorbed by leaves; I am saturated with blue, blue thinks itself within me. I decay, am consumed by fungi, dissolve to elements, to water; mycorrhizal threads weave through me, absorb my oxygen and nitrogen, my hydrogen, my carbon.

---

66 Abram, *The Spell of the Sensuous*, 46.

Abram writes, we are "corporeally embedded . . . a vast, interpenetrating webwork of perceptions and sensations borne by countless other bodies":

> [This] intertwined web of experience is, of course, the "life-world" to which Husserl alluded in his final writings, yet now the life-world has been disclosed as a profoundly *carnal* field, as this very dimension of smells and tastes and chirping rhythms warmed by the sun and shivering with seeds. It is, indeed, nothing other than the biosphere—the matrix of earthly life in which we ourselves are embedded . . . Yet this is not the biosphere as it is conceived by an abstract and objectifying science, not that complex assemblage of planetary mechanisms presumably being mapped and measured by our remote-sensing satellites; it is, rather, the biosphere as it is experienced and *lived from within* by the intelligent body—by the attentive human animal who is entirely a part of the world that he, or she, experiences.[67]

La chair, the flesh, designates for Merleau-Ponty this entangled body, not bodies, but contiguous flesh, a "mysterious tissue or matrix that underlies and gives rise to both the perceiver and the perceived as independent aspects of its own spontaneous activity."[68] This idea of *la chair* is bound up with the concept of *le chiasme*.

In "The Intertwining—The Chiasm," the final chapter of his unfinished book, Merleau-Ponty introduces the term "intertwining": "Intertwining [*entrelacs*] here translates Husserl's *Verflechtung*, entanglement or interweaving, like the woof and warp of a

---

67 Abram, *The Spell of the Sensuous*, 65.

68 Abram, *The Spell of the Sensuous*, 66.

fabric."[69] Chiasmus comes from the Greek *χίασμα*, or "crossing," and ultimately from the Greek, *χιάζω*, meaning "to shape like the letter X."[70] The term refers to the rhetorical device of reversing grammatical structures in an A-B-B-A configuration, but technically without repetition of words—although this is often how we think of chiasmus: *Live simply so that others might simply live*. In physiology, the optic chiasm is a region of the brain where the optic nerves cross. Merleau-Ponty takes up both the symbolic chiasm (language, abstractions, the "invisible") and physiological (the flesh, the crossing of bodies, the "visible"). Toadvine notes that Merleau-Ponty borrowed the term originally from Paul Valéry with reference to the crossing of glances, the opening of perspectives.[71]

Merleau-Ponty offers the example of a handshake in thinking of chiasm, as described here by Toadvine:

> The generality of flesh embraces an intercorporeity, an anonymous sensibility shared out among distinct bodies: just as my two hands communicate across the lateral synergy of my body, I can touch the sensibility of another: "The handshake too is reversible."[72]

In the realm of the visible, I can be seen, touched, heard; from within my body, within the realm of the invisible, I see, I touch,

---

69 Toadvine, "Maurice Merleau-Ponty."

70 Wikipedia, "Chiasmus," accessed July 30, 2022, https://en.wikipedia.org/wiki/Chiasmus.

71 Toadvine, *Merleau-Ponty's Philosophy of Nature*, 110. "Valéry's term *chiasma*, in its literal anatomical usage, refers to the crossing of two or more nerves or ligaments, and especially to the *X* formed where the optic nerves cross at the base of the brain, allowing for images from the right visual field to be processed in the left visual system of the brain and vice versa."

72 Toadvine, "Maurice Merleau-Ponty."

I hear. Merleau-Ponty provides the example of the touch of tree bark, of sight, of the Koyukon people in a "forest of eyes."[73] Renaud Barbaras observes that "[i]t is necessary... to picture the universe as intuited by Merleau-Ponty as a proliferation of chiasms that integrate themselves according to different levels of generality."[74] Toadvine takes this concept of chiasm and argues for its application to an ecophilosophical consideration of humans in nature, beyond the "positivist ontology of the natural sciences."[75]

The gap or *écart* appears here also: In Merleau-Ponty's terms, it is "dehiscence," as in a surgical complication where the ragged edges of a wound no longer meet. An example of this would be in the relationship between language and silence, the aseity (that essence or property by which a being exists in and of itself) of nature being located in its silence.[76] The philosophical task then, according to Toadvine's discussion of Merleau-Ponty, is to seek to express the being of nature, while preserving its silence. This is a variation of Heidegger's project of creating a clearing, of creating space for letting things be. Here is Merleau-Ponty on dehiscence:

> A sort of dehiscence opens my body in two... between my body looked at and my body looking, my body touched and my body touching, there is overlapping or encroachment, so that we must say that the things pass into us as well as we into things.[77]

---

73 Merleau-Ponty quoted in Abram, *The Spell of the Sensuous*, 187.

74 Quoted in Toadvine, "Maurice Merleau-Ponty."

75 Toadvine, *Merleau-Ponty's Philosophy of Nature*, 107.

76 Toadvine, *Merleau-Ponty's Philosophy of Nature*, 107.

77 Merleau-Ponty, *The Visible and the Invisible*, 123.

So, as Toadvine has noted, for Merleau-Ponty, the "gap" or slippage between sentient and sensible is "not a failure" but "precisely the disclosure of the world"[78]—that is, necessary even for the very perception of the world. Merleau-Ponty writes, "We situate ourselves in ourselves and in the things, in ourselves and in the other, at the point where, by a sort of chiasm, we become the others and we become world."[79] Toadvine:

> The "good error" of *écart* pushes us past the opposition between the pure original and the mediated by recognizing that the originary is already and from the first mediated. Thus it is that "language realizes, by breaking the silence, what the silence wished and did not obtain." Language that is "operative," truly active and creative, is "open upon things, called forth by the voices of silence, and continues the effort of articulation which is the Being of every being."[80]

Silence opens into language, and words slip back into the silent realm. Merleau-Ponty writes of language, "We need only take language too in the living or nascent state, with all its references, those behind it, which connect it to the mute things it interpellates... Language is a life, is our life and the life of the things."[81] Of note, Merleau-Ponty says that philosophy "does not seek a verbal substitute for the world we see, it does not transform it into something said, it does not install itself in the order of the said or of the written as does the logician in the proposition, the poet in the word, or the musician in the music. It is the things

78 Toadvine, *Merleau-Ponty's Philosophy of Nature*, 115.

79 Quoted in Toadvine, *Merleau-Ponty's Philosophy of Nature*, 115.

80 Toadvine, *Merleau-Ponty's Philosophy of Nature*, 128–29.

81 Merleau-Ponty, *The Visible and the Invisible*, 125.

themselves, from the depths of their silence, that it wishes to bring to expression."[82] I disagree with him here; surely it is the poet or the musician who, far from seeking a verbal substitute for the world she sees, seeks to bring the things themselves "from the depths of silence," far moreso than philosophy. Harman develops this argument in his discussion of metaphor.

The privileged trope in *The Visible and the Invisible*, as suggested by the title, is that of sight, which inevitably privileges distance between subject and object, and then seeks resolution to this binary. Touch is closer, more intimate, and I will look shortly at how Levinas develops the concept of touch in relation to the thing in itself, the Other; sound is closer still, because we resonate, taking up the soundwaves into our flesh and bones. Bruns addresses sound in relation to Levinas and poetry, but again presents this as invasion, alien and hostile. Merleau-Ponty does touch upon sound, which is also a form of touch, when he writes about the cry and the voice:

> Like crystal, like metal and many other substances, I am a sonorous being, but I hear my own vibration from within; as Malraux said, I hear myself with my throat... my voice is bound to the mass of my own life as is the voice of no one else. But if I am close enough to the other who speaks to hear his breath and feel his effervescence and his fatigue, I almost witness, in him as in myself, the awesome birth of vociferation. As there is a reflexivity of the touch, of sight, and of the touch-vision system, there is a reflexivity of the movements,

82 Merleau-Ponty, *The Visible and the Invisible*, 4.

> of phonation and of hearing: they have their sonorous inscription, the vociferations have in me their motor echo.[83]

While Bruns describes sound as invasion, Merleau-Ponty here describes sound as inscription, a form of touch. As with qualia, as in the colour blue, but even more profoundly, sound saturates the body. The embryo is enveloped by fluid and flesh; the mother's voice and the rhythms of her heartbeat, her lungs, the swish of blood in circulation through her arteries and veins, the digestive gurglings and creak of bones, all saturate the unborn child, just as the sound of its heartbeat amplified by ultrasound fills the mother's ears, breast, and belly. Words emerge out of silence, newborn out of liquid flesh, monarch out of chrysalis with its splash of meconium, poem out of clearing. Sound saturates, is tactile, resonates, is profound.

I take this sonorous being, that rings like crystal, that hums like a bee, to Levinas, the face, and the voice.

LEVINAS | ALTERITY OF SOUND

The thing in itself, *das Ding an sich,* the Other, *Autrui,* calls to us from across an untraversable gap (*écart,* dehiscence, darkness). Gerald Bruns explores the ethical call of the other presented in Levinas, the call to attend that comes with an ethical responsibility: "as a subject I have been turned inside out and exposed to the other with nothing to fall back on that will exempt me from my responsibility. As Levinas says, 'The word "here I am" (*me voici*), answer[s] for everything and for

83 Merleau-Ponty, *The Visible and the Invisible,* 145.

everyone.'"[84] Bruns explicates the distinction Levinas makes between seeing and hearing as forms of perception. Levinas observes that to "see is to be in a world that is entirely here and self-sufficient";[85] that is, sight offers separation and gestalt, a grasping of the Other at a distance, as object of cognition. But sound is transcendent. Sound enters me as subject, permeates corporeal boundaries, and saturates me:

> In sound, and in the consciousness termed hearing there is in fact a break with the self-complete world of vision. In its entirety, sound is a ringing, clanging scandal. Whereas, in vision, form is wedded to content in such a way as to appease it, in sound the perceptible quality overflows so that form can no longer contain its content. A real rent is produced in the world, through which the world that is here prolongs a dimension that cannot be converted into vision.[86]

What Levinas calls a rent produced in the world resonates with Merleau-Ponty's dehiscence: a tear, the lips of a gaping wound. Bruns describes sound in this way:

> Sound decomposes the self-identity of the subject, a self-identity that is the first principle of rationality. Sound is invasive; ears are porous in a way that eyes are not. Sound fills the subject with foreign things at a distance and in perspective . . . transforms the *I* of cognition and representation into the *me* whose existence is exposed and vulnerable. Sound bleeds the self.[87]

---

84 Levinas, "Language and Proximity," 42.

85 Levinas quoted in Bruns, *The Material of Poetry*, 44.

86 Levinas quoted in Bruns, *The Material of Poetry*, 44–45.

87 Bruns, *The Material of Poetry*, 45.

As such, Bruns links poetry to the call of the Other as poetry requires attentive listening, a relinquishing of rational control, an openness. As a form of listening and receptivity, poetry then, he argues, is "a mode of responsibility, taking this word, as Levinas does, in its literal sense of responsiveness and receptivity, as well as in its ethical sense of answerability."[88] Bruns describes Plato's expulsion of the poets from his Republic "not just because they traffic in images but because they are noisy and heterogeneous"; their voices hint at schizophrenia; the sounds of their words attack the singular, rational *cogito*—sound "decomposes," is "invasive," "bleeds the self." There is an unwillingness in Plato to embrace this alterity and respond to its ethical call.[89] By contrast, Bruns writes,

> Responsiveness to others and to things *in their irreducible singularity* calls for an intimacy that cognition rules out. The "I" or "me" in responsibility is in the unabstracted, undetached condition of nonindifference. Levinas calls this condition "proximity" and also "sensibility," where we exist in the mode of being touched rather than in the cognitive mode of grasping or appropriation. Hearing or listening is perhaps the most inescapable way of dwelling in this anarchic condition.[90]

Regarding poetry, Bruns points to Levinas's depiction of words as transcendent—that is, words as sounds, which are in excess of symbolic or semantic meaning, as an alterity that is analogous to the alterity of the other human who is "emphatically not an object of my cognition, representation,

---

88 Bruns, *The Material of Poetry*, 43.
89 Bruns, *The Material of Poetry*, 43.
90 Bruns, *The Material of Poetry*, 43.

or conceptual control . . . a mode of radical exteriority,"[91] and I would extend this to the alterity of our more-than-human kin. As Toadvine observes, "Does Levinas's sensibility to the face of the other human being deafen him to another, different, if quieter, call?"[92] Little brother, little sister.

I walk into Salmon camp, off Granite Main, to the high bank overlooking Renfrew Creek—the water flows past, wide, slow-moving, an opaque chalk green, slate in the shadows. I am distinct from it, I see it in an instant, see the shape of its banks, the water's chiaroscuro. At night in my one-person tent, the sound of the creek rises, flows through huckleberry and salal, seeps through thin nylon, flesh, bone. I am awash with creek. World pours in.

OOO | MUTUAL DARKNESS

From my discussion with several philosophers who are also friends, I know that object-oriented ontology, or OOO, is a branch of philosophy subject to suspicion and dismissal. It is not surprising to me, however, that OOO has found a listening ear among those who create—architects, sculptors, musicians, poets—as it speaks to our experience of artistic practice.

OOO builds from Heidegger and subsequent phenomenological theories, with a particular focus on Heidegger's tool analysis. In his book *Tool-Being*, Graham Harman elaborates upon the thing in and for itself, expanding Heidegger's model to consider the perspective of objects—Harman prefers

---

91 Bruns, *The Material of Poetry*, 44.

92 Toadvine, "Ecophenomenology in the New Millenium," 82.

the term "object" over "thing"—as they presence to, and interact with, not only humans but also other objects.[93]

Objects can be both real and imaginary: this science-fiction paperback I hold in my hand; the character of Takvar in *The Dispossessed*; her moon world of Anarres; her mobiles—the occupations of uninhabited space. Harman rejects undermining (the tendency to reduce objects to their constituent parts—molecules, atoms, quarks, stardust) and overmining (the tendency to reduce objects to their function, to what they do). There can be what one might think of as a traditional material object—an acoustic guitar—and a compound object: His typical example is the Dutch East India Company; I suggest the constantly fluctuating membership and tactics of Save Old Growth and the dispersed A22 Network.[94]

His definition of an object, then, is "anything that cannot be entirely reduced either to the components of which it is made or to the effects that it has on other things,"[95] a definition that challenges the assumption that "everything must be able to be stated accurately in literal propositional language."[96] This is true as much for describing a salmonberry leaf down to its apparent constituent parts (chloroplasts → chlorophyl → $C_{55}H_{72}O_5N_4Mg$ → Carbon → Group 14, Atomic No. 6, Mass 12.011) as for the use of "literal" language to describe it: "alternate . . . dark green . . . composed of three sharply-toothed

---

93 Harman, *Tool-Being*.

94 "A22 Network." The A22 Network is self-described as "a group of connected projects engaged in a mad dash to try and save humanity." It has comprised, at various times, Save Old Growth (BC, Canada), Just Stop Oil (UK), Letzte Generation (Germany), Ultima Generazione (Italy), Dernière Rénovation (France), among others.

95 Harman, *Object-Oriented Ontology*, 43.

96 Harman, *Object-Oriented Ontology*, 35.

leaflets [that] form an elongated maple leaf-like shape."[97] Harman gives the example of Dan Dennett rejecting the phenomenological assertion that there might be a specific conscious human experience of a phenomenon. Harman writes, "the claim of OOO is that literal language is *always* an oversimplification, since it describes things in terms of definite literal properties even though *objects are never just bundles of literal properties*."[98] Harman therefore prioritizes poetic over literal language, as did Heidegger in his later writings, as poetic language might be better able to express the polysemous nature of objects; even in the above "literal" description of a salmonberry leaf, it is already in the realm of metaphor ("sharp-toothed") and analogy (in the shape of a maple leaf).

And because human consciousness cannot ever fully access the thing in itself,[99] no matter how carefully the salmonberry leaf is scrutinized, described, tasted, drawn, placed on a glass slide and slipped under a microscope, the object is said to be withdrawn—not only withdrawn from human consciousness but from other objects. In this way, OOO attempts to move beyond Heidegger, theorizing autonomy of objects as "mutually 'withdrawn'" from each other.[100] This places OOO within earshot of "thing-power materialism"—Jane Bennett's *Vibrant Matter*, in which she outlines a "political ecology of things"—and Bruno Latour's actor-network theory, although OOO does not suggest that objects exist only in their constantly shifting relationships with other objects. OOO also posits a flat ontology, an initial attempt to consider all objects—salmonberry leaf, my paperback copy of *The Dispossessed*,

97 Fretwell and Starzomski, "Salmonberry / *Rubus spectabilis*."

98 Harman, *Object-Oriented Ontology*, 37. Emphasis in original.

99 Although I would ask, Why should it want to fully access a salmonberry leaf? And why is there so much concern to create a "theory of everything"?

100 Harman, *Object-Oriented Ontology*, 12.

Takvar—the same, "rather than assuming in advance that different types of objects require completely different ontologies."[101] Harman

---

101 Harman, *Object-Oriented Ontology*, 54. In his provocative essay, "Object-Oriented Ontology and the Other of We in Anthropocentric Posthumanism," Yogi Hale Hendlin elides—and at times misrepresents—various forms of OOO and new materialism, but nonetheless argues there are two deeply ethical problems with OOO that must be addressed: (1) that "OOO's 'ontological flattening' of all life (e.g., humans, rhinoceroses, orchids, amoebas), things (artifacts and ecological features), ideas and fantasies into one lumped group of 'objects' inexorably involves an ethical flattening" and (2) that "OOO focuses on a 'gap between all beings/objects… unassailable and untraversable. Perhaps it is the focus—and obsession—with gaps (and by implication, purity), which is the problem" (Hendlin, 328).

Regarding ontological flattening, my reading of Harman is that such an ontological flattening is only a starting point and allows for a reframing of enlightenment humanism that has centred the human—that is, positing an ontological flatness is a tool for rejecting human exceptionalism; as such, it does not involve an ethical flattening but rather the reverse, as in my discussion of the rights of Pachamama, of bees considered as citizens, of the Fraser River as a person that must be accorded rights. Hendlin's second concern is predicated again on a misreading of Harman—the acknowledgement of a "gap" never implies an obsession with "purity," nor does it preclude what Hendlin himself argues for, that is, approaches towards the Other, whether as a poet or as a scientist like Alexandra Morton who is so intimately immersed in the orca realm that she becomes attuned to their way of being, if also knowing that at a fundamental level they are unknowable, and honoring that darkness. Hendlin: "[B]acteria disclose the world in ways we cannot understand. But in understanding bacteria (say, biologically), we can catch glimpses of its world-disclosing work. When we become aware of the agency of other organisms and how this expresses in detectable changes in ecosystems and organisms that humans can (via multiple methods) grok" (Hendlin, 333).

I don't believe Harman's version of OOO would dispute this; what is useful in Harman's and Morton's elaboration of OOO is their focus on the methods of the artist in seeking attunement with other beings, whether oldgrowth specklebelly lichen or orca, and in particular, Harman's focus on the role played by metaphor. Hendlin criticizes OOO for its belief that "[e]pistemic finitude [as in, knowledge is finite, unable to ever fully grasp or describe reality] leads to epistemic humility"…

contrasts this with Descartes or Kant, who privilege human beings (the cogito, the transcendental correlationist) as the privileged lens that brings the world into focus, perhaps even into being. By contrast, OOO, Harman argues, is a realist philosophy, taking the concept of the thing in itself, from Kant, via Heidegger, and embracing the reality of dark noumena outside of human consciousness and perception.

Harman writes of OOO's "commitment to the mutual darkness of objects," which are always "withdrawn" or "withheld."[102] Any approach, any attempt at description is always mediated or translated; therefore, "an indirect or oblique means of access to reality is in some ways a wiser mode of access than any amount of literal information about it."[103] His argument is that in the contemporary world, in Western developed countries in particular, there is too much value placed on literal, rational, scientific knowledge of a thing, "while ignoring cognitive activities that do not translate as easily into literal prose terms." Art, as with philosophy, he points out, does not have as its primary aim the desire "to communicate knowledge about its subject";[104] although a drawing or a poem is still only one attempt to access, one translation or mediation, it can offer something different, particularly in its use of metaphor.

... (318). I think it does lead to epistemic humility, as a starting point. Hendlin suggests other ways in which to approach the withdrawn Other: attention, attunement, biosemiotics, "phylogenetic humility" (Robert Sapolsky), enlivenment (Andreas Weber), nonscalability (Anna Tsing). I've addressed some of these throughout my book; none of these are incompatible with a beginning in epistemic humility, as laid out by Harman.

102 Harman, *Object-Oriented Ontology*, 12.

103 Harman, *Object-Oriented Ontology*, 40. Tim Lilburn describes such attempts in *Living in the World as If It Were Home*: "You lie down with what is ignored. You are beyond the gravity of the mind's propriety and caught in the gravity of things. Consciousness becomes feral" (44).

104 Harman, *Object-Oriented Ontology*, 44.

It is the focus in OOO on less-easily translated cognitive activities that is relevant to ecopoetry. Literal prose terms are bypassed by the figurative mechanisms of metaphor, metonymy, analogy, metaphysical conceit, allusion, and an array of aural effects—assonance, consonance, slant rhyme, rhythm—all gesturing towards the semiotic over the symbolic. Words become concrete and material beings, constructed of ink, shapes, alphabets, fonts, all physical instantiations of shaped breath—fricatives, velars, plosives, glottal stops, trills, and tongue roots. The poem, as made of words, playful in its making, points to the nature of language and meaning-making itself and is self-aware and self-questioning; it becomes a means of *thinking with,* as Morton describes of Coleridge's "Effusion 35," glimpses its own ontology and epistemological methods. With each reading of the poem, a new translation or mediation is carried out, contingent on what the reader brings to it; it is never exhausted and cannot ever be translated into literal prose terms or propositional language. The poem then with such varied tools can offer an oblique approach to the Other.

There is a sincere commitment in OOO to the independent existence of the thing in itself, to objects, which will always withdraw. For a human,

> [n]o access mode will work properly: thinking, stabbing with scissors, eating, ignoring, writing a poem about, crawling across (if you are a fly), kicking (if you are a football player), eating (if you are a dog), irradiating (if you are a gamma ray) . . . nothing can be accessed all at once in its entirety.[105]

And by access, as glossed here by Timothy Morton, Harman means not simply thinking but all kinds of access: "any way of grasping a thing: brushing against, thinking about, licking, making a

105 Morton, *Being Ecological,* 33.

painting of, eating, building a nest on, blowing to bits."[106] Morton's inclusion of "writing a poem about" in his list of modes of access seems inconsistent with his praise of the serpent poetry as a way to think into the future in *Dark Ecology*; similarly, Harman will embrace metaphor, which Adrienne Rich once described as the engine of poetry, as offering a unique mode of approach.

Morton uses the term "grasping"—that ur-metaphor of the handedness of *Homo sapiens*, which McGilchrist associates with the left hemispheric domain that sorts, processes, categorizes, but ultimately recirculates dead information if not flooded with new data and sensations gathered by the right. In Harman's writing, there is also less focus on more-than-human kin, such as plants, trees, crows, mosses; when he provides examples of objects, he tends to favour inanimate objects, including composite human objects and imaginary ones. This is a deliberate attempt by Harman to challenge our ideas of what an object is, to not undermine or overmine; there may also be a concern on his part not to favour animate over inanimate. When I discuss panpsychism, which posits a continuum of consciousness in all matter, I will return to this idea, as our ethical relationships with other beings seems contingent (again from a Western enlightenment perspective) on a certain level of consciousness that can be assumed in such beings, counter to a concept such as *tsawalk*, which sees everything as connected.

Consider Ecuador, as I noted previously, which enshrines the rights of Pachamama, "Mother Earth," in its constitution—that is, its very right to exist and to "maintain and regenerate its cycles, structure, functions and evolutionary processes."[107] These rights were upheld in December 2021, in Ecuador's Constitutional Court, forcing the Ecuadorian government

106 Morton, *Being Ecological*, 33.
107 Surma, "Ecuador's High Court."

to revoke mining grants that had been issued to both Ecuador's state mining company, along with its Canadian partner, Cornerstone Capital Resources. The companies had planned to conduct exploratory operations within the Los Cedros protected area; in a majority decision, the court ruled that "the risk in this case is not necessarily related to human beings... but to the extinction of species, the destruction of ecosystems or the permanent alteration of natural cycles."[108]

As opposed to grasping or accessing, I prefer Heidegger's language of attending, of letting something dwell or come into its own being by creating space for it, analogous to Weil's concept of negative attention. Despite the use of "access"—words matter, to grasp versus to touch, to hold, to carry, to cradle—I like that OOO offers, as described by Morton,

> a marvelous world of shadows and hidden corners, a world in which things can't ever be completely irradiated by the ultraviolet light of thought, a world in which being a badger, nosing past whatever it is that you, a human being, are looking at thoughtfully, is just as validly accessing that thing as you are.[109]

Its focus on emotional, visceral, musical forms of "cognition" are all foundational to poetry. This world of shadows and mystery echo John Keats's observations on negative capability, to be "capable of being in uncertainties, Mysteries, doubts, without any irritable reaching after fact and reason."[110] It suggests a similar interest in rejecting the more traditional cognitive grasping after "fact and reason," while embracing

---

108 Judge Agustín Grijalva Jiménez quoted in Surma, "Ecuador's High Court." I've noted previously the campaign to assign legal personhood to the Fraser River estuary.

109 Morton, *Being Ecological*, 34.

110 Keats, *Selected Letters of John Keats*, 60.

darkness; when Keats describes seeing a sparrow, he associates with it, as if also pecking about the gravel, becoming for a moment this little bird.

ORTEGA Y GASSET | *THE BEAUTIFUL CELL (LA CÉLULA BELLA)*

At the heart of object-oriented ontology is the belief that objects are mysterious, "in a radical and irreducible way."[111] And while there is no single technique that can fully access the thing in itself, the object, Harman places great emphasis on metaphor as theorized in a short essay by José Ortega y Gasset, "An Essay in Esthetics by Way of a Preface" (1914). He describes this essay as a radical assertion of realism that acknowledges objects as holding "equally rich independent lives."[112] In this short essay, Ortega y Gasset writes:

> There is the same difference between a pain that someone tells me about and a pain that I feel as there is between the red that I see and the being red of this red leather box. Being red is for it what hurting is for me... Just as there is an I-John Doe, there is also an I-red, an I-water, and an I-star. Everything, from a point of view within itself, is an "I."[113]

Not only objects but qualities are described as "I"s; Harman observes that this is not contingent on a being or object having what we might consider to be consciousness, but simply that each being or object *is* a thing; as a human, I can self-reflect on my own consciousness, but I am still not capable of completely exhausting my knowledge of what

---

111 Morton, *Being Ecological*, 47.

112 Harman, *Object-Oriented Ontology*, 67.

113 Ortega y Gasset, "An Essay in Esthetics," 134.

it is to be this particular "I." Similarly, Harman argues, "it follows that every non-human object can also be called an 'I' in the sense of having a definite inwardness that can never fully be grasped."[114]

Ortega y Gasset, Harman asserts, places emphasis on art that seeks not to provide us with knowledge of a thing but to present the thing to us in the act of executing itself while simultaneously preserving its inwardness, a "touching without touching."[115] Metaphor, Ortega y Gasset writes, is central to this presentation; metaphor is an "elementary aesthetic object, the beautiful cell [*la célula bella*]."[116] Art, Harman argues, seems to present to us the "inwardness of things … the *executant* reality of things in their own right, quite apart from how they are seen or used."[117] More recently, the biologist and philosopher Andreas Weber, in his book *Enlivenment: Towards a Poetics for the Anthropocene* (2019), makes a similar argument for the important role of art where each artistic work "is an act of aliveness. It cannot be demonstrated or represented; it can only be shared."[118] This is a variation of Harman's concept of metaphor's executant function. Weber writes that the promise of such art is that it speaks to "a mesh of existential relationships—a quite real 'web of life.'"[119] He contrasts "objective" or "inductive" logic with "subjective," "abductive" logic, the "poetic argument" that rests upon "speculative insight."[120] Here he veers towards Harman's discussion of metaphor.

Similarly, Tim Lilburn, often in consort with philosopher/poet Jan Zwicky, poets Robert Bringhurst and Don McKay, explored

---

114 Harman, *Object-Oriented Ontology*, 90.

115 Harman, *Object-Oriented Ontology*, 82.

116 Ortega y Gasset, "An Essay in Esthetics," 140.

117 Harman, *Object-Oriented Ontology*, 78.

118 Weber, *Enlivenment*, 46.

119 Weber, *Enlivenment*, 48.

120 Weber, *Enlivenment*, 86.

in the 1980s and '90s and beyond, the idea of poetry as a way of knowing. In *Living in the World as If It Were Home*, Lilburn writes, "[poetry's] curiosity yearns beyond this barrier of intelligibility to know the withinness of things."[121] Their body of work hums all around but is beyond the scope of this little book.

Consider a metaphor such as "the blue gas flame of a crocus."[122] As readers, Harman argues, we take the place of the real object, the crocus, in a theatrical gesture, and embrace the qualities of a blue gas flame. Harman puts it this way: "metaphor uses a different method than digging downward to the things themselves. Instead, it replaces the absent [crocus] with *us ourselves* as the real object that embraces the qualities of the flame."[123] To what extent is Harman's emphasis here on the theatricality of metaphor, where the human reader of the metaphor substitutes herself for the crocus, much different from Kantian correlationism, which posits a human interpreter or correlator? The only real object we have any access to is oneself—I am still required to take the place of the crocus and experience the nature of the blue gas flame, which has been transferred over to me as crocus. However, there is an important sympathetic element here, a variant of Keats's sparrow. We imagine ourselves as a crocus, slim and blue as a gas flame, piercing earth to emerge, burning in the spring light. Metaphor functions as bridge (carries us over, as its etymology suggests) to experience in a theatrical ("executant") exchange what it is like to be the crocus, aspects of the blue gas flame transferred to that of the emerging

---

121 Lilburn, *Living in the World as If It Were Home*, 6.

122 I have used one of my own metaphors from *Karyotype* (Brick Books, 2015), similar to the one presented by Ortega y Gasset as it is less complicated; Harman discusses the metaphor employed by Ortega y Gasset (cypress as ghost of a dead flame).

123 Harman, *Object-Oriented Ontology*, 83.

flower. The poem is always executant, latent until read or performed by the reader; so, too, is the crocus as it becomes blue gas flame.

Harman argues there are five important features of metaphor, as he extrapolates from Ortega y Gasset's essay:

1. metaphor gives us something *like* the thing in itself, in its own right;
2. metaphors are non-reciprocal (the crocus does not lend something to the flame);
3. metaphors are asymmetrical (the focus is on the crocus, not the flame);
4. the only real object available is the self; and
5. "metaphor is an act of coupling rather than uncoupling."[124]

On this last point, he means that metaphor provides a more intimate form of experience—a sympathetic kind of knowing—while cognition is most typically cooler and more distant (subject/object; sight over the intimacy of hearing). He argues we are not undermining the object, the crocus, because we have attached ourselves to it; again, this is negative capability, sympathetic attachment. He also asks, as I have, Might this simply be another version of correlationism? No, he concludes, because it's a "new amalgamated reality formed from the reader (who poses as a [crocus] object) and the qualities of the

124 Harman, *Object-Oriented Ontology*, 87. I would disagree with Harman that metaphors are non-reciprocal and asymmetrical; I believe they are far more porous and witchy than his typology suggests.

flame."[125] That is, it is a compound, not a correlative, relationship; the reader forms a compound with the object metaphorized. Ultimately, it seems to come down to the idea that OOO and metaphor are more sincere in their dedication to the independent existence of the thing in itself, capable of existing in uncertainty and doubt.

PANPSYCHISM | *RAINFOREST TEAMING WITH CONSCIOUSNESS*

> Panpsychism has the potential to transform our relationship with the natural world. If panpsychism is true, the rain forest is teeming with consciousness. —PHILIP GOFF, *Galileo's Error: Foundations for a New Science of Consciousness* (2019)

I am lying in a tent in Casx'ou, which means "sea foam" in the Pacheedaht / Ditidaht language; this is a camp formerly known as R+R at Fairy Creek. It is almost 7 pm, a beautiful, sometimes sunny, sometimes spitting-with-rain day on a Tuesday in early May 2022. Indigenous organizers and land defender allies are gearing up for a third season at Fairy Creek. My colleague Foxtrot and I drove in yesterday: a ferry from Tsawwassen to Schwarz Bay, a two-hour drive along Pacific Marine to Port Renfrew, then past what used to be Roadside and HQ at Granite Main, where only the Teal-Jones guards remain in place; no land defender camp, no watch, no fire. We turned at last onto Lens Main, a forest service road, then Bear Creek Main, to this camp near San Juan Creek. We were met at the entrance by Tall-Tree and others, on watch, sitting around the fire inside a makeshift tarpee shelter and a shorn log erected as a barrier to cars. I rolled down my window, said that I was Crow, with

---

125 Harman, *Object-Oriented Ontology*, 88.

Foxtrot. We had let them know via Signal that we'd be arriving on the one o'clock ferry. Tall-Tree pulled aside the barrier and we drove in, parked. Introductions were made. *Crow. Foxtrot. Flying Squirrel. Sunshine. Tall-Tree.* We sat on the ground in a circle by the gate, and Tall-Tree went through the protocols: the well-being and protection of Indigenous hosts and BIPOC land defenders; how many queer, BIPOC, Indigenous folk were alienated over the last two years at Fairy Creek. That we are here on Pacheedaht land, at the invitation of Elder Bill Jones. That when Bill Jones or Whale Tail speaks, we listen; that their word is the closest we have to law here on this land. To make connections to this land—to the rocks, to the trees. To listen.

Flying Squirrel arrived a few days ago from Ontario; Sunshine has medical skills and has been around since the beginning of the protests. There aren't many people here in the camp, but perhaps there are more out on the mountain, in the injunction zone, preparing for the long summer ahead. We are all here because we want to protect the old-growth forest and all the creatures sustained within it. An old-growth yellow cedar is an elder, not a resource worth a stumpage fee of $80.87 per cubic metre. Grandmother Tree. Oldgrowth specklebelly lichen. Screech owl.

Last night I fell asleep to the calls of the Pacific tree frogs, my heartbeat synchronizing to their call. They are invisible in nearby pools of standing water, singing through the night. And I woke to birdsong, a scatter of amorous frogs still awake, the steady drilling of a sapsucker not far off. I am one of many species, living, breathing, withdrawn, dark.

Panpsychism has recently come back into favour in philosophical theories of consciousness and seems complementary to object-oriented ontology, in that it also questions the scientific focus on quantitative method and displaces *human* consciousness as central to ontology. Philip Goff, a contemporary philosopher of panpsychism, observes that the scientific revolution "was premised on *putting consciousness outside of the domain of scientific inquiry*."[126] His book, *Galileo's Error*, identifies the crucial flaw in Galileo's insistence on the language of mathematics as the only valid language to describe the nature of the universe while deliberately ruling out consciousness and qualia—as Descartes observed, "Nothing is more certain than consciousness, and yet nothing is harder to incorporate into our scientific picture of the world."[127] The easiest way to deal with the unruliness of qualia was to deem it unmeasurable and beyond the scope of science. Galileo argued that philosophy (natural science)

> is written in this grand book, the universe, which stands continually open to our gaze, but it cannot be understood unless one first learns to comprehend the language and read the letters in which it is composed. It is written in the language of mathematics . . . without them, one wanders about in a dark labyrinth.[128]

That is, Galileo denied sensory qualities (qualia) within his world view, as qualia could not be "captured in the purely quantitative language of mathematics." Goff observes, "How could an equation ever explain to someone what it's like to see red, or to taste paprika? How could an abstract mathematical description convey the sweet smell of flowers?"[129] Galileo's reimagining of the material world necessarily severed sensory qualities from objects because these qualities could not be quantified:

---

126 Goff, *Galileo's Error*, 13. Emphasis in original.

127 Descartes quoted in Goff, *Galileo's Error*, 5.

128 Galileo quoted in Goff, *Galileo's Error*, 16.

129 Goff, *Galileo's Error*, 16.

"Paprika isn't really spicy, flowers don't really smell of anything and objects aren't really coloured. In Galileo's reimagined world, material objects have only the following characteristics: size, shape, location, motion."[130] Galileo believed that the qualia are in the "soul," and that the material world and the soul constitute two radically distinct entities: material objects with size, shape, location, motion; and souls, which are conscious and capable of receiving rich sensory perception.

This radical fiat—qualia cannot be quantified and therefore cannot be included in a scientific description of the material world—severs much of our experience and relationship to the world from our scientific understanding of it. Goff argues, "the basic reality of consciousness is a datum in its own right."[131]

The implications of panpsychism for ecological thought are clear. As Goff observes, with specific reference to the climate emergency, if consciousness is the intrinsic nature of matter, then this necessarily transforms our relationships within the natural world:

> If panpsychism is true, the rain forest is teeming with consciousness. As conscious entities, trees have value in their own right: chopping one down becomes an action of immediate moral significance. Moreover, on the panpsychist worldview, humans have a deep affinity with the natural world: we are conscious creatures embedded in a world of consciousness.[132]

---

130 Goff, *Galileo's Error*, 16–17.
131 Goff, *Galileo's Error*, 11.
132 Goff, *Galileo's Error*, 191.

Goff asks how might children's perceptions of the forest change if they were raised to "accept the tree as an individual locus of sentience."[133] Indigenous cultures that have managed to remain with some traditions intact already know this. *Grandmother Tree. Grandfather Tree.* He references UBC Forestry professor Suzanne Simard's work on what she has called "mother trees": those trees (such as her initial experiments with Douglas fir and paper birch) linked by mycorrhizal networks, where a mother tree might share elements to those in greater need and bequeath her own nutrients to her offspring upon expiration. Plants, Goff further argues, have been observed to communicate via chemical signals, to learn to grow towards resources, to remember seasons of drought and prepare accordingly for future seasons. He observes, "On the basis of all this, we now know that plants communicate, learn, and remember. I see no reason other than anthropic prejudice not to ascribe to them a conscious life of their own."[134] Consciousness, then, must be seen as a continuum that runs through all matter, all being.

It is Thursday night, May 12, 2022. 10:58 pm. Casx'ou. Droplets of rain. The frogs sing off and on. Humans, distant: a cough, rasp of a tent closure. We had a circle meeting around the fire this afternoon to address the movement going forward. There are still so few of us. How do we maintain a culture of security yet also welcome newcomers; how can the long-timers acknowledge the newcomer presence, yet protect themselves, within a culture of RCMP surveillance, and with a sense of deep urgency to protect the trees? It was observed that the snow will soon be gone high on the mountain, at Heli, at Ridge, and the logging will begin; how many trees will be lost while

133 Goff, *Galileo's Error*, 191.

134 Goff, *Galileo's Error*, 194.

we wait for reinforcements? Someone says the students are waiting to come in the summer months, in July and August. Matihi says *no, no*—it will be too late then, the trees will already have fallen.

Industry has no trouble; the NDP government, Teal-Jones, the forestry lobby—all are organized hierarchically, determined by the bottom line. Capitalism requires growth, profit, stockpiling, the churning up of natural resources into more capital. But here, we are individuals, Indigenous, settler allies, many broken, survivors, neurodivergent, some systematically targeted by the justice system and the RCMP, but all with a commitment to a non-hierarchical, consensus-based model, struggling to maintain some form of guerilla-style organization while hamstrung by the need for secrecy and personal safety.

Tonight, there are twelve of us around the fire. The rain comes down steadily. We collect it in pans and buckets for dishwater, which we heat on the campfire. We acknowledge the flying beings, the ones with sharp teeth, the ones who swim, the stones around the fire, the trees, the rain. We leave an offering for the mice, who come to scoop up lard with tiny nails. We place scraps of our food on the fire, for the Creator. We are here not for ourselves but for Ada'itsx, for Grandfather Tree, for Grandmother Tree. For oldgrowth specklebelly lichen, for raven, for tree frog.

Here we stand by the river
through the wind, the rain, and snow.
In the wind our branches may quiver
we may sway but we will stay.
And one day, when we fall
we will rot and we will crumble.
But we know that we have given our all
and we will feed the seeds of tomorrow.

POSTSCRIPT: SOME NOTES ON AN OLDGROWTH SPECKLEBELLY LICHEN POEM

How might the microecosystem of the poem feel and sound? What will be its acoustic niche? What rhythm? What form? How will I stitch the poem's ecosystem into its seams, make audible its dehiscence, trace the externalities, bear furious witness, fight for life on this Earth for the next seven generations of human and more-than-human kin?

I sift through my scribbled notes, my leaf-green notebooks, camp journals, iNaturalist maps, and photographs. I'm still looking. But as I have written and revised this manuscript, I have the glimmer of a process going forward—a score, a poem composed like a Miebach sculpture, the raw data of citizen scientists, a lichenous form.

1. There's tension between elegy, one of the oldest lyric forms, and the urgent need to channel grief into rage in order to fight for the survival of oldgrowth specklebelly lichen and yellow cedar and red sapsucker and marbled murrelet. Elegy is an inadequate response to the sixth mass extinction. Elegy is one of the oldest forms and has always incorporated rage; resist the urge to mourn and resolve.

2. Karl Marx wrote of the "metabolic rift" that occurred when humans shifted to industrial agriculture in the nineteenth century, characterizing it as a kind of severing of humans from older agricultural methods that had participated in a reciprocal cycle of moving matter and energy through form, in which all kinds of beings participated in making the layered earth and its formations. Marx was thinking of soil depletion, the draining of key minerals from fields, leaving formerly fertile soil barren (everything taken, nothing returned to the land), which became even more starkly

apparent with the depletion of guano, rich in phosphate and nitrogen, which was initially used to replenish the soil.[1]

I like the analogy of metabolism in relation to the intermeshing of human and other makers with the elements of the world—in fact, it is not analogy so much as literal description, as metabolism refers to the transformation of energy into food, which is then turned into energy again and so on through trophic levels. From sunlight and carbon, everything flows. Earlier, I've quoted Bateson's beautiful and startling observation: "We commonly think of animals and plants as matter, but they are really systems through which matter is continually passing."[2] I'd like to think of a lyric ecopoem in this way as well, as a system through which materials and energy (words, information, ideas, song) pour. The lyric ecopoem approaches the metabolic rift as a making, a restitching.

3. I asked at the beginning of this little book, What tools might lyric poetry bring to a project of co-making the world with our more-than-human kin, in the face of breached planetary boundaries, global heating, insectageddon, a slow-burning ecological catastrophe? What furious witness might poetry offer? What shining and lichenous form? My answers must come in the form of poetry, of poems and books of poetry by perhaps me, and by many others.

---

1 Initially, guano, packed with phosphate, nitrates, potassium-rich kainite, and coprolites, allowed "industrial civilization to escape the limitations imposed by nutrient recycling" (Cushman, *Guano and the Opening of the Pacific World*, 40). Yet when guano began to run out, it led to trade battles and wars. Cushman attributes the beginnings of US imperialism to the drive to secure sources of guano for agricultural production.

2 Bateson quoted in Goward, Essay v, "Twelve Readings," 1.

4. I recall my list of key elements. *The lyric ecopoem I seek to write*:

- is an aperture, a clearing, and seeks attunement: with the world as it currently exists in its fractured and desolate being, and with other beings.

- is medial and recalls its material being: paper, ink, tent, nest, shell, clay; a poem is a made thing and takes cues from the chickadee nest and the snail shell; it is an act of co-making this world; it is an ecosystem, self-aware of and displaying the externalities that produced it.

- is vigilant; uses the right hemispheric forms of broadband attention; is alert, vigilant, practises a sustained attention; is open to new possibilities, sights and sounds, so as to participate in a redistribution of sentience.

- is an ecological witness, in the manner of field notes.

- is open to listening and imagining the *Umwelt* of other beings and our more-than-human kin; will carry the music of these *Umwelten*.

- will acknowledge and draw strength from Indigenous models of grounding song in specific place, in the knowledge that "everything is one."

- will respect the darkness of other beings, in their withdrawing.

5. As I revise this postscript, Nathalie Miebach writes in an Instagram post, "Something also happens when you allow data to build its own metaphor, driven by

the human experiences it is connected to."[3] Timothy Morton writes, in *Being Ecological* (2018),

> Art is important to understanding our relationship to nonhumans, to grasping an object-oriented ontological sense of our existence. Art fails in this regard when it tries to mimic the transmission of sheer quantities of data; it's not artful enough. This isn't just a matter of effective persuasion. As a matter of fact, that's the trouble with ecological data art. The aesthetic experience isn't really about data—it's about data-*ness*, the qualities we experience when we apprehend something... The aesthetic experience is about *solidarity* with what is given.[4]

I am not suggesting that the two of them agree on what might be "successful" ecological data art.[5] Morton describes with approval a glacial installation in Paris, in which participant-observers were invited to interact with a piece of melting ice. This is quite unlike the meticulous attention Miebach pays to data points in her own sculptures, which draw out more explicit stories from data. Yet Miebach's sculptures, as with the artwork Morton describes, both engage in solidarity with respect to what is "given" by the data. And they each raise important questions about such

---

3 Nathalie Miebach (@miebachsculpture), "What Is Data?," Instagram post, February 4, 2024.

4 Morton, *Being Ecological*, 121.

5 Morton aligns failed "ecological data art" with "ecological writing" that "has the same format, roughly speaking, as information dump mode," which can be overwhelming and alienating. *Being Ecological*, 28.

art and have guided my own thinking about what happens when data is translated into the language of poetry.

What might it mean to allow form to be determined by data, in a poem, whose materials are words? What would it mean to be true to the data, where data is a portion of a poem's materials, data which I have been steadily assembling, on a lichen I have not yet seen in situ? Photographs. Diagrams. Government monographs. Instagram posts. Messages on Signal. More searching. This past weekend (November 2023), Foxtrot and I returned to Fairy Creek. Before we left, I poured over Gaia GPS topographical maps, iNaturalist observations of oldgrowth specklebelly lichen, satellite images on Google Earth. I began at Port Renfrew and zoomed in, slowly, slowly—Pacific Marine road, Five Mile FSR, Fairy Creek FSR, the faintly greened-over track of an old logging road. New cutblocks. Older cutblocks with a fuzz of new growth. Many of the original sightings of oldgrowth specklebelly in Upper Granite Creek are gone; the pink markers of observations superimposed on satellite images show where the clear cuts destroyed whole communities of lichen.

I wondered if it might be possible to hike up to the two southern-most sightings, which still seemed untouched and were originally observed on August 6, 2022, by Natasha Lavdovsky. Would they still be there, over a year later?

Our first day, after a ferry from Tsawwassen to Nanaimo and a two-hour drive across the island to Lake Cowichan and then along Pacific Marine, we parked at the gate that blocks access to Five Mile Road. The FSRs along Pacific Marine are still blocked by gates controlled by Teal-Jones, barring public access; these are supposed to be removed when the injunction expires at the end of 2023. We parked Foxtrot's car and hiked up Five Mile Road until we reached the juncture with Fairy Creek Road. A sign warned that the road had been decommissioned and to proceed at our own risk. Vines had begun to reach across the roadway; spikes of green at intervals; a green resurgence.

At dusk we stopped, pitched our tents, and made a small campfire that struggled to burn in the wind. The next day we continued, leaving most of our gear and bringing only survival essentials. We found a much older logging road overtaken by tall slim alders that shone like a cathedral's pillars in the second-growth forest's darkness. The undergrowth grew thicker and became more difficult to traverse. Occasionally we'd find the stump of an old-growth cedar, or an ancient giant cut down but never retrieved, its torso strewn across the steeply canted mountain and softened with rot. We came to within perhaps a kilometre and a half of our destination, which I'd programmed into Gaia GPS—48.632738, -124.322992—before deciding to turn back, not having time to go farther and return before nightfall. At camp, we ate hummus and pita, drank tea, and agreed we would come back again, that we would keep looking.

6. And even as I write this, I receive a Signal from Rutabaga, asking how our trip went and letting me know of some oldgrowth specklebelly lichen he found off Gordon Main:

> *Yeah, it can be tricky to determine from a distance how bushwacky a forest "shortcut" will be. I usually aim for forests with tall trees, as sparsely placed as possible*

(forests of new-growth trees seem to have taller shrubs). How far along the road did you get with your vehicle?

The photos include:

- *The one hemlock we saw the specklebelly on, which is at: 48.XXXXX, -124.XXXXX*[6]
- *Some of the boundary tags in the area*
- *A screenshot of the logging road, where the dotted line I drew is my best guess re the newest extension of the road (not depicted yet on googlemaps or applemaps), the red star is the new end of the road, and the dot is the specklebelly, 30–40 ft into the forest south of the road.*

It's at the end of a logging road that's off of Gordon River Rd, a few km south of Truck Rd 11 (where a recent front-line camp was). Re vehicle access, along the new extension, there are some very steep areas, with big chunky gravel, and there's no turnaround at the end. If you were to park 1 km before the new end of the road, you could avoid 1 or 2 sketchy stretches. This is an approved cutblock, so unlikely it would get shut down due to the specklebelly sighting. Would be great to know though how much more specklebelly is in that area besides that one tree, and whether it is within the approved cutblock.

The next time you go searching, if you go on a weekend,

---

6 I have redacted the specific coordinates to safeguard the lichen—an abundance of caution, perhaps unnecessary; these have not yet been identified on iNaturalist and may already be gone, having been within the boundaries of an approved cutblock.

is there by chance any space for 1 more in your vehicle?
If yer full, that's cool, I've already been there :)[7]

His hope is to find more oldgrowth specklebelly lichen on not-yet-approved cutblocks in order to save the trees. I write back, yes, yes, 100%.

7. I am still at the beginning of my journey to learn about the morphology, anatomy, physiology, phylogeny of lichens, about their symbiotic and communal ways of being in the world, about oldgrowth specklebelly lichen and its beautiful, retreating, ancient presence. I have not even begun to approach other oldgrowth lichens, mosses, ferns, and organisms in their myriad variations and ways of being. I'm still thinking about a lichenous sympoietic form, in poetry, and how my poem on oldgrowth specklebelly lichen might rest within the larger ecosystem of a book that is rooted in Ada'itsx / Fairy Creek. These questions float nearby, subconscious, retreating: How might the microecosystem of the poem feel and sound? What will be its acoustic niche? What rhythm? What form? How will I stitch the poem's ecosystem into its seams, make audible its dehiscence, trace the externalities, bear furious witness, fight for life on this Earth for the next seven generations of human and more-than-human kin?

8. What will I carry in my backpack? All the necessary gear—my one-person tent and my sleeping bag, hatchet and multitool, notebook, compass, flint, whistle—all these small, crucial tools for basic survival. I'll carry the idea of a Miebach sculpture, its textural complexity, where each bead, dowel, and ribbon

7 Private communication with author, November 3, 2023.

is a datapoint, form determined by the tensions inherent in the data as her reeds respond to the numbers. I will try to fail with the material a thousand times; I will keep searching; I will test its strengths, its flexibilities and weaknesses so as to understand it. I will carry Seamus Heaney's idea of a documentary adequacy, Fred Wah's search for the "right words" so that he can speak to the river, Rita Wong's reminder of reciprocity and humility, a reminder to ask, *What can my poem give back*? I'll carry Robin Wall Kimmerer's discussion of the voices of mosses: "The names we give ourselves are a powerful form of self-determination, of declaring ourselves sovereign territory. Outside the circle, scientific names for mosses may suffice, but within the circle, what do they call themselves?"[8] I will carry Trevor Goward's beautiful observations on lichen, his reading of the lichen thallus that embodies these and other concepts—community, conversation, scale-free network, transcription, microecosystem, portal, technology for thinking; his search for terms to describe these ideas, aware of our conceptual limitations and our "overwhelming allegiance to words."[9] I will carry the desire to respect the reality of the oldgrowth specklebelly lichen, in its own being, outside of the conceptual, verbal, narrative mapping of the human poet.

Thinking of Simone Weil's conception of *le vide*, I'll make space within myself. I'll wait, patiently. I'll be vigilant. I'll attend.

8 Kimmerer, *Gathering Moss*.

9 Goward, Essay VII, "Twelve Readings," 2.

ACKNOWLEDGEMENTS

I'm grateful to live in the rainforest on the edge of the Salish Sea, on the unceded, traditional territories of the Coast Salish Peoples, including the land of the q̓íc̓əy̓, q'ʷa:n̓ƛ̓ən̓, kʷikʷəƛ̓əm, xʷməθkʷəy̓əm, qiqéyt, Skwxwú7mesh, scəw̓aθən, and səlilwətaɬ Peoples.

My deep gratitude to Oskana Poetry & Poetics / University of Regina Press and in particular to Randy Lundy, editor of the Oskana series; acquisition editors Karen Clark and Rachel Stapleton; managing editor Shannon Parr; copy-editor Kelly Laycock; proofreader Crissy Boylan; John van der Woude, who designed the book; and David Fassett for the elegant cover design. My gratitude to Natasha Lavdovsky for providing the image of oldgrowth specklebelly. You have all been so generous and kind. My thanks to Douglas College for providing a four-month education leave during the writing of this book, and to the anonymous readers who provided such thoughtful feedback on an early draft.

This book is seeded with some beautiful poems. Every effort has been made to secure permissions for those not in the public domain. The excerpt from "Hotline to the Gulf" is reproduced by kind permission of Pat Lowther's daughters, Beth and Christine. "Negative Space" is reproduced courtesy of Lorna Crozier. Poetry on pages 87 and 88 are from Ariel Gordon's *TreeTalk* and are used with kind permission from At Bay Press. Poems quoted from *Elegies of Rotting Stars* are courtesy of Tiffany Morris. The song "Here We Stand" was "caught from the trees" in the Walbran and is kindly shared here, along with the story of its origin, by Ayden Craty-Bauer. Permissions to reproduce the excerpt from Ted Hughes's *Moortown Diary* have been kindly granted by Faber, and permissions to reproduce the excerpt from *The Poems of Emily Dickinson: Reading Edition* by Harvard University Press.

I am also grateful for conversations on aspects of ecology, art, activism, music, and myriad other things with Hazel Fairbairn, Amy-Claire Huestis, and Noah Quastel. And a heartfelt thank-you to Trevor Goward, Natasha Lavdovsky, Nathalie Miebach, and Derek Woods for their generosity of time in discussing their beautiful, important work with me. I have no formal training in biology, botany, or ecology, so any wild misunderstandings expressed here of lichens and old-growth forests are my own.

Early versions of this book were drafted while staying at various house and yurt sits organized by Naava Smolash on Cortes Island. I'm grateful to have been introduced to this beautiful island (and its tiny green inchworms) through her warm gatherings of like-minded friends and writers.

Foxtrot (aka Ivana Čikeš)—this book would not exist without you: Steadfast comrade and friend, you are always ready to pack a bag and head into the forest with me when the trees call.

My respect and love to everyone who offered their time and care at Ada'itsx / Fairy Creek over the years: Pacheedaht Elder Bill Jones, the matriarchs, the builders, the makers, the dishwashers, the arrestees, Grandmother Tree, Grandfather Tree, and all the many defenders whom I will never know beyond a camp name, a voice in the dark, a linked arm bracing mine on the barricade.

"A22 Network." Accessed May 1, 2023. https://a22network.org/en/#declaration.

Abbott, Amory, and Liz Toohey-Wiese, eds. *Fire Season.* 3 vols. https://fireseason.org.

"About." iNaturalist. Last updated September 10, 2024. https://www.inaturalist.org/pages/about.

"About." Lobe Studio. Accessed April 23, 2025. https://lobestudio.ca/about.

Abram, David. *The Spell of the Sensuous: Perception and Language in a More-Than-Human World.* Vintage, 1997.

Acker, Maleea. "Artist Finds New Population of Rare Imperiled Lichen at Fairy Creek." *Focus on Victoria,* August 3, 2021. https://www.focusonvictoria.ca/forests/87.

Adamatzky, Andrew. "Language of Fungi Derived from Their Electrical Spiking Activity." *Royal Society Open Science* 9, no. 211926 (2022). https://doi.org/10.1098/rsos.211926.

Aisch, Gregor, Sarah Almukhtar, Jeremy Ashkenas, Matthew Bloch, Audrey Carlsen, Jose A. Delreal, Ford Fessenden, K.K. Rebecca Lai, Adam Pearce, Anjali Singhvi, and Karen Yourish. "Thousands Cried for Help as Houston Flooded." *The New York Times,* August 30, 2017. https://www.nytimes.com/interactive/2017/08/30/us/houston-flood-rescue-cries-for-help.html.

Anonymous. *Desert.* The Anarchist Library, 2011. https://theanarchistlibrary.org/library/anonymous-desert.

Aschenbrenner, Ines A., Tomislav Cernava, Gabriele Berg, and Martin Grube. "Understanding Microbial Multi-Species Symbioses." *Frontiers in Microbiology* 7 (2016). https://doi.org/10.3389/fmicb.2016.00180.

Avery, Dan. "Apple Breaks Ties with 12 Suppliers over Concerns About 'Conflict Minerals' Violations." *CNet,* February 10, 2022. https://www.cnet.com/tech/apple-breaks-ties-with-12-suppliers-over-concerns-about-conflict-minerals-violations.

Bartlett, Cheryl, Murdena Marshall, and Albert Marshall. "Two-Eyed Seeing and Other Lessons Learned Within a Co-Learning Journey of Bringing Together Indigenous and Mainstream Knowledges and Ways of Knowing." *Journal of Environmental Studies and Sciences* 2 (2012): 331–40. https://doi.org/10.1007/s13412-012-0086-8.

Bawaka Country, Sarah Wright, Sandie Suchet-Pearson, Kate Lloyd, Laklak Burarrwanga, Ritjilili Ganambarr, Merrkiyawuy Ganambarr-Stubbs, Banbapuy Ganambarr, Djawundil Maymuru, and Jill Sweeney. "Gathering of the Clouds: Attending to Indigenous Understandings of Time and Climate Through Songspirals." *Geoforum* 108 (2020): 295–304. https://doi.org/10.1016/j.geoforum.2019.05.017.

BC RCMP. "Critical Response Unit—British Columbia (CRU-BC)." Royal Canadian Mounted Police. Last updated September 10, 2024. https://rcmp.ca/en/bc/police-services/critical-response-unit-british-columbia.

Beiler, Kevin J., Daniel M. Durall, Suzanne W. Simard, Sheri A. Maxwell, and Annette M. Kretzer. "Architecture of the Wood-Wide-Web: *Rhizopogon* spp. Genets Link Multiple Douglas-Fir Cohorts." *New Phytologist* 185, no. 2 (2010): 543–53. https://doi.org/10.1111/j.1469-8137.2009.03069.x.

Bennett, Jane. *Vibrant Matter: A Political Ecology of Things*. Duke University Press, 2010.

"Blaauw Eco Forest." Blaauw Eco Forest. Accessed November 17, 2023. http://blaauwecoforest.ca.

Blasing, Mutlu Konuk. *Lyric Poetry: The Pain and the Pleasure of Words*. Princeton University Press, 2007.

Bloch, Julia. *Lyric Trade: Reading the Subject in the Postwar Long Poem*. University of Iowa Press, 2024.

Blumenau, Ralph. "Kant and the Thing in Itself." *Philosophy Now* 31 (2001). https://philosophynow.org/issues/31/Kant_and_the_Thing_in_Itself.

Borodale, Sean. *Bee Journal*. Cape Poetry, 2012.

Bourgon, Lyndsie. "How Thousand-Year-Old Trees Became the New Ivory." Future of Conservation Special Report. *Smithsonian Magazine*, May 22, 2017. https://www.smithsonianmag.com/science-nature/how-thousand-year-old-trees-became-new-ivory-180963365.

Bringhurst, Robert, and Jan Zwicky. *Learning to Die: Wisdom in the Age of Climate Crisis*. University of Regina Press, 2018.

Broadland, David. "Teal Cedar's Big, Dirty Secret." *Focus on Victoria*, June 29, 2021. https://www.focusonvictoria.ca/forests/81.

Bruns, Gerald L. *The Material of Poetry: Sketches for a Philosophical Poetics*. University of Georgia Press, 2012.

———. *Modern Poetry and the Idea of Language*. Yale University Press, 1974.

Bureau of Land Management. "Management Recommendations for *Pseudocyphellaria rainierensis* Imshaug, Version 2.0." US Department of the Interior. https://www.blm.gov/or/plans/surveyandmanage/MR/Lichens/PSRA_V2.pdf. (No longer available.) Accessed August 4, 2023.

Burke, Kathryn. "The Sami Yoik." Sami Culture. Accessed August 16, 2023. https://www.laits.utexas.edu/sami/diehtu/giella/music/yoiksunna.htm.

Calvo, Paco. "What Is It Like to Be a Plant?" *Journal of Consciousness Studies* 24, no. 9–10 (2017): 205–27.

Calvo, Paco, František Baluška, and Anthony Trewavas. "Integrated Information as a Possible Basis for Plant Consciousness." *Biochemical and Biophysical Research Communications* 564 (2021): 158–65. https://doi.org/10.1016/j.bbrc.2020.10.022.

Chan, Adam. "BC Heat Dome Led to 48 Deaths on Vancouver Island: Coroners." *CTV News*, November 1, 2021. https://www.ctvnews.ca/vancouver/vancouver-island/article/bc-heat-dome-led-to-48-deaths-on-vancouver-island-coroners.

Chiu, Allyson. "An Orca Calf Died Shortly After Being Born, Her Grieving Mother Has Carried Her Body for Days." *The Washington Post*, July 27, 2018. https://www.washingtonpost.com/news/morning-mix/wp/2018/07/27/an-orca-calf-died-shortly-after-being-born-her-grieving-mother-has-carried-her-body-for-days.

Close, Hannah. "The Poetics of Ecology: A Conversation with Andreas Weber." The Dark Mountain Project. February 23, 2022. https://dark-mountain.net/the-poetics-of-ecology.

Coles, Sidney. "BC Extends Old Growth Deferral in Fairy Creek." *Capital Daily*. February 4, 2025. https://www.capitaldaily.ca/news/bc-extends-old-growth-deferral-fairy-creek.

Collis, Stephen. *Once in Blockadia*. Talonbooks, 2016.

Committee on the Status of Endangered Wildlife in Canada. "COSEWIC Assessment and Status Report on the Oldgrowth Specklebelly *Pseudocyphellaria rainierensis* in Canada." In *Special Concern 2010*. COSEWIC, 2010. https://www.sararegistry.gc.ca/virtual_sara/files/cosewic/sr_Oldgrowth%20Specklebelly_0810_e.pdf.

Cordasco, Laura. "BC Judge Refuses to Extend Court Injunction at Fairy Creek." *Vancouver Sun*, September 29, 2021. https://vancouversun.com/news/local-news/b-c-judge-refuses-to-extend-the-injunction-at-fairy-creek.

Corey, Joshua. "The Challenge of Francis Ponge." Introduction to *Partisan of Things* by Francis Ponge. Translated by Joshua Corey and Jean-Luc Garneau. Kenning Editions, 2018.

Cowasuck Band of the Pennacook Abenaki. "Lesson 10—Animal Names." The Abenaki Language. Accessed June 10, 2023. https://www.cowasuck.org/language/lesson-10.html.

Crawford, Lars. "Killer Whales Are Non-Human Persons." Greymattersjournal.org, December 7, 2013. https://greymattersjournal.com/killer-whales-are-non-human-persons.

Cushman, Gregory T. *Guano and the Opening of the Pacific World: A Global Ecological History*. Cambridge University Press, 2013.

Dearing, Jessey, dir. "At War for the Forest: On the Front Lines at Fairy Creek." Brut America. YouTube, December 18, 2021. 14 min., 56 sec. https://www.youtube.com/watch?v=GrXoFoARi9g.

Derdeyn, Stuart. "From Mushroom Jazz to Bark-Rocking Beats, Bio-sonification Suits Ruby Singh's Sound." *Vancouver Sun*, November 16, 2023. https://vancouversun.com/entertainment/from-mushroom-jazz-to-bark-rocking-beats-bio-sonification-suits-ruby-singhs-sound.

Descartes, René. "Animals Are Machines." In *Animal Rights and Human Obligations*. Edited by Tom Regan and Peter Singer. 2nd ed. Prentice Hall, 1989.

Desjardins, Jeff. "The Extraordinary Raw Materials in an iPhone 6s." *Visual Capitalist*, March 8, 2016. https://www.visualcapitalist.com/extraordinary-raw-materials-iphone-6s.

Des Pres, Terrence. *Praises & Dispraises: Poetry and Politics, the 20th Century*. Penguin, 1989.

Dickinson, Adam. *Anatomic*. Coach House Books, 2018.

———. "'The Human Endocrine System Represents a Kind of Poetics': Adam Dickinson on His Poetic, Chemical Autobiography." *Open Book*. May 24, 2018. https://open-book.ca/News/The-Human-Endocrine-System-Represents-a-Kind-of-Poetics-Adam-Dickinson-on-his-Poetic-Chemical-Autobiography.

Dickinson, Darci, and Glenn R. Kohler. "Western Hemlock Looper." *Forest Insect & Disease Leaflet* 186 (April 2020). US Department of Agriculture, Forest Service. https://www.fs.usda.gov/sites/default/files/users/user3914/FHP-files/FIDL-186-WesternHemlockLooper.pdf.

Dickinson, Emily. "Essential oils are wrung." Poems: Loose sheets, MS Am 1118.3 (249)—J675, Fr772. The Emily Dickinson Collection. Houghton Library, Harvard University. Emily Dickinson Archive online. http://www.edickinson.org.

"Ditidaht-Pacheedaht Language Circle Survival Conversations." Resources on Ditidaht and Pacheedaht. October 16, 2019. https://kwistuup.net/d/files/DPLC-SCs-2p-dtd.pdf.

Egan-Elliott, Roxanne. "RCMP Has Spent Nearly $9 Million Enforcing Fairy Creek Injunction." *Vancouver Sun*, December 29, 2021. https://vancouversun.com/news/local-news/rcmp-has-spent-nearly-9-million-enforcing-fairy-creek-injunction.

———. "Teal-Jones Wins Appeal, Injunction Against Fairy Creek Old-Growth Protests Extended." *Times Colonist*, January 26, 2022. https://www.timescolonist.com/local-news/teal-jones-wins-appeal-to-have-fairy-creek-injunction-extended-4995921.

Fairbairn, Hazel. "'Everything Is Interconnected': Creating the Soundscape for 'Hwlhits'um | signs.'" In *walk quietly / ts'ekw'unshun kws qututhun: walking with respect and honour along the shore: a guided walk at Hwlhits'um (Canoe Pass / Brunswick Point) Ladner, British Columbia*. COHAB Press, 2023. https://walkquietly.ca/assets/walk_quietly.pdf.

Fatur, Miranda. "Looper Moth Outbreak Taking Over Metro Vancouver." *Vancouver CityNews*, September 10, 2020. https://vancouver.citynews.ca/2020/09/10/looper-moth-outbreak-taking-over-metro-vancouver.

Feld, Steven. *Sound and Sentiment: Birds, Weeping, Poetics, and Song in Kaluli Expression*. 3rd ed. Duke University Press, 2012.

———. "Sound Worlds." In *Sound*. Edited by Patricia Kruth and Henry Stobart. Cambridge University Press, 2000.

Fischer, Thilo C., Artur Michalski, and Axel Hausmann. "Geometrid Caterpillar in Eocene Baltic Amber (*Lepidoptera, Geometridae*)." *Nature* 9, no. 17201 (2019). https://doi.org/10.1038/s41598-019-53734-w.

Foltz, Bruce V. *Inhabiting the Earth: Heidegger, Environmental Ethics, and the Metaphysics of Nature*. Humanity Books, 1995.

Foster, John Bellamy. *Marx's Ecology: Materialism and Nature*. Monthly Review Press, 2000.

Franklin, R.W. "The Emily Dickinson Fascicles." *Studies in Bibliography* 36 (1983): 1–20. https://www.jstor.org/stable/40371771.

Franklin, R.W., ed., *The Poems of Emily Dickinson: Reading Edition*. Belknap Press of Harvard University Press, 1999.

Fretwell, Kelly, and Brian Starzomski. "Salmonberry / *Rubus spectabilis*." Biodiversity of the Central Coast. Accessed May 7, 2022. https://www.centralcoastbiodiversity.org/salmonberry-bull-rubus-spectabilis.html.

Garrard, Greg. *Ecocriticism*. 2nd ed. Routledge, 2012.

Gay'wu Group of Women. *Songspirals: Sharing Women's Wisdom of Country Through Songlines*. Allen & Unwin, 2019.

Goff, Philip. *Galileo's Error: Foundations for a New Science of Consciousness*. Pantheon, 2019.

Gordon, Ariel. *TreeTalk*. At Bay Press, 2020.

Goward, Trevor. "Twelve Readings on the Lichen Thallus, I–XII." *Enlichenment*. https://www.waysofenlichenment.net/ways/readings/index. Originally published as "Twelve Readings on the Lichen Thallus XI. Preassembly." *Evansia* 28, no. 1 (2011): 1–17, https://doi.org/10.1639/0747-9859-28.1.1.

Gray, Patricia, Bernie Krause, Jelle Atema, and Roger Searle Payne. "The Music of Nature and the Nature of Music." *Science* 291, no. 5501 (2001): 52–54. https://doi.org/10.1126/science.10.1126/SCIENCE.1056960.

Greene, Roland, Stephen Cushman, Clare Cavanagh, Jahan Ramazani, and Paul Rouzer, eds. "Environment and Poetry." *Princeton Encyclopedia of Poetry and Poetics*. 4th ed. Princeton University Press, 2012.

———. "Lyric." *Princeton Encyclopedia of Poetry and Poetics*. 4th ed. Princeton University Press, 2012.

Greenfield, Patrick. "'Sweet City': The Costa Rica Suburb That Gave Citizenship to Bees, Plants, and Trees." *The Guardian*, April 29, 2020. https://www.theguardian.com/environment/2020/apr/29/sweet-city-the-costa-rica-suburb-that-gave-citizenship-to-bees-plants-and-trees-aoe.

Gunn, Kate. "Injunctions as a Tool of Colonialism." *First Peoples' Law*, July 30, 2022. https://www.firstpeopleslaw.com/public-education/blog/injunctions-as-a-tool-of-colonialism.

Haigney, Sophie. "The Lessons to Be Learned from Forcing Plants to Play Music." NPR Music. NPR, February 21, 2020. https://www.npr

.org/2020/02/21/807821340/the-lessons-to-be-learned-from-forcing-plants-to-play-music.

Hall, Rachel. "Simon Armitage: Poets Can Fight Climate Crisis by Making Us Spellbound by Nature." *The Guardian*, June 2, 2024. https://www.theguardian.com/books/article/2024/jun/02/simon-armitage-poets-can-fight-climate-crisis-by-making-us-spellbound-by-nature.

Haraway, Donna J. *Staying with the Trouble: Making Kin in the Chthulucene.* Duke University Press, 2016.

Harman, Graham. *Object-Oriented Ontology: A New Theory of Everything.* Pelican, 2018.

———. *Tool-Being: Heidegger and the Metaphysics of Objects.* Open Court, 2002.

Hatfield, Gary. "René Descartes." In *Stanford Encyclopedia of Philosophy Archive*, summer 2018 ed. Last updated January 16, 2014. https://plato.stanford.edu/archives/sum2018/entries/descartes.

Heaney, Seamus. *Crediting Poetry: The Nobel Lecture.* Farrar, Straus & Giroux, 1995.

Heidegger, Martin. *Poetry, Language, Thought.* Translated by Albert Hofstadter. Harper and Row, 1971.

———. *The Question Concerning Technology and Other Essays.* Translated by William Lovitt. Harper Perennial, 1982.

Hendlin, Yogi Hale. "Object-Oriented Ontology and the Other of We in Anthropocentric Posthumanism." *Zygon* 58, no. 2 (2023): 315–39. https://doi.org/10.1111/zygo.12864.

"Here We Stand—Frontline Song Circle." Ada'itsx/Fairy Creek Blockade. Facebook video, July 17, 2021. 1 min., 48 sec. https://www.facebook.com/watch/?v=145343591006448.

Hore, Peter J., and Henrik Mouritsen. "How Migrating Birds Use Quantum Effects to Navigate." *Scientific American*, April 1, 2022. https://www.scientificamerican.com/article/how-migrating-birds-use-quantum-effects-to-navigate.

Houston Center for Contemporary Craft. "Nathalie Miebach: The Water Line." Exhibition, September 28, 2019, to January 5, 2020. https://crafthouston.org/exhibition/nathalie-miebach-the-water-line.

Huestis, Amy-Claire. "Co-making This World." Unpublished draft. College Art Association 2021, panel session. https://www.amyhuestis.com/nest-works.

Hughes, Ted. *Moortown Diary*. Faber and Faber, 1979.

Hume, Mark. "Writers Hang Poems in Trees in Bid to Save Langley Land Parcel." *The Globe and Mail*, December 5, 2012. https://www.theglobeandmail.com/news/british-columbia/writers-hang-poems-in-trees-in-bid-to-save-langley-land-parcel/article5983994.

Hummingbirds Plus. "Hummingbird Nest Facts." Accessed November 16, 2023. https://www.hummingbirdsplus.org/hummingbird-nest-facts.

"Interactive Polyphonic Garden." *Signals Creative Tech Expo*. Accessed May 10, 2025. https://signals.digibc.org/digibc_projects/polyphonic-garden.

Irwin, Aisling. "World's Tiniest Snail Is So Small That 10 Fit in a Needle's Eye." *New Scientist*, September 28, 2015. https://www.newscientist.com/article/dn28248-worlds-tiniest-snail-is-so-small-that-10-fit-in-a-needles-eye.

Jabr, Ferris. "How Emily Dickinson Grew Her Genius in Her Family's Backyard." *The Slate Book Review*, May 17, 2016. https://www.slate.com/articles/health_and_science/books/2016/05/every_single_living_creature_in_emily_dickinson_s_complete_works_cataloged.html.

Janik, Vincent M. "Whale Song." *Current Biology* 19, no. 3 (2009): R109–R111. https://doi.org/10.1016/j.cub.2008.11.026.

"Judge Grants Temporary Injunction at Fairy Creek, Citing Economic Harm to Logging Company." *CBC News*, October 8, 2021. https://www.cbc.ca/news/canada/british-columbia/fairy-creek-injunction-appeal-1.6204905.

Kant, Immanuel. *Critique of Pure Reason*. Translated and edited by Paul Guyer and Allen W. Wood. Cambridge University Press, 1998. https://cpb-us-w2.wpmucdn.com/u.osu.edu/dist/5/25851/files/2017/09/kant-first-critique-cambridge-1m89prv.pdf.

Kara, Siddharth. *Cobalt Red: How the Blood of the Congo Powers Our Lives*. St. Martin's Press, 2023.

Katwala, Amit. "A Gene-Tweaked Jellyfish Offers a Glimpse at Other Minds." *Wired*, December 13, 2021. https://www.wired.com/story/gene-tweaked-jellyfish-neurology.

Keats, John. "Ode to a Nightingale." In *The Poetical Works of John Keats*. Edited by H. Buxton Forman. Oxford University Press, 1908.

———. *Selected Letters of John Keats*. Rev. ed. Edited by Grant F. Scott. Harvard University Press, 2005.

———. "To Benjamin Bailey." Letter, November 22, 1817. https://en.wikisource.org/wiki/Letter_to_Benjamin_Bailey,_November_22,_1817.

Kimmerer, Robin Wall. *Gathering Moss: A Natural and Cultural History of Mosses*. Oregon State University Press, 2003.

———. "P-Values and Cultural Values: Creating Symbiosis Among Indigenous and Western Knowledges to Advance Ecological Justice." ESA Videos. YouTube, August 15, 2019. 1 hr, 8 min, 20 sec. https://www.youtube.com/watch?v=xKmKFJzvizo.

Kingsnorth, Paul. "Dark Ecology: Searching for Truth in a Post-Green World." *Orion Magazine*, December 21, 2012. https://orionmagazine.org/article/dark-ecology.

Kingsnorth, Paul, and Dougald Hine. *Uncivilization: The Dark Mountain Manifesto*. The Dark Mountain Project, 2009. https://dark-mountain.net/about/manifesto.

Koep, Gregg, and Linda Hughes. "World's Largest Yellow Cedars are on Vancouver Island." *Vancouver Island Big Trees* (blog). March 5, 2013. https://vancouverislandbigtrees.blogspot.com/2013/05/worlds-largest-yellow-cedars.html.

Koren, Marina. "Transforming Raw Scientific Data into Sculpture and Song: Artist Nathalie Miebach Uses Meteorological Data to Create 3D Woven Works of Art and Playable Musical Scores." *Smithsonian Magazine*, March 1, 2013. https://www.smithsonianmag.com/science-nature/transforming-raw-scientific-data-into-sculpture-and-song-235223.

Kostadinov, Peter. "The Cobalt Rush: Here's How Apple Wants to Safeguard Its Future iPhone Batteries." *Phone Arena*, February 21, 2018. https://www.phonearena.com/news/Apple-iPhone-battery-cobalt-miners_id102648.

Kristeva, Julia. *Desire in Language: A Semiotic Approach to Literature and Art*. Columbia University Press, 1980.

Kulkarni, Akshay. "What Happens After the Donnie Creek Wildfire, Now Larger than PEI, Stops Burning?" *CBC News*, July 3, 2023. https://www.cbc.ca/news/canada/british-columbia/donnie-creek-wildfire-aftermath-1.6892294.

Kunuk, Zacharias, and Ian Mouro, dirs. *Qapirangajuq: Inuit Knowledge and Climate Change*. IsumaTV, February 4, 2011. Video, 54 min. 7 sec. https://www.isuma.tv/inuit-knowledge-and-climate-change/movie-no-subtitles.

Lavdovsky, Natasha. "Lichen Acid Noise Soundscapes (In Progress)." Projects. Accessed August 15, 2023. http://www.natashalavdovsky.com/works#/sound-of-lichens. (No longer available.)

———. "Music for Lichens (In Progress)." Projects. Accessed April 12, 2025. http://www.natashalavdovsky.com/projects#/music-for-lichens.

———. "The Sound of Lichen Chemistry: An Old-Growth Cedar Branch." Bandcamp. May 3, 2022. Digital track, 3 min., 19 sec. https://natashalavdovsky.bandcamp.com/track/the-sound-of-lichen-chemistry-an-old-growth-cedar-branch.

Leahy, Stephen. "If the Hardiest Species Are Boiled Alive, What Happens to Humans?" *The Atlantic*, July 31, 2021. https://www.theatlantic.com/ideas/archive/2021/07/billions-victims-heat-dome/619604.

Levinas, Emmanuel. "Language and Proximity." *Collected Philosophical Papers*. Translated by Alphonso Lingis. Martinus Nijhoff Publishers, 1987.

Lewis, Tim. "'It Always Hits Me Hard': How a Haunting Album Helped Save the Whales." *The Guardian* (Australia), December 6, 2020.

Liebich, Katrina. "'Tshcick-a-dee-dee' Chickadees: Sounds and Songs from the Northern Forests." US Fish & Wildlife Service. Accessed April 12, 2025. https://www.fws.gov/story/tshcick-dee-dee-chickadees.

Lilburn, Tim. *Living in the World as If It Were Home*. Cormorant Books, 1999.

Livingston, David. "It's Canada's Worst Fire Season in Modern History, as Smoke Fills Skies." *The Washington Post*, June 26, 2023. https://www.washingtonpost.com/weather/2023/06/26/canada-wildfire-worst-season-quebec-ontario-smoke.

Loeffelholz, Mary. "What Is a Fascicle? Reading Emily Dickinson's Manuscript Books." *Harvard Library Bulletin* 10, no. 1 (Spring 1999): 23–41. https://nrs.harvard.edu/URN-3:HUL.INSTREPOS:37363504.

Logan, Cloe. "Hummingbirds Put a Temporary Halt on Trans Mountain." *Canada's National Observer*, April 27, 2021. https://www.nationalobserver.com/2021/04/27/news/hummingbirds-temporary-halt-trans-mountain-stop-work-order.

Lokhorst, Gert-Jan. "Descartes and the Pineal Gland." In *Stanford Encyclopedia of Philosophy Archive,* Winter 2021 ed. Last updated September 18, 2013. https://plato.stanford.edu/archives/win2021/entries/pineal-gland.

Lovelace, Joyce. "Composing Chaos." *American Craft,* December–January 2014. https://www.craftcouncil.org/magazine/article/composing-chaos. (No longer available.)

Lowther, Christine, ed. *Worth More Standing: Poets and Activists Pay Homage to Trees.* Caitlin Press, 2022.

Lowther, Pat. "Hotline to the Gulf." *A Stone Diary.* Oxford University Press, 1977.

"Lyric Crow—A Deep Dive into the BC 'Justice' System." *Arrest Stories.* Podcast, season 1, episode 11, 45 min. December 4, 2022. https://podcasts.apple.com/ca/podcast/arrest-stories/id1609863177?i=1000588702442.

"'Lytton Is Gone': Wildfire Tears Through Village After Record-Breaking Heat." *The Guardian,* July 1, 2021. https://www.theguardian.com/world/2021/jul/01/lytton-wildfire-heatwave-british-columbia-canada.

Margulis, Lynn, and Dorion Sagan. "The Beast with Five Genomes." *Natural History Magazine,* June 2001. https://www.naturalhistorymag.com/htmlsite/0601/0601_feature.html.

Mason, Herbert. *Gilgamesh: A Verse Narrative.* New American Library, 1972.

McGilchrist, Iain. *The Master and His Emissary: The Divided Brain and the Making of the Western World.* Yale University Press, 2012.

———. *Ways of Attending: How Our Divided Brain Constructs the World.* Routledge, 2018.

"Meet the Sonic Artist Making Music with Plants: Sound Builders." Motherboard. YouTube, September 16, 2014. 9 min. https://www.youtube.com/watch?v=wYU18eiiFt4.

Merchant, Brian. "Op-Ed: Were the Raw Minerals in Your iPhone Mined by Children in Inhumane Conditions?" *Los Angeles Times,* July 23, 2017. https://www.latimes.com/opinion/op-ed/la-oe-merchant-iphone-supplychain-20170723-story.html.

Merleau-Ponty, Maurice. *Phenomenology of Perception.* Translated by Colin Smith. Routledge & Kegan Paul, 1962.

———. *The Visible and the Invisible*. Translated by Alphonso Lingis. Northwestern University Press, 1969.

Miebach, Nathalie. *The Burden of Every Drop*. 2018. Watercolor on paper, 16 x 20 in. https://www.nathaliemiebach.com/work/new-portfolio-item.

———. *The Burden of Every Drop*. 2018. Wood, paper, rope, data, 17 x 10 x 1 ft. https://www.nathaliemiebach.com/work/crystals-ye5wt.

———. *Harvey's Twitter SOS*. 2018. Watercolor on paper, 16 x 20 in. https://www.nathaliemiebach.com/work/new-portfolio-item.

———. "Keynote—Expanding the Reach and Meaning of Data Through Art and Science." field.work. YouTube, May 5, 2015. 34 min., 43 sec. https://www.youtube.com/watch?v=_hrRfAqkWNs.

Morin, Brandi. "'We're Not Going Anywhere': Inside the Latest RCMP Raid at Fairy Creek." *IndigiNews*, August 23, 2023. https://indiginews.com/features/were-not-going-anywhere-inside-the-latest-rcmp-raid-at-fairy-creek.

Morris, Tiffany. "Decolonizing the Apocalypse Through Etuaptmumk." *The Town Crier* (blog). *The Ex-Puritan*, April 9, 2020. https://ex-puritan.ca/blog/tiffany-morris-decolonizing-apocalypse-etuaptmumk.

———. *Elegies of Rotting Stars*. Nictitating Books, 2022.

Morton, Alexandra. *Listening to Whales: What the Orcas Have Taught Us*. Ballantine Books, 2004.

Morton, Timothy. *Being Ecological*. Pelican, 2018.

———. *Dark Ecology: For a Logic of Future Coexistence*. Columbia University Press, 2018.

———. *The Ecological Thought*. Harvard University Press, 2012.

———. *Ecology Without Nature: Rethinking Environmental Aesthetics*. Harvard University Press, 2007.

———. *Hyperobjects: Philosophy and Ecology After the End of the World*. University of Minnesota Press, 2013.

———. "Of Matter and Meter: Environmental Form in Coleridge's 'Effusion 35' and 'The Eolian Harp.'" *Literature Compass* 5, no. 2 (2008): 310–35. https://doi.org/10.1111/j.1741-4113.2007.00520.x.

Nagel, Thomas. "What Is It Like to Be a Bat?" *The Philosophical Review* 83, no. 4 (October 1974): 435–50. https://doi.org/10.2307/2183914.

Nao. "The Poetry and Brief Life of a Foxconn Worker: Xu Lizhi (1990–2014)." libcom.org. October 29, 2014. https://libcom.org/blog/xulizhi-foxconn-suicide-poetry.

Nassar, Dalia, and Margaret M. Barbour. "Rooted." *Aeon*, October 16, 2019. https://aeon.co/essays/what-can-an-embodied-history-of-trees-teach-us-about-life.

Natural Resources Canada. "Phantom Hemlock Looper." Government of Canada. Accessed April 1, 2022. https://tidcf.nrcan.gc.ca/en/insects/factsheet/1000004?wbdisable=true.

Neilson, John, Loys Maingon, and Natasha Lavdovsky. "Without an Over-Arching Biodiversity Protection Act, What Protections Exist for Biodiversity in British Columbia? A Case Study of Oldgrowth Specklebelly Lichen." *Canadian Field-Naturalist* 136, no. 2 (2022): 192–96. https://doi.org/10.22621/cfn.v136i2.3105.

Nicholson, Marcy. "British Columbia Tree Costs Surge as Lumber Makers Move South." *BNN Bloomberg*, June 30, 2021. https://financialpost.com/pmn/business-pmn/british-columbia-tree-costs-surge-as-lumber-makers-move-south.

Omstead, Jordan. "Environmental Groups Celebrate Court Ruling as a Win for At-Risk Birds in B.C. and Beyond." *CBC News*, February 6, 2024. https://www.cbc.ca/news/canada/british-columbia/birds-old-growth-court-murrelet-1.7107092.

"The Order of the Burial of the Dead," *Anglican Book of Common Prayer*. 1662.

Ortega y Gasset, José. "An Essay in Esthetics by Way of a Preface (1914)." In *Phenomenology and Art*. Translated by Philip W. Silver. W.W. Norton, 1975.

Pacheco, Agatha. "Seattle's Contribution to Standing Rock: A Twist on the Teepee." *The Seattle Globalist*, November 13, 2016. https://seattleglobalist.com/2016/11/30/standing-rock-seattle-tarpees-winter/59706.

Palmer, A. Laurie. *The Lichen Museum: Art After Nature*. University of Minnesota Press, 2023.

Parfitt, Ben. "Leaked Data Reveals New Threat to BC's Old Growth Forests." Canadian Centre for Policy Alternatives, March 7, 2024. https://www.policynote.ca/old-growth-leak.

Pasternak, Avery, and Kristin Walters. *Rights of Nature: Pathways to Legal Personhood for the Fraser River Estuary*. Raincoast Conservation Foundation, 2023. https://www.raincoast.org/reports/fraser-personhood.

Pawson, Chad. "Money Trees: The Struggle Over What's Ancient, Giant, Valuable, and Dwindling in BC's Coastal Forests." CBC *News*, November 13, 2018. https://newsinteractives.cbc.ca/longform/the-hunt-for-b.c-coastal-giant-trees.

Payne, Katharine. "A Change of Tune." *Natural History* 100, no. 3 (1991): 44–46.

Payne, Roger S., and Scott McVay. "Songs of Humpback Whales." *Science* 173, no. 3997 (1971): 585–97. https://doi.org/10.1126/science.173.3997.585.

"Planetary Boundaries." Stockholm Resilience Centre, Stockholm University. Accessed October 21, 2024. https://www.stockholmresilience.org/research/planetary-boundaries.html.

Ponge, Francis. *Partisan of Things*. Translated by Joshua Corey and Jean-Luc Garneau. Kenning Editions, 2018. Originally published in 1942.

Preminger, Alex, ed. "Elegy." *Princeton Encyclopedia of Poetry and Poetics*. 2nd ed. Princeton University Press, 1974.

Proppe, D.S., L.L. Bloomfield, and C.B. Sturdy. "Acoustic Transmission of the Chick-a-dee call of the Black-Capped Chickadee (*Poecile atricapillus*): Forest Structure and Note Function." *Canadian Journal of Zoology* 88, no. 8 (2010): 788–94. https://doi.org/10.1139/Z10-047.

"Province Extends Fairy Creek Old-Growth Deferral." BC Government, June 2, 2023. https://news.gov.bc.ca/releases/2023FOR0033-000860.

Rabie, Passant. "Why Tardigrades Spilled All Over the Moon in 2020." *Inverse*, December 24, 2020. https://www.inverse.com/science/tardigrades-may-have-taken-over-the-moon.

Rantanen, Mika, Alexey Yu Karpechko, Antti Lipponen, Kalle Nordling, Otto Hyvärinen, Kimmo Ruosteenoia, Timo Vihma, and Ari Laaksonen. "The Arctic Has Warmed Nearly Four Times Faster Than the Globe Since 1979." *Communications Earth & Environment* 3, no. 168 (2022). https://doi.org/10.1038/s43247-022-00498-3.

Ratcliffe, Mitch. "The Leaked IPCC Report Spells Disaster: What to Do Now." earth911.com, June 28, 2021. https://earth911.com/business-policy/the-leaked-ipcc-report-spells-out-disaster-what-to-do-now.

Rauhala, Emily. "The Poet Who Died for Your iPhone." *Time*. Accessed April 12, 2025. http://time.com/chinapoet.

Renner, Serena. "The Deep Roots of BC's Old Growth Defenders." *The Tyee*, September 16, 2020. https://thetyee.ca/News/2020/09/16/Movement-In-Woods.

Review Panel for the Roberts Bank Terminal 2 Project. "Summary of Key Findings." In *Federal Review Panel Report for the Roberts Bank Terminal 2 Project*, 1–3. Impact Assessment Agency of Canada, March 27, 2020. https://iaac-aeic.gc.ca/050/evaluations/document/134507.

Rilke, Rainer Maria. *The Duino Elegies and The Sonnets to Orpheus: A Dual Language Edition*. Translated by Stephen Mitchell. Vintage International, 2014.

Rozelle-Stone, A. Rebecca, and Benjamin P. Davis. "Simone Weil." In *Stanford Encyclopedia of Philosophy Archive*, summer 2022 ed. https://plato.stanford.edu/archives/sum2022/entries/simone-weil.

Russell, Rachel. "Satellite Images Show Canadian Wildfire Smoke over UK." *BBC News*, June 29, 2023. https://www.bbc.com/news/uk-66058108.

Saklikar, Renée Sarojini. *The Heart of This Journey Bears All Patterns (THOT J BAP)*. Projected 3 vols. Harbour Publishing, 2021–.

Scarry, Elaine. *The Body in Pain: The Making and Unmaking of the World*. Oxford University Press, 1985.

Schwartz, Jeremy. "How Five Common Birds Got Their Names." Medium, July 3, 2017. https://medium.com/@jschwartz1124/how-five-common-birds-got-their-names-3aa377607483.

Scranton, Roy. *Learning to Die in the Anthropocene: Reflections on the End of a Civilization*. City Lights Books, 2015.

Sheldrake, Merlin. *Entangled Life: How Fungi Make Our Worlds, Change Our Minds & Shape Our Futures*. Random House, 2020.

Shelley, Percy Bysshe. *Adonais*. 2nd ed. Edited by William Michael Rossetti and A.O. Prickard. Oxford University Press, 1903. Originally published in 1821.

Shivaram, Deepa. "Heat Wave Killed an Estimated 1 Billion Sea Creatures, and Scientists Fear Even Worse." NPR Environment. NPR, July 9, 2021. https://www.npr.org/2021/07/09/1014564664/billion-sea-creatures-mussels-dead-canada-british-columbia-vancouver.

Singh, Ruby. "After the Fires | Ruby Singh's Polyphonic Garden Suite II | 2023." YouTube, November 15, 2023. 4 min., 35 sec. https://www.youtube.com/watch?v=deF5nDUsXR8.

———. "Fairy Creek Lament | Ruby Singh's Polyphonic Garden | 2023." YouTube, October 16, 2023. 6 min., 23 sec. https://www.youtube.com/watch?v=_MdnotsGDv8&list=TLPQMjgxMTIwMjPbzGM3LhyQoQ&index=3.

———. *Polyphonic Garden Suite II*. Bandcamp. Digital album, 10 min., 6 sec. https://rubysingh.bandcamp.com/album/polyphonic-garden-suite-ii.

"Sitka Spruce." BC Government. Last updated January 25, 2024. https://www2.gov.bc.ca/gov/content/industry/forestry/managing-our-forest-resources/silviculture/tree-species-selection/tree-species-compendium-index/sitka-spruce.

Sloan School of Music. "The Fundamentals of Pitch Versus Tone." Last updated on December 27, 2023. https://sloanschoolofmusic.com/pitch-vs-tone/#elementor-toc__heading-anchor-2.

Smailbegović, Ada. *Poetics of Liveliness: Molecules, Fibers, Tissues, Clouds*. Columbia University Press, 2021.

Snyder, Gary. *The Practice of the Wild*. Counterpoint, 2010.

"Species at Risk." Biodiversity of the Central Coast. Accessed August 7, 2023. https://www.centralcoastbiodiversity.org/species-at-risk.html. (No longer available.)

"Species Profile: Oldgrowth Specklebelly Lichen." Government of Canada. Last updated December 23, 2024. https://species-registry.canada.ca/index-en.html#/species/126-423.

Spribille, Toby, Veera Tuovinen, Philipp Resl, Dan Vanderpool, Heimo Wolinski, M. Catherine Aime, Kevin Schneider et al. "Basidiomycete Yeasts in the Cortex of Ascomycete Macrolichens." *Science* 353, no. 6298 (2016): 488–92. https://doi.org/10.1126/science.aaf8287.

Stein, Vicky. "How a Snail's Shell Gets Its Twist." *PBS News*, May 14, 2019. https://www.pbs.org/newshour/science/how-a-snails-shell-gets-its-twist.

Stonich, Kathryn. "Hummingbird Nests 101: A Beginner's Guide." *Bird Calls Blog*. American Bird Conservancy. May 6, 2021. https://abcbirds.org/blog21/hummingbird-nests.

"Strawberry's Arrest Police Britality Ada'itsx Fairy Creek August 20th, 2021." Love and the Multiverse. YouTube, August 30, 2021. 2 min., 58 sec. https://www.youtube.com/watch?v=S6kBSmY-PKg.

Strongman, Phil. "Forgotten Audio Formats: The Flexi Disc." *Ars Technica*, April 15, 2017. https://arstechnica.com/gadgets/2017/04/forgotten-audio-formats-flexi-disc.

Surma, Katie. "Ecuador's High Court Affirms Constitutional Protections for the Rights of Nature in a Landmark Decision." *Inside Climate News*,

December 3, 2021. https://insideclimatenews.org/news/03122021/ecuador-rights-of-nature.

Tatham, Kelly. "The Human Cost of Defending Forests at Ada'itsx Fairy Creek." *Rabble*, September 1, 2021. https://rabble.ca/environment/human-cost-defending-forests-adaitsx-fairy-creek.

Tierney, Orchid. *looking at the Tiny: Made lichen on the surfaces of reading*. Essay Press, 2023.

Timber Pricing Branch. *Coast Appraisal Manual*. Effective 15 December 2021. BC Government. Accessed July 30, 2022. https://www2.gov.bc.ca/assets/gov/farming-natural-resources-and-industry/forestry/timber-pricing/coast-timber-pricing/coast-appraisal-manual/cam_2021_amend_master_b.pdf.

———. "Coast Average Stumpage Rates: Effective March 1, 2021." Accessed May 11, 2025. https://www2.gov.bc.ca/assets/gov/farming-natural-resources-and-industry/forestry/timber-pricing/coast-timber-pricing/coast_stumpage_2021.pdf.

———. "Coast Log Market Reports: One Month Ending May 31, 2023—Old-growth." BC Government. Accessed July 30, 2022. https://www2.gov.bc.ca/assets/gov/farming-natural-resources-and-industry/forestry/timber-pricing/coast-timber-pricing/coast-log-reports/1mc_may_23.pdf.

Toadvine, Ted. "Ecophenomenology in the New Millenium." In *The Reach of Reflection: Issues in Phenomenology's Second Century*. Edited by Steven Crowell, Lester Embree, and Samuel J. Julian. Center for Advanced Research in Phenomenology, 2001.

———. "Maurice Merleau-Ponty." In *Stanford Encyclopedia of Philosophy Archive*, Spring 2019 ed. September 14, 2016. https://plato.stanford.edu/archives/spr2019/entries/merleau-ponty.

———. *Merleau-Ponty's Philosophy of Nature*. Northwestern University Press, 2009.

Trainor, Kim. "An Anthropocene Poetics: A Review of Adam Dickinson's *Anatomic* (Coach House Books, 2018)." *Arc Poetry Magazine* 90, October 2019.

———. *A blueprint for survival*. Guernica Editions, 2024.

———. "documentary adequacy & poetic form." Kim Trainor (blog), July 31, 2014. https://kimtrainor.ca/2014/07/31/documentary-adequacy-poetic-form.

———. "'the idyllic era of cushions was at an end': 20th century lyric genres." Kim Trainor (blog), June 19, 2013. https://kimtrainor.ca/2013/06/19/the-idyllic-era-of-cushions-was-at-an-end-20th-century-lyric-genres.

———. "poem as trace of an event 1." Kim Trainor (blog), February 19, 2013. https://kimtrainor.ca/2013/02/19/the-poem-as-trace-of-an-event-1.

———. "We Will Feed the Seeds of Tomorrow: Kim Trainor at Fairy Creek: 2." *Faculty Matters* no. 18 (Spring 2022). https://dcfa.ca/wp-content/uploads/2022/04/2022-Spring-issue.pdf.

Traubeck, Bartholomäus. "Interview: Bartholomäus Traubeck on 'Years.'" Interview by Joe Patitucci. Data Garden. February 14, 2012. https://www.datagarden.org/post/2018/9/18/interview-bartholomus-traubeck-on-years.

———. *Years*. Bandcamp. June 26, 2013. Digital album, 5 min., 21 sec. https://traubeck.bandcamp.com/album/years.

Trower, Shelley. "Nerves, Vibration, and the Aeolian Harp." *Romanticism and Victorianism on the Net* 54 (May 2009). https://doi.org/10.7202/038761ar.

Tsing, Anna Lowenhaupt. *The Mushroom at the End of the World: On the Possibility of Life in Capitalist Ruins*. Princeton University Press, 2015.

Tsoulis Reay, Alexa. "What It's Like to See 100 Million Colors." *The Cut*, February 26, 2015. https://www.thecut.com/2015/02/what-like-see-a-hundred-million-colors.html.

Turner, Nancy J. *Ancient Pathways, Ancestral Knowledge: Ethnobotany and Ecological Wisdom of Indigenous Peoples of Northwestern North America*. McGill-Queen's University Press, 2014.

Umeek (E. Richard Atleo). *Tsawalk: A Nuu-chah-nulth Worldview*. University of British Columbia Press, 2004.

United Nations. "Secretary-General Calls Latest IPCC Climate Report 'Code Red for Humanity,' Stressing 'Irrefutable' Evidence of Human Influence." UN Press Release, August 9, 2021. https://press.un.org/en/2021/sgsm20847.doc.htm.

US Forest Service. "About Lichens." US Department of Agriculture. Accessed April 15, 2025. https://www.fs.usda.gov/wildflowers/beauty/lichens/about.shtml.

Vancouver Fraser Port Authority. "Roberts Bank Terminal 2 Receives Approval from the Government of Canada." Cision, April 20, 2023.

https://www.newswire.ca/news-releases/roberts-bank-terminal-2-receives-approval-from-the-government-of-canada-846173579.html.

Van Dooren, Thom. *Flight Ways: Life and Loss at the Edge of Extinction.* Columbia University Press, 2014.

Vendler, Helen. *Our Secret Discipline: Yeats and Lyric Form.* Belknap Press, 2007.

Wah, Fred, and Rita Wong. *beholden: a poem as long as the river.* Talonbooks, 2018.

Wainwright, Joel, and Geoff Mann. *Climate Leviathan: A Political Theory of Our Planetary Future.* Verso, 2018.

Watts, Johnson. "We Have Twelve Years to Limit Climate Change Catastrophe, Warns UN." *The Guardian,* October 8, 2018. https://www.theguardian.com/environment/2018/oct/08/global-warming-must-not-exceed-15c-warns-landmark-un-report.

"The Weather Artist: Chasing Storms with Sculpture." Great Big Story. YouTube, March 15, 2016. 2 min., 10 sec. https://www.youtube.com/watch?v=1ES4Ds7ApQw.

Weber, Andreas. *Enlivenment: Toward a Poetics for the Anthropocene.* MIT Press, 2019.

Weil, Simone. *Waiting for God.* Translated by Emma Craufurd. Harper & Row, 1992. Originally published in 1951.

"Whose Police?: RCMP Unit Acts as a Private Security Force, Critics Say." *The Fifth Estate,* CBC. YouTube, November 3, 2023. 42 min., 30 sec. https://www.youtube.com/watch?v=kQO2RIytszY.

"Who We Are: History." Data Garden. Accessed April 23, 2025. https://www.datagarden.org/who-we-are.

Williams, Bob. "Restoring Forestry in BC: The Story of the Industry's Decline and the Case for Regional Management." Canadian Centre for Policy Alternatives, January 2018. https://policyalternatives.ca/sites/default/files/uploads/publications/BC%20Office/2018/01/CCPA-BC_RestoringForestry_web.pdf.

Williams, Jared Qwustenuxun. "Hul'q'umi'num—ts'ekw'unshun qututhun." COHAB. YouTube, February 5, 2023. 5 min., 22 sec. https://www.youtube.com/watch?v=-3G47uO059Q.

Wolfe, Joe, Maëva Garnier, and John Smith. "Voice Acoustics: An Introduction." *Music Acoustics.* University of New South Wales. http://www.phys.unsw.edu.au/jw/voice.html.

Wong, Rita. *forage*. Blew Ointment Press, 2007.

"Wood Types on Pianos: What They Mean and Why They Matter." *The Piano Space* (blog). Millers Music. March 10, 2021. https://millersmusic.co.uk/blogs/blog/wood-types.

Woods, Derek. "Prosthetic Symbiosis." *CR: The New Centennial Review* 22, no. 1 (Spring 2022): 157–86. https://doi.org/10.14321/crnewcentrevi.22.1.0157.

Yong, Ed. *An Immense World: How Animal Senses Reveal the Hidden Realms Around Us*. Random House, 2022.

Zhong, Raymond. "Geologists Make It Official: We're Not in an 'Anthropocene' Epoch." *The New York Times*, March 20, 2024. https://www.nytimes.com/2024/03/20/climate/anthropocene-vote-upheld.html.

Zimmerman Smith, Bet. "All About Black-Capped Chickadees (*Poecile atricapillus*)." Sialis. Accessed May 20, 2021. http://www.sialis.org/chickadee.htm.

ᐅᐢᑲᓇ

OSKANA POETRY & POETICS

BOOK SERIES

Publishing new and established authors, Oskana Poetry & Poetics offers both contemporary poetry at its best and probing discussions of poetry's cultural role.

PREVIOUS BOOKS IN THE SERIES:

Something for the Dark, by Randy Lundy (2025)

Dog and Moon, by Kelly Shepherd (2025)

The Salmon Shanties: A Cascadian Song Cycle, by Harold Rhenisch (2024)

Into the Continent, by Emily McGiffin (2024)

Wrack Line, by M.W. Jaeggle (2023)

Dislocations, by Karen Enns (2023)

The History Forest, by Michael Trussler (2022)

Synaptic, by Alison Calder (2022)

Shifting Baseline Syndrome, by Aaron Kreuter (2022)

Pitchblende, by Elise Marcella Godfrey (2021)

Red Obsidian, by Stephan Torre (2021)

Burden, by Douglas Burnet Smith (2020)

Field Notes for the Self, by Randy Lundy (2020)

Live Ones, by Sadie McCarney (2019)

Forty-One Pages: On Poetry, Language, and Wilderness, by John Steffler (2019)

Blackbird Song, by Randy Lundy (2018)

The House of Charlemagne, by Tim Lilburn (2018)

Cloud Physics, by Karen Enns (2017)

The Long Walk, by Jan Zwicky (2016)

Measures of Astonishment: Poets on Poetry, presented by the League of Canadian Poets (2016)